Babies and Bosses: Reconciling Work and Family Life

AUSTRALIA, DENMARK AND THE NETHERLANDS

Volume 1

OECD

ORGANISATION FOR ECONOMIC CO-OPERATION AND DEVELOPMENT

ORGANISATION FOR ECONOMIC CO-OPERATION AND DEVELOPMENT

Pursuant to Article I of the Convention signed in Paris on 14th December 1960, and which came into force on 30th September 1961, the Organisation for Economic Co-operation and Development (OECD) shall promote policies designed:

- to achieve the highest sustainable economic growth and employment and a rising standard of living in Member countries, while maintaining financial stability, and thus to contribute to the development of the world economy;
- to contribute to sound economic expansion in Member as well as non-member countries in the process of economic development; and
- to contribute to the expansion of world trade on a multilateral, non-discriminatory basis in accordance with international obligations.

The original Member countries of the OECD are Austria, Belgium, Canada, Denmark, France, Germany, Greece, Iceland, Ireland, Italy, Luxembourg, the Netherlands, Norway, Portugal, Spain, Sweden, Switzerland, Turkey, the United Kingdom and the United States. The following countries became Members subsequently through accession at the dates indicated hereafter: Japan (28th April 1964), Finland (28th January 1969), Australia (7th June 1971), New Zealand (29th May 1973), Mexico (18th May 1994), the Czech Republic (21st December 1995), Hungary (7th May 1996), Poland (22nd November 1996), Korea (12th December 1996) and the Slovak Republic (14th December 2000). The Commission of the European Communities takes part in the work of the OECD (Article 13 of the OECD Convention).

Publié en français sous le titre :
Bébés et employeurs : comment réconcilier travail et vie de famille
AUSTRALIE, DANEMARK ET PAYS-BAS – Volume I

Foreword

Family-friendly policies help parents, and potential parents, to match their care commitments to young children with their own preferences for participating in the labour market. Family-friendly policies, including improved access to affordable and quality childcare, arrangements to take leave to care for children, flexibility in workplace arrangements, financial incentives to work, and, employment support for jobless parents, provide a key to better employment opportunities for families with young children. As such, family-friendly policies help both fathers and mothers to simultaneously increase the living standards of the family, fulfil individual aspirations to have both a career and a family, and give their children the care and support they need. Hence, the reconciliation of work and family life is an important goal in itself.

But the importance of the reconciliation of work and family life also lies in the fact that getting the right policy balance will promote other societal goals. Aggregate labour supply and employment will be increased; stable, secure sources of income for families fostered; gender equity facilitated; child development supported; and independence promoted.

This first OECD review of the reconciliation of work and family life analyses the existing mix of family-friendly policy measures in Australia, Denmark, and the Netherlands and explores how this policy balance contributes to different labour market and other societal results in these three countries. The review is based on visits to the three countries that took place in August/September 2001, and the analysis concerns the situation at that time. The review was discussed by the Working Party on Social Policy of the Employment, Labour and Social Affairs Committee in April 2002. The report was prepared by Willem Adema, Donald Gray and Mark Pearson, assisted by Cécile Cordoliani and Maxime Ladaique. This volume is published under the responsibility of the Secretary-General of the OECD.

Table of Contents

List of Charts

Introduction to the Review

The reconciliation of work and family life directly involves two goals that are important both to individuals and societies: the ability to participate fully in the labour market, generating income but also seeking fulfilment in the most important social activity of modern life, and to provide the best for one's own children, giving them the care and nurturing they need. These aspirations need not be mutually exclusive.

If a suitable balance of work and care commitments cannot be achieved this has implications for either labour force or family decisions, or both. Parents or potential parents who, rightly or wrongly, perceive their desired work-family balance to be unachievable, may adjust their family behaviour and decide to have children at a later age, not as many as desired, or to not have children at all. Alternatively, parents may opt to alter their labour market behaviour. Indeed, many parents are not part of the labour force, either temporarily or on a long-term basis. Sometimes, this is because they prefer to provide full-time care for their children, whatever their employment opportunities. Other parents would like to work, or to work more hours, but are not doing so because resource constraints in terms of time and access to services restrict their labour force participation. Still others spend so much time working that families may be put under strain, leaving societies as a whole to help pick up the pieces of broken relationships and young people who have not received the nurturing they need.

Work and family decisions are being made in the context of a broad set of interacting factors including individual preferences, opportunities and aspirations, future prospects and wider family relations. A whole gamut of social policies impinge on the work and family life balance, including retirement, elderly care and health policies, schooling and education policies, as well as employment, gender equity, childcare and income policies. Taken together, these factors influence individual decisions on labour force participation but also on family formation, parenthood, and family dissolution. These decisions in turn influence how future society will evolve and function and has implications for a wide range of public policy concerns. For example, if current fertility and demographic trends were to continue, future working age populations will be smaller (and older) relative to populations of non-working age than they are today (Chapter 2), with obvious implications for future labour supply, health, education, retirement and other public policies. Thus, the importance of the reconciliation of work and family life also lies in the fact that getting policy right will promote other societal goals and contribute to the sustainable development of societies (OECD, 2001).

This volume focuses on the challenges that *parents of young children* face when trying to square their work and care commitments, and the implications this has for social and labour market trends. In coming to a decision as to how to balance work and family life, parents have to consider a great many issues, including the availability of flexible workplace arrangements, possible childcare solutions and the implications for child development, access to child-related leave programmes, and net family income in-and-out of work. Whether or not parents decide to combine their work and care commitments, and in what way, largely depends on their access to *family-friendly policy* measures, the provision of which is largely determined by government policy and the outcome of industrial bargaining processes.

What are family-friendly policies?

Family-friendly policies are those policies that facilitate the reconciliation of work and family life by fostering adequacy of family resources and child development, that facilitate parental choice about work and care, and promote gender equality in employment opportunities. For the purpose of the review the "families" and "reconciliation" policies are defined as follows:

Families: "Each household of one of more adults living together with and taking responsibility for the care and rearing of one or more children". It follows that,

Reconciliation policies: include "All those measures that extend both family resources (income, services and time for parenting) and parental labour market attachment".

Not all parents face constraints in realising their preferences with regard to labour force participation or caring responsibilities. The reviews will pay particular attention to those parents that do.

Since it would have required a comprehensive analysis of long-term care systems (OECD, 1996), pensions (OECD, 1998, 2000 and 2001a), and health policies (OECD/Health Canada, 2002) this review does not directly consider the role of families in caring for disabled or older family members, though of course many of the issues are the same as for children.

The main findings of this study are presented in the first chapter, followed by an overview of the current situation of families in society and parental labour market outcomes in particular. The subsequent chapters examine various aspects of family-friendly policies: childcare (Chapter 3); leave arrangements (Chapter 4); female employment (Chapter 5); and workplace practices (Chapter 6). More detailed information on social programmes and leave arrangements can be found in the Background Annex to the review.

Chapter 1

Main Findings

This chapter contains the main findings of the review of policies supporting the reconciliation of work and family life in Australia, Denmark and the Netherlands.

1.1. Policy objectives

There is a well-known principle in economics that in order to achieve one policy target you need at least one policy instrument. If there are two policy targets, but only one policy, then achieving both goals is a matter of pure luck.

The reconciliation of work and family life is in part a goal in itself. There is a belief that people should not have to choose between pursuing a career – because work is, after all, the main way in which many people express themselves, their main forum for social interaction, and the main source of material resources – and their family life (including whether, when and how many children to have). If that were all that public policy was concerned with, it would be hard enough to achieve. But in fact the reason why the reconciliation of work and family life is increasingly important to so many governments is that it is hoped that getting the right balance will promote all sorts of other goals of society. Increasing aggregate labour supply and employment (so increasing national income); families with more stable and secure sources of income; families better able to stand the strains of modern life, and if relationships do break down, better able to move on in their lives; better child development outcomes; less public expenditures; higher fertility (or at least, enabling families to have their desired number of children) and more gender equity are all often primary governmental objectives.

Given so many objectives, the policy challenge is not how to achieve them all, as this is not likely to be feasible. Rather, it is about aiming at an appropriate balance among them. In the three countries under review, this balance has had to change – rapidly, in some cases – because greater priority is given now to goals such as increased labour supply and gender equity, that were not considered that important thirty or so years ago. Because measures to attain policy goals in one area often make attaining goals in other areas harder to achieve, there is a potential escalation of public intervention. This may not be a bad thing, but it is neces-

13

sary as well that the process is understood and acknowledged, rather than treated as some unexpected surprise. These "findings" are therefore in three parts. The first summarises the *main trends* in working life and family formation. The second describes the main features of *where policy is now*. The third looks at *how these policies are likely to interact* with social and labour market trends to see where pressures for further changes in policies will possibly develop in the future.

1.2. Work and families

Changing female behaviour has contributed to structural changes in the labour market over the last 40 years. These days, younger women are more able to work and to have a career than women of the same age in the 1960s. In all three countries, the male breadwinner remained the predominant notion until at least the beginning of the 1970s as reflected in the outcomes of industrial bargaining processes, tax/benefit systems and parental work patterns.[1] In Australia and the Netherlands a considerable part of the population still considers it appropriate that mothers with young children do not work or work part-time. This was an issue in Denmark in the 1970s. Since then, the share of female full-time employment increased in Denmark, and societal preferences changed as well (although many Danish women say they prefer to work on a part-time basis). Societal preferences are bound to have some impact on labour market outcomes and policy, but they are not independent from policy.

In the beginning of the 1970s, female employment rates were about 30% in the Netherlands, 45% in Australia, and close to 60% in Denmark, while at the turn of the millennium, female rates were about 75% Denmark and almost reaching 70% in both Australia and the Netherlands. At the same time, men do not appear to have changed their behaviour markedly. Although the prevalence of long working hours varies across the three countries (in Australia, a quarter of the labour force works over 50 hours per week as opposed to 10% in Denmark), those long hours are mainly worked by men. Indeed, male behaviour remains largely traditional in all three countries: take-up rates of parental leave among men are low, and although the gender gap in unpaid housework is smaller in Denmark than in the other two countries, caring remains primarily a female activity.

The broad story about labour markets is nevertheless one of achievement. More people are working than before. Women in particular, who were denied the chance to pursue achievement through labour market careers, with the financial independence that work brings, face vastly improved life chances than previously.

Closer-up, there are blemishes that can be discerned: *inter alia*, low rates of employment and high rates of poverty of lone-parent households in Australia and the Netherlands; a gender wage gap which remains stubbornly wide: and women are at a greater risk of being "trapped" in jobs which do not giver career progression. There are still labour market objectives which remain some way from being achieved.

The broad story in terms of family developments is less positive. The age at first childbirth has been increasing over the last 30 years, while completed fertility rates for age cohorts of women born in 1930 to 1965 have fallen continuously in Australia and the Netherlands. Completed fertility rates were lowest for Danish women born in 1955, but have since edged up. Family formation is being deferred, if not postponed indefinitely, until parents have completed more years of education and when one or both members of a couple are more securely established in their careers, possibly with access to parental leave and/or childcare support. The implications for the age structure of the populations are significant, with smaller working age populations.

1.3. Comparison of current policies to reconcile work and family life

1.3.1. *The overall policy stance*

In Australia, the avowed policy objective is to give parents a *choice* about whether they work or care for children. Social support is targeted on low-income families, and includes benefits for work-poor low-income parents with lone parents being exempt from mandatory job-search until their child is 16, thus allowing them to choose to stay at home and care for their children. Recent policy changes put greater emphasis on work than previously and childcare support is most generous to low-income workers.

In the Dutch policy model part-time work solutions play a central role, and part-time workers have equals rights as full-time employees. The previous tax system with considerable individual transfers and the limited family benefits and childcare support limitations contributed to the common establishment of the "one-and-a-half earner" model. Gender equity objectives underlie a desire for a more equal distribution of paid work across both parents. The recent individualisation of the tax/benefit system and the projected increase in childcare support do not necessarily underlie a political objective for a full-time dual earner model; rather, a "two two-thirds earners model" has made inroads in policy debate. But such a solution is likely to remain illusory for the near future, as it would require a fundamental change in male labour market behaviour, evidence for which is lacking.

The Danish policy model is aimed towards gender-equitable labour force participation on a full-time and universal basis. To that aim comprehensive family support is provided, workers can access generous child-related leave programmes and childcare is accessible to almost all children as from the age of 6 months. The tax/benefit system generates a high degree of horizontal equity with a strong emphasis on activity testing for those on benefit. Surprisingly perhaps, the tax sys-

15

tem is not fully individualised since considerable individually transferable allowances continue to exist, and *paid* parental leave is a family entitlement. Nevertheless, the Danish policy model generates the highest degree of equity in employment across the genders. Interestingly, the new Danish government stresses the need for parents to have a real choice about whether they work with good quality childcare, or whether they stay at home with their children. A new payment to families making the latter choice may be introduced at the discretion of local governments.

1.3.2. Employer-provided family benefits

There are three major areas of policy – childcare, leave and part-time work – about which employers and employees may bargain or which may be taken over as public policy concerns. In addition, there are a number of issues – flexible working hours, days off to care for sick children, teleworking etc. – which may contribute to helping families combine work and family life.

In Denmark, childcare is all-but-entirely a matter of public policy, not industrial relations. Paid leave is extensive, though is often topped-up by employers in line with collective agreements. Part-time work is pushed by neither employers nor unions. Other family-friendly work practices have gained some prevalence, but are by no means general. In the Netherlands, the distinction between what is left to the social partners for negotiation and what is the concern of public policy is more fluid than in the other countries. The government specifies issues that it thinks should be the topics under discussion in industrial bargaining. If the outcomes are unsatisfactory – as they have been over leave, working time flexibility and childcare, to some extent – it may then consider imposing legislation. Maternity leave is paid at a high rate by government, though with some role for employer top-ups. Part-time work, already prevalent, has received further legal backing through the Adjustment of Working Time Act, which gives employees the right to change their working hours, unless the employer can prove this to be a problem for the business. The penetration of other family-friendly work practices (flexitime, time off for sick children, etc.) is high.

In Australia, the role of government in ensuring family-friendly work practices is less than in the other two countries. It neither legislates for standard provisions, beyond a minimum, as is the case in both other countries but Denmark in particular, nor does it "direct" industrial bargaining as is the case in the Netherlands. This reflects constitutional limits on the jurisdiction of the federal government. This makes the outcome of industrial bargaining far more important in determining how work and family life can be reconciled (Chapter 6).

Some family friendly policies are advantageous to both employer and employee, or do not involve direct costs on the employer (*e.g.* flexitime). There is a mild paradox in this area, namely that some companies which have introduced such practices (and some of those who study the topic) report extraordinarily high returns to the policies, yet the coverage of many schemes is at best patchy, even low. There are a number of possible explanations, ranging from an inability of businesses to take a global view of the possible gains, differences in size, skill mix and extent of female employment in industries, union conservatism in being attached to regular full-time work as an ideal, and even that the underlying demand by workers for some of these practices is actually not that high.

But does this variety in work practices matter? It rather depends on the objectives in question. The low penetration of family-friendly work practices in Australia may lead to increased gender segregation, with women working in areas of the economy where such schemes are more common. This is both good (the more are occupations segregated, the more likely will employers be sensitive to the needs of mothers) and bad (reducing occupational mobility).

Furthermore, women, rather than men, are the main users of many family-friendly work practices. This could alter employment practices of employers. For example, paid maternity leave increases employers' costs. Some studies suggest that employer-financed paid leave can nevertheless improve "the bottom line" by attracting good quality workers, increasing retention rates after childbirth and improving productivity. If these gains are not realised, then these benefits give an incentive for employers to hire men, rather than women. In practice, this cost is passed onto women in the form of lower wages. In effect, unless the costs of these provisions are either taken by men as well as women, apply across all industries (including those which are male dominated) and/or are financed by levies on men as well as women, they act as a tax on being a female worker. The financing of continued (partial) wage payments during child-related leave serves as an example, potentially imposing considerable costs on employers. The Dutch maternity payment system is largely "gender neutral" as employers get reimbursed for the continued wage payment up to a high level. But as shown in Chapter 4, redistribution of costs associated with child-related leave among employers in Denmark is more limited. Costs are only distributed within industrial sectors, and where these are male dominated, unions are not keen to share costs with sectors with a larger proportion of female workers, thereby deterring a comprehensive pooling of resources across all sectors. All costs associated with child-related leave in Australia and a significant proportion of those costs in Denmark are borne by individual employers, who thus face incentives not to hire women of childbearing age. Non-discrimination legislation, important though it is, is only ever likely to prevent the most blatant abuses of the law.

Hence, there appear to be limits to the extent to which a family-friendly policy can be pursued through industrial bargaining alone. The outcome of such an approach appears to put the onus of balancing work and family life on women to organise their working life around their family responsibilities, unless they are highly skilled, working in a large company and/or the public sector. For the rest, part-time work and (in the Australian context) casual work is apparently the way in which women square the circle. There is nothing inherently unsustainable about this, but such a solution does risk maintaining a lack of gender and social equity.

1.3.3. Tax/benefit systems and financial incentives to work

No other area of policy is so quickly confusing as looking at the effects of the tax/benefit system on the incentives to work facing a second earner in a two-adult household. As a rule of thumb, it is widely assumed that individual taxation of the two spouses is likely to promote two-earner households. Indeed, this is the case, but whether it matters in practice depends also on the detailed operations of the social security system and family transfers. The Danish tax structure with its transferable allowances appears to favour one-earner households, but in practice the high average tax rates on all families and the limitation on the transferability of the allowance for high-income earners means that it does not. Australia has a benefit system that appears to favour one-earner households, but the progressivity of the individual-based tax system means that two-earner couples who "split" their income evenly save at least as much tax as they lose in means-tested benefits. The Dutch system has (after a long peregrination) settled on individual taxation, but the credit structure and that of social security contributions leaves the system fairly neutral as to the distribution of earnings across the two adults.

Despite these complications, some indicative facts do come through. The Danish tax/benefit system generates marginal effective tax rates (after child support) that are lower for full/time workers with children on average earnings, than (part-time) workers with children with up to two-thirds of average earnings. In other words, the returns to part-time work are limited, and once working, the incentive to choose full-time rather than part-time work is high. The Australian means and income-tested benefit system inevitably generates high marginal tax rates at the earnings range where such support is phased out. Recent reforms have improved the marginal effective tax rate structure to the extent that many of the highest rates have been reduced. One effect has been to leave precisely the opposite incentive structure to that in Denmark – movement into part-time work has been made more attractive than previously, but the spouse of a low-income earner faces disincentives in moving from part-time work to full-time work.

For potential dual earner couples with children with good access to childcare, the net gains of dual earnership appear largest in Australia and the Netherlands with effective net *average* tax rates at about 25 to 30%, whereas in Denmark these are highest at 50%. Hence, at first sight it appears that having a second earner in the family is financially more worthwhile in Australia, and the Netherlands than in

Denmark. The reality is, however, that female employment rates in Denmark are higher than in Australia and the Netherlands, and this is particularly so when full-time employment rates are considered. There is some evidence that an income or resource effect associated with high average tax rates generated by the tax/benefit system contributes to this high rate of female employment. Richer families can afford to have only one earner or a second part-time earner, despite the *prima facie* relatively high returns to dual earnership. Furthermore, because childcare is available at a highly-subsidised rate, failure to use childcare is in effect throwing away an all-but-free good. The two key features which encourage labour force participation of mothers in Denmark are therefore high taxation and childcare, the price of which to parents does not vary much by whether they work, nor for how long they work.

1.3.4. *Access to affordable childcare*

Government policies influence both quantity and quality of formal childcare facilities as well as the costs to parents, and thus the extent to which childcare is used. In Denmark, public expenditure on childcare and the number of very young children in formal childcare is much higher than in the other two countries. Public childcare expenditure is widely considered as "an investment in the future", contributing to better outcomes across a range of factors, including child development, educational achievement, gender equality and future labour supply. In Australia too, childcare expenditure is seen as contributing to future family and community functioning, while in the Netherlands public spending (and that of employers) is largely related to labour market considerations.

Parents in Denmark at all earnings ranges have access to subsidised childcare which facilitates their full-time labour force participation. Parents in full-time work use full-time care. The average level of public spending per child in the childcare system is also much higher than in the other two countries – around US$6 300 per year, compared with US$2 200 in Australia and US$1 500 in the Netherlands. However, as shown in Chapter 3 the fee structure of the Danish childcare system is not always sensitive to the number of hours of care actually used. This means that in some cases parents reserve more care than they need or use, and if fees and use of care were better aligned, this would enhance efficiency in supply and in utilisation.

Compared to Denmark, formal childcare capacity is relatively limited in Australia and the Netherlands, particularly for children aged 0 to 2. This feature is related to underlying cost and pricing structures, the preferences for parental and/or informal care and labour market opportunities to work part-time (Chapter 2). In Australia, Child Care Benefit (CCB) is paid to parents to subsidise the cost of childcare: it is an income-linked payment most generous to low-income workers and is phased out at earnings close to twice the average earnings levels (Chapters 3 and 5). In recognition of the significant proportion of women who work part-time, the CCB structure includes a higher rate for part-time use of formal childcare services. This is to take account of the different fee structure for part-time care. However, the CCB structure does not match the age-related cost-structure underlying the provision of childcare, which is one factor that contributes to fewer places for 0-2-year-olds and some unmet demand for this age group.[2] Both the higher rates for part-time care and the capacity considerations for 0-2 years help explaining the prevalence with which formal care for very young children is used on a part-time basis.

In the Netherlands, childcare capacity, particularly for very young children is constrained and if unsubsidised, prohibitively expensive when it concerns more than one child. This helps explain why in the Netherlands, the likelihood that mothers are in part-time work and out of the labour force increases with the number of children. Part-time employment in the Netherlands remains popular among women with older children. To some extent this reflects satisfaction with being in part-time work, but also the knowledge that school-hours are unreliable, particularly on Fridays, and in any case require a search for additional out of school hours care facilities that are limited at present.

Much more than in Denmark, parents of younger children in both Australia and the Netherlands have to rely on informal care solutions. Parents may actually prefer trusting their infant to wider family members and friends, which is cheaper than formal childcare unless the latter is fully subsidised. However, informal care solutions are more available on a part-time rather than a full-time full-week basis, further contributing to parents seeking part-time solutions. But where part-time solutions in the Netherlands are often of long duration, it appears that in Australia being in part-time work makes it easier for mothers to return to full-time work when children grow up.

1.3.5. Choice for parents in childcare

In all three countries, parents are able to choose to use childcare or to care for their children at home. This choice is constrained by costs to parental and available capacity. The Australian and Danish systems appear to satisfy current demand (albeit at different levels), but supply constraints are significant in the Netherlands. However, normal patterns of use differ across countries, with almost all parents choosing to use childcare (and full-time childcare) in Denmark, while in the Netherlands and in Australia young children are more likely to be cared for at home, or be in part-time rather than full-time childcare.

The proposed new Dutch childcare support programme will provide choice to parents. Hence, like the Australian reform some years ago, financial support will be redirected from providers to parents. The aim is to increase parental choice both in terms of type and quantity of providers, rather than the current situation where most parents are unsure of being able to obtain a place in a subsidised (municipal) centre.

Another aspect of the projected Dutch policy reform is that it will simplify the organisational provision of childcare, and the accompanying multitude of financing streams. In future, all public subsidies will directly go to parents (via the tax system), rather than involving two different ministries and about 500 local governments. Moreover, all workers will have access to this benefit rather than only those covered by collective agreements that include employer-provided childcare support (about 60% of all workers).

The Danish childcare system, in contrast, relies almost completely on public providers, as many Danes dislike the idea of having their children looked-after by a commercial provider.

Both the Australian and Danish systems rely to a large extent on formal family day care (especially for very young children in the case of the latter), a care option which is often cheaper than centre-based care and is preferred by a considerable number of parents. The Netherlands could look into a further use of family day care as a lower-cost way of increasing supply.

In Australia, occasional care and family day care can often be bought by the hour, while both Australian and Dutch providers generally allow parents to buy centre-based childcare at half a day at the time. As noted above, the Danish system does not always offer parents the possibility of buying childcare on a part-time basis. The lack of choice over time in childcare is a major barrier for those wishing to work part-time.

Much more than in the Netherlands, which appears at an earlier stage in developing its childcare services, in both Denmark and Australia, concerns about the availability of childcare places are giving way to concerns about quality and child development. Quality is critical if parents are going to be willing to use childcare. Parent involvement in Denmark is important, and quality is required by law, but with no external benchmarking, the system is open to over-reliance on local childcare professionals. The Australian quality assurance systems offer a model, including the use of peer reviews as an innovative way of monitoring quality, and helps support a very large and successful involvement by the private sector in providing care services. Although this system appears to be working well at the moment, care is needed to avert the risk that over-reliance on other childcare professionals may create a profession more concerned about defending its collective interests, rather than promoting wider societal objectives. However, the system of licensing of services and accreditation for funding purposes, with responsibilities resting at both state and federal levels, results in some duplication and higher compliance costs for providers than is necessary. The issue of quality is linked to that of child development. At least in Denmark, the consensus is that formal child-care is beneficial to children, provided the care is of appropriate quality.

1.3.6. Work, care for children, schools and shop-opening hours

Out-of-school care is a policy issue in all countries under review. In Denmark, 80% of children aged between 6-9 use after-school centres; the Australian government is increasing investment in out-of-school care facilities, while in the Netherlands projects are undertaken to optimise the use of school facilities for out-of-school care purposes. The use of school facilities for out-of-school care purposes seems entirely logical but is not always feasible as educational authorities (or independent school boards as in the Netherlands) are not keen on their school being used for that purpose (apart from problems with existing insurance regulations). Parents in the Netherlands have an additional problem; they are not all that certain of school-hours. Teacher-shortages frequently force schools to close for a day (or half a day) at short notice, leaving parents having to find care solutions. In the school year 2000/2001, 35% of primary schools in the Netherlands sent their children home at least once. The fact that school teachers do not consider themselves childminders, and resent the implication that this is one of the purposes of formal education systems, is clearly a barrier for parents who need stable and predictable school hours if they are to work.

In line with long-standing practice in Australia, recent product market deregulation in Denmark and the Netherlands has made shop-opening hours more conducive to working parents, but such flexibility does not yet apply to public services. To improve overall coherence in service delivery the Dutch government is financing local experiments on for example, the co-location of various services to find best practices that may be suitable to a wider application.

1.4. Emerging pressures for the reconciliation of work and family life

1.4.1. How important is encouraging more labour supply?

Reasons for wishing to increase labour supply fall into two broad groups. First, increased labour supply is in the interests of individuals and families which have low labour supply. The family becomes richer; it becomes less vulnerable to labour market shocks (*i.e.* if one partner loses their job, the family still has some income from work); family dissolution is less catastrophic for the partner who becomes the main carer for the children if she has income from work. These are important reasons for preferring that parents retain some labour force attachment. It is incumbent on governments to eliminate barriers to work, so that families can realise these gains. The second set of reasons for wishing to increase labour supply are more general. Higher labour supply reduces wage pressure, increases wealth, and leaves countries in a better position to cope with population ageing.

Female participation rates in Australia and the Netherlands are now 65%, with a strong cohort effect, which suggests that further increases in participation will take place irrespective of government policy. Even with the extensive range of policies in place now for many years, the female participation rate in Denmark is 76%. Assuming Denmark represents something of an upper bound on female participation rates, then the scope for further gains in participation rates in the other two countries are significant, but not dramatic.

In fact, universal Danish childcare coverage, extensive leave rights, individual benefits, etc., did *not* precede the achievement of high participation rates in that country. Rather, these were the demands made by women who found that they had entered the labour market as desired by government, but who faced great demands on their time. They found themselves being forced to rely on informal care or lost a high proportion of their wages in paying for formal childcare, or were trapped in part-time work when they wanted full-time careers.

A similar stage now appears to be reached in Australia and the Netherlands. Female labour force participation is now quite high, and will get higher. Families have found ways of using friends and relatives to help with care, or to pick children up from childcare centres. Second earners in the household have chosen jobs which are often part-time, or which are in the public sector or other sectors which give them the flexibility to be able to fit their work around their caring activities. More family-friendly policies are not necessary to get them into work because they already, in overwhelming numbers, do work. Rather, the demands for policies which help reconcile work and family life reflects dissatisfaction with the returns to choosing to work.

In other words, there is often confusion about the underlying dialectic between family policies and the labour market. Greater labour force participation itself creates the demand for more family policies to help reconcile work and family life. The fact that such policies themselves promote further labour force participation is a secondary factor in their introduction.

This is not the full story, of course. More highly subsidised childcare will increase the labour supply of some groups, particularly those for whom labour force participation is marginal because they are low skilled and cannot expect to earn much. Furthermore, working part-time is a principal means used in Australia and the Netherlands to ensure that there is time available for caring for children. More extensive childcare provision and other rights may make full-time work viable for more people. This might not affect labour force participation rates, but would help overcome occupational segregation and improve gender equality, as well as increasing overall labour supply.

23

These distinctions have consequences for what can realistically be expected from policy reforms. For example, given that only 20% of Dutch families use formal childcare at the moment and there are capacity constraints, the move to subsidising parents rather than providers is likely to lead to very heavy substitution from informal and unsubsidised childcare, and possibly enable some who are currently working part-time to consider working full-time. It is very unlikely to dramatically expand labour force participation of mothers. If the latter were the dominant objective of policy, then it is very difficult to avoid the conclusion that other methods might be a lot more effective or less expensive – general wage subsidies, for example (see Powell, 2002), or targeted interventions to promote employability.

Whilst the likely direction of Dutch reforms and participation rates seems relatively clear, where Australia is in this cycle of higher female participation generating a demand for more family-friendly policies is less certain. There have been, indisputably, greater efforts to get family-friendly provisions for employees, but the emphasis on the central role of workplace practices in achieving these goals is greater than in the other two countries.[3] This reflects two traditions in Australian public life. First, many goals often pursued through social policies in other countries have, for constitutional and other reasons, always been left to the particularistic industrial relations institutions in Australia. Second, benefits have generally been means-tested and targeted on low-income groups. Australian social policy over the last half century has deliberately avoided "middle class welfare" in order to keep overall tax rates low. The union movement has supported this approach. Hence, the European Social and Christian democratic traditions of solidarity across income groups through social insurance have never taken root. It is therefore at least possible that the circle of greater female labour force participation, leading to demands for greater *public* expenditures on helping people to reconcile their work and family lives, may be avoided.

1.4.2. How much compulsion about labour force participation should governments apply?

If, despite all the advantages attached to labour force participation, families nevertheless have one partner *not* working, it implies that either the preference for caring is very strong indeed, or that there are serious barriers to participation in the labour market. The former may sometimes be the concern of governments to change, but the latter certainly is.

This sort of logic has led all three countries under review to intervene heavily in reducing barriers to labour supply of parents. This is particularly true of lone parents, who are overwhelmingly more at risk of poverty than two-adult households. For lone parents in the three countries under review, work dramatically reduces the chances of poverty (though even when working, lone parents are more at risk of poverty than the "average" household in each country).

Few aspects of Danish tax, benefit, childcare or labour market policy can be interpreted as anything other than a concerted and consistent effort to ensure that all adults have an employment contract. The benefit system is (broadly) based on the individual. Those on benefit cannot use caring responsibilities as a reason for not searching for work beyond the end of one year of leave. The tax system might not be fully individualised, but it is not far off, and the income effect of high rates of taxation appears to be a major reason for all adults to work.

It is not that long ago that the Netherlands had a system strongly based around the one-earner household than Australia. Those on benefit, including lone parents, were not required to look for work if they had caring responsibilities. The tax (and even the social security) systems were based on the family, so had an in-built bias against second earners in a household. There was little publicly-financed childcare worth speaking of.

In an extraordinarily short space of time, this picture has been made obsolete at least so far as the policy direction is concerned. Parents are expected to seek work from when the youngest child is 5. The tax and large parts of the benefit system are more individualised than previously. Childcare provision is being expanded. And the rights to change working hours to suit family circumstances are far more extensive than in any other country.

That said, practice has not kept up with theory. The pressure on benefit recipients to work is not applied in practice. Childcare provision is expanding, but with school hours short and variable, society is not set up to cope with all adults working full-time. Hence, the Dutch system is one in transition. The legal provisions increasingly seem to suggest that work by all adults is the norm (while acknowledging that much of that work will be part-time), but the practice falls some way short of this.

The broad direction of policy in Australia is not so very different from that in the Netherlands. As in the Netherlands, the tax/benefit system now makes part-time work financially viable, and this opens up participation possibilities for mothers who previously considered that their caring responsibilities meant labour force participation was not feasible. However, up until very recently, public policy has stopped short of *requiring* any parents responsible for children and in receipt of public income support to participate in the labour market. This is changing, albeit in a very marginal way (requiring just a few hours participation from those with older children). For a number of reasons, not least being the difficulty of motivating and reskilling people who have been out of the labour force for so long, it is difficult to imagine that this is anything other than a transitional policy which will have as its end point something akin to the Dutch policy (in theory, if not in practice) of requiring participation of all parents with children of school age. However, to be meaningful, as the Dutch experience shows, this requires a commitment of resources and the incentives on those administrating benefit systems to apply them.

1.4.3. The role of leave

Notwithstanding the marked differences in the design of leave programmes, in all three countries leave benefits have recently been and/or are an issue in policy debate. The Dutch debate recently led to the establishment of the Work and Care Act introduced on 1 December 2001: an encompassing framework covering different types of leave. In Australia and Denmark, policy debate concerns the design of income support provisions during leave periods to care for children not yet one year of age. The Danish system is being reformed to give parents the opportunity to care for their child until the first birthday, and possibly for longer, depending on local government policy. In Australia, the absence of a public maternity/parental leave payment for eligible workers recurrently leads to discussion on the desirability of such a programme.

Some period of recovery after childbirth (and repose beforehand) is medically desirable, but there are wider societal concerns to do with labour supply, gender equity, income support and child development that influence policy regarding the optimal amount of paid leave. There may also be a case for some period of paid leave if it reduces demand on otherwise hard-pressed and highly subsidised childcare systems (Chapter 3). All these factors affect leave policy but these measures need careful balancing against other uses of public funds that may be more effective in achieving the relevant policy goals.

There is a business case for employers introducing paid leave, to the extent that it improves motivation, increases retention rates of highly-skilled employees, even reduces sickness. It transpires that such considerations have not been sufficient to lead to extensive use of maternity pay in Australia, although demands for such pay do appear to be mounting. In the other countries, employers are not expected to pay full pay during leave as there are public benefits, but they often do top-up these payments, though again their coverage is less than universal, generating inequitable outcomes among workers.

In all three countries, governments provide income support to sustain income levels of families with children. Averting poverty during periods of leave is an objective in all three countries, and benefit systems are in place to cope with this. Paid leave also helps redistribute household income from periods when it was high to when the need to devote resources to caring for children means that it is low. This is one of the traditional functions of social insurance systems, and it is no surprise to find such paid leave schemes in the Netherlands and Denmark, but not in Australia where this tradition never took root.

The effective extension of paid parental leave in Denmark is motivated in part by providing parents (usually the mother) a continuous earnings stream for about one year before returning to their previous employer. Other new government proposals allow (not mandate) local governments to pay the equivalent of childcare subsidies to parents who care for their child at home for 12 months (Chapter 3). This will help local governments (in particular, Copenhagen) that, because of supply constraints, are unable to guarantee a childcare place for all children as from their first birthday to reduce demand for formal childcare. This choice of solving the "problem" through extending leave and effectively giving parents, usually the mother, the right to care for their own children for a prolonged period of time or pay for childcare at home rather than expanding formal childcare does imply a preference for home-based care for young children that has not been present in public policy for some years.

The Danish reform of leave arrangements is designed to be neutral in terms of labour supply, but this abstracts from the pressure employers may face to extend the period during which they top up benefits to full wages, which would inevitably raise labour costs. This would reduce labour demand, unless the effectively higher hourly wages attract additional labour supply. However, that seems unlikely in the Danish context, as female employment rates are already high. Similarly, extension/introduction of paid leave around childbirth in the other two countries is unlikely to attract additional labour supply, as so many non-mothers of childbearing age are already in employment.

There are other considerations to be considered. If employers are expected to finance payments during leave, then the cost of hiring women will rise relative to men, potentially affecting employment rates or (more likely) widening the pay gap between men and women. The Dutch financing system of pay during leave is more gender equitable than the Danish because the costs do not fall on the employers of mothers to the same extent. Furthermore, long leave periods may lead women to lose labour market skills, damaging their income prospects over their lifetimes.

The programme of the Australian government includes a commitment to introduce the First Child Tax Refund, which in many respects mimics the effects of an insurance-type system, albeit with a low level of benefits. Beyond this, the Australian government continues to believe that financial support for most workers should be determined through negotiation between employers and employees, and as described above such paid leave is in practice only available to a limited group of workers. However, the debate is ongoing (HREOC, 2002) and there have been signs that more employers are thinking of introducing paid maternity leave, while the Australian Council of Trade Unions (ACTU) has been campaigning for the introduction of a case for the Australian Industrial Relations Commission to consider for the introduction of 14 weeks paid maternity leave.

27

It is perhaps surprising that leave arrangements attract so much attention and effort. After all, discussions about payments and duration generally refer to a few extra weeks here and there. If these weeks are critical, in that without (paid) leave women (in particular) would be forced to exit the labour force, then perhaps the concern would be understandable. In practice, it seems hard to believe that this is often the case (though the meshing of the childcare guarantee and parental leave in Denmark, as described above, does perhaps fall into this category). Generally, the problems parents face in balancing their work and family life go far beyond the period when their children are very young, and so policy solutions should perhaps concentrate on these more general issues. To that extent, the approach in some Dutch agreements facilitating part-time work without the equivalent loss in wages for a period, looks strategically coherent.

1.4.4. *Gender equity*

Paid work in all three labour markets is unequally distributed across the genders. Many households in Australia and the Netherlands distribute paid work along a "one and a half dual earner model" in terms of hours in paid employment, while in terms of contribution to household income a "one and a quarter model" appears a better description. The distribution of full-time work is more equally distributed in Denmark, but even there, men work longer hours than women. And although men are contributing more to unpaid household work than previously, caring predominantly remains a female activity in all three countries under review.

Gender employment and wage gaps remain considerable, especially in the Netherlands. To a considerable extent these are related to female employment being concentrated in sectors, where wage gains in recent years have been relatively limited. Part-time employment for longer duration as in the Netherlands does often not facilitate career progress into senior management positions. And prolonged use of parental leave in Denmark seems to contribute to difficulties high-skilled female workers have in breaking through the glass ceiling.

To some extent current gender employment and wage gaps reflect the employment pattern of older cohorts of female employees that had lower participation rates and/or dropped out of the labour force for a considerable period of time to care for children. As educational attainment of female workers entering the labour market now is on par or even above the level of skills of male labour market starters, gender wage gaps could possibly be smaller in future.

Nevertheless, it seems unrealistic to be overly optimistic in this regard. Today's new parents still behave fairly traditionally, as suggested by the gender discrepancies in the use of leave benefits. When payments during child-related leave are paid to either parent at the previous level of earnings, in theory it does not matter to households which of the parents uses the leave entitlement. But in

28

reality it does. As long as men (rightly) feel that using family-friendly benefits damages their career prospects, the long-run household opportunity costs will be lowest when the mother uses the benefits. The existing workplace culture still places a penalty on fathers using family-friendly benefits, especially when it concerns longer term leave. Without a shift in workplace culture, "providing *choice* to parents" will more often than not contribute to perpetuating existing gender inequalities at the labour market.

Notes

1. For example, Denmark abolished joint taxation and higher unemployment benefits for married males in 1970, family taxation in the Netherlands reformed in the mid-1970s and in 1974 the minimum wage set by the Industrial Relations Commission in Australia for the first time equally applied to male and female employees.

2. In childcare centres (in line with regulations) the number of staff attending 0-2 year olds is about twice the number of staff caring for children in the age group 3 to 5. The CCB payment, however, does not vary with the age of the child. As staff costs constitute about 80 to 90% of all costs of childcare centres, providers need to pool resources from one age group to another, and most centres do this by having fewer places for 0-2 to years olds than for older children.

3. Industrial relations are central in the Dutch model, as many family-friendly policies including childcare subsidies for parents are subject to negotiation between employees and employers. However, the Dutch authorities play a leading role in this process, in that they will indicate to the social partners that they wish to have an agreement on a topic, leaving it up to negotiation as to how the policy is implemented.

Chapter 2

Families and Work: How Are Families Doing?

This chapter provides an overview of how families are doing in terms of work and family decisions. It shows population characteristics and household compositions as well as parental labour force outcomes.

During the last quarter of the 20th century, profound social changes took place that have considerably changed family life. Patterns of family formation, dissolution and fertility have changed, as has the gender division of paid work. To a large extent these changes reflect changing individual aspirations, and in particular women have been at the forefront of these societal changes. But other factors are also changing the work and care balance.

Economic and labour market developments and the nexus of industrial relations, government policies, and parental choices all play a part in determining societal outcomes. This chapter describes these outcomes in the three countries under review. It starts with a summary view of macroeconomic indicators and public social spending, followed by a brief overview of population and fertility patterns, and changes in household composition and observations on the compatibility of work and family formation. The remainder of the chapter describes in detail the labour market outcomes for men and women and parents, mothers in particular, and the impact of employment outcomes on poverty.

2.1. Macroeconomic indicators

Of the three countries covered in this review, Australia has the largest economy, being almost 15% larger than that of the Netherlands. The Danish economy is less than half the size of the Dutch economy (Table 2.1). The three countries are among the most affluent in the OECD with per capita GDP exceeding US$26 000 (with the cost of living in Denmark being relatively high for OECD countries: see third column Table 2.1). Over the last five years the economies of all three countries grew considerably, with average annual growth rates of 2.5 to 3.8% in real terms. Growth of the Danish and Dutch economies declined in the second part of 2001, and is projected to be modest at just over 1% of GDP in 2002. By contrast,

Table 2.1. **Main economic indicators**

Percentages

	GDP (current prices)	GDP per capita (current prices)	Comparative price levels for GDP	GDP (real)	Employment rate	Standardised unemployment rate	Percentage annual wage growth	Percentage annual growth in consumer prices	General government outlays	General government receipts
	Billion US$ PPP[a] 2000	US$ PPP[a]		Annual average growth rate 1996-2001	2000	2000	2001	2001	Percentage of GDP, 2001	
Australia	507.6	26 495	81	3.8	69.1	6.6	4.4	3.8	33.3	33.4
Denmark	157.4	29 495	109	2.5	76.4	4.7	3.9	2.1	49.4	51.4
Netherlands	443.2	27 836	88	3.4	72.9	2.8	4.9	4.6	41.3	42.4
OECD	26 177.7[b]	24 746[b]	100	2.8	65.7	6.4	..	..	37.2	36.4

.. Not available.
a) PPP: Purchasing power parities.
b) Excluding the Czech Republic, Hungary, Poland and the Slovak Republic.
Source: OECD (2001b, 2002 and 2002a).

the Australian economy slowed down in late 2000 but rebounded in 2001, and GDP growth is projected to be 3.2% in 2002 (OECD, 2001b).

Strong economic growth has contributed to the higher employment rates and lowest unemployment rates since 1990. After a prolonged period of wage moderation and low inflation, annual wage growth and inflation rates were highest in the Netherlands in 2001 (OECD, 2002b). Wage growth and low labour productivity in the Netherlands have led to rapidly increasing unit labour costs: higher than all its main trade partners (OECD, 2001b). This is important given the intention of the government to use employers in financing leave and childcare benefits (Chapters 4 and 6).

2.2. Government intervention with a social purpose

General government outlays account for half of GDP in Denmark and one-third in Australia. Over the last five years trends in tax receipt related to GDP were fairly flat (OECD, 2001c), while public spending as a proportion of GDP declined (OECD, 2001d). Indeed, having been in deficit for most of the 1990s, government financial balances were in surplus at the turn of the millennium. Denmark and the Netherlands have accrued considerable public debts (about 50% of GDP) in the past, and without the resultant interest payments the financial public surplus in 2001 would have been about 3.5% of GDP in both countries (OECD, 2001b).

Since, the mid-1980s the decline of the ratio of public social spending to GDP in the Netherlands has been more pronounced than in Denmark, although since 1994 the public spending to GDP ratio has declined at similar rates in both countries (Chart 2.1). Dutch spending declined rapidly due to a reduction of generosity in disability spending, the mandatory privatisation of sickness benefits and a more pronounced decline in unemployment-related spending (OECD, 2001d). By 1998, public social expenditure amounted to 29.8% of GDP in Denmark, 24.5% in the Netherlands and 17.8% in Australia.

Public spending in Australia on income transfers to the working age population is about half of that in Denmark and the Chart 2.1 Netherlands (Table 2.2). This has two main reasons. First, entitlement to public benefits in Australia is generally subject to income testing, and benefit levels are generally below benefit

Chart 2.1. **Trends in total public social expenditure, 1980-99**
Percentage of GDP

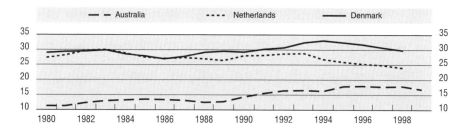

Source: OECD (2001d).

Table 2.2. **Public social expenditure by broad social policy area, 1998**
Percentage of GDP

	Health	Family cash benefits and services	Support for those on retirement[a]	Support for the working age population[b]	Total
Australia	6.0	2.6	5.3	3.9	17.8
Denmark	6.8	3.8	9.8	9.5	29.8
Netherlands	6.0	1.4	8.3	8.8	24.5

a) Old age and survivors cash benefits, and services to the elderly and disabled.
b) Disability, occupational injury, sickness, unemployment, labour market programmes, housing and other.
Source: OECD (2001d).

levels in Denmark and the Netherlands, which are more generally based on work-history and contributory records. Second, public cash transfers in Denmark and the Netherlands are taxed heavily: the ratio of tax to gross spending on cash transfers is close to 25% in Denmark and the Netherlands, while in Australia it is less than 3%. Accounting for the overall impact of the tax system on public spending (Adema, 2001), the differences in overall public spending are relatively limited. In 1997, public social effort *after tax* amounted to 22.9% of GDP at factor cost in Denmark compared to 18.2% for the Netherlands and 16.6% for Australia.

In view of the relative importance of public social spending, it is not surprising that private spending is least important in Denmark. At about 4-5% of GDP, private spending in the Netherlands and Australia is rather similar, and in both countries includes private social health benefits, employer-provided sick pay and pension benefits (accruing from occupational plans in the Netherlands and "superannuation" in Australia; see Adema, 2001).

The three countries have different approaches to the role of the state in assisting families with children. Australia spends about 2.2% of GDP on cash payments to families with children (not including specific benefits for lone-parent families), while Denmark and the Netherlands spend less than half of that. Public spending on childcare support (Chapter 3) is largest in Denmark at 2% of GDP while this is much lower in both Australia and the Netherlands. Public maternity/parental leave payments do not exist in Australia, while they amount to 0.2% of GDP in the Netherlands and 0.5% of GDP in Denmark (Chapter 4). Spending on general family support services (not including day care) is limited in all three countries under review (Table 2.3).

Table 2.3. **Public spending on child benefits, 2001**
Percentage of GDP

	Australia	Denmark	Netherlands
Family services (not including childcare)[a]	0.2	0.1	0.1
Family cash benefits[b]	2.2	1.0	0.7
Chilcare	0.3	2.1	0.2
Pay during leave	..	0.5	0.2
Total	2.7	3.7	1.2

a) 1998 figures.
b) Does not include benefit to low income families with or without children.
Source: Information provided by national authorities. OECD (2001d) and national authorities for spending a childcare and pay during leave.

2.3. Population characteristics

2.3.1. *Population size*

Australia is a vast country but its population at 19.2 million is only a little larger than the Netherlands with about 16 million inhabitants. Denmark's population is smallest at 5.3 million. The Netherlands has an extremely high population density, so that few people are very far from urban services, while Denmark has a moderate population density – with a mix of urban and rural. Australia's average population-density is low, but as it is a highly urbanised country, 90% of the total population lives in just 2.6% of the land area. This means that some part of the country have a much lower population density than the average suggests – resulting in serious challenges in terms of service provision.

2.3.2. *Ethnic diversity*

Denmark is the most homogenous in terms of ethnicity, with small populations of "New Danes". Immigrants and their descendants number just under 400 000 representing about 7.4% of the total population (mostly from Turkey, and former Yugoslavia). The Netherlands is more diverse with 18% of the population being of foreign origin. The largest ethnic communities are from Turkey, Morocco, the Netherlands Antilles, and Surinam. Australia also has a diverse population, with nearly a quarter being foreign or foreign born – of whom 39% come from non-English language countries. There is also a small but significant population of indigenous peoples (Aboriginal and Torres Strait Islanders), who represent about 2.1% of the population.

2.3.3. *Population growth and fertility patterns*

All three countries have experienced significant population growth since the 1950s, because of the natural increase, net immigration, increases in life expectancy, and reductions in infant mortality. Net migration to Australia and the Netherlands throughout the 1990s was 0.4% of the population per annum. Danish net migration was not that different during the first part of the 1990s, but there was a hike in net immigration (as in the Netherlands) during the second part of the 1990s because of successful asylum applicants from the former republic of Yugoslavia (OECD, 2000c).

Fertility patterns have changed significantly over the last 30 years because women *a)* have postponed the age at which they have their first child and *b)* have fewer children than in the past. The mean age for mothers having their first child has risen in each country from 23-24 in the early 1970s, to around 28-29 of age in 2000. The completed fertility rate (CFR) dropped most sharply in Australia, from three children for the 1930-cohort to just over two for mothers born in 1965. For this cohort the estimated CFR is lowest in the Netherlands at about 1.7 (Charts 2.2 and 2.3).

Chart 2.2. **Mean age of women at first birth, 1970-2000**

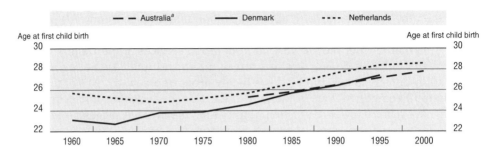

a) Australia: 1990 is a mid-point estimation between 1985 and 1995.
Source: Council of Europe (2001); ABS (2001).

Chart 2.3. **Evolution of completed and total fertility rates**

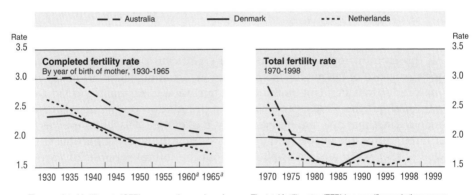

The completed fertility rate (CFR) measure the number of children that a cohort of women who have reached the end of their childbearing years had in the course of their reproductive life. The CFR is measured by cumulating age-specific fertility rates in a given cohort as they aged from 15 to 49 years.

The total fertility rates (TFR) in a specific year is the average number of children who would be born to a synthetic cohort of women whose age-specific birth rates were the same as those actually observed in the year in question.

a) Estimations.
Source: ABS (2001) ; and EUROSTAT, New Cronos database, Theme 3.

The different patterns in the completed fertility rate and the mean age of women at first childbirth underlie differences in the total fertility rate trends. The decline in total fertility rates was most pronounced in Australia and the Netherlands during the 1970s. Since 1985 total fertility rates remain largely the same in Australia and the Netherlands, but increased from about 1.5 to 1.8 in Denmark. In the Netherlands, there is a relatively high birth rate among younger women of the immigrant population (CBS, 2001). This is likely to be a temporary effect, however, as fertility rates among new migrants rapidly adjust to fertility behaviour of the existing population (OECD, 2000c).

In all, these patterns point to an ageing population, with expected smaller cohorts of children, and smaller working age populations. Chart 2.4 shows the effect of this on the age structure of the population in the three countries over the next 50 years. In the future a significantly greater share of the working age population will be 45 plus. At the same time the population of retired people will have grown substantially in all three countries, with the most significant growth being in the "oldest cohorts" of the population, which is likely to increase demand for health and long-term care services. These demographic trends also have consequential implications for the labour market: increasing the need to encourage a greater aggregate participation rate from people of working age, including those with dependent children.

2.3.4. *Children and households*

With the growth in the number of households, average household size in all three countries under review has fallen since the 1980s to 2.6 persons per household in Australia and just over 2 persons per household in Denmark and the Netherlands (Table 2.4). Over the last 20 years, the proportion of households without children has grown as more young people live longer on their own deferring family formation, while increased life expectancy contributed to the ageing population phenomenon (OECD, 2001e). Hence, there has been a significant decline in the proportion of households with children in all three countries over the last 20 years, and the decline (13 percentage points) was particularly pronounced in the Netherlands.

The proportion of lone-parent families in all households remained stable in Denmark and the Netherlands, and increased to just over 6% in Australia. Indeed, compared to families with children the proportion of lone-parent families increased in all three countries to about 15% in Denmark and the Netherlands, while by 2000 one in five families with children were lone-parent families in Australia.

Most children live with both their parents, although the likelihood of doing so decreases with the age of children.[1] In Australia by 1996 16% of children were raised in one-parent families, as against 12% in 1980. In Denmark in 1999, 75% of

37

Chart 2.4. **Total population by age group, 2000 and 2050**

In thousands

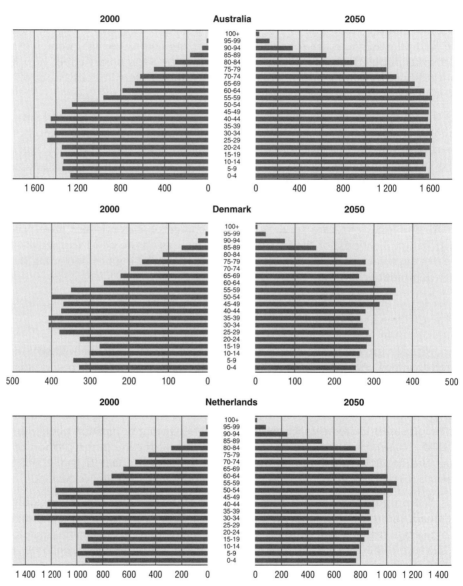

Note: Data for 2000 are mid-year estimates; data for 2050 are medium variant population projections.
Source: United Nations (2001).

© OECD 2002

Table 2.4.   **Trends in household size and composition,**[a] **1980-2000**

Percentages

	1980[b]	1985[c]	1990[c]	1995	2000
Australia					
Average number of persons per household	..	2.8	2.7	2.7	2.6
Share of families with children in all households	..	34.8	32.4	31.5	30.0
Share of one parent families in all households	..	4.8	4.8	5.8	6.3
Share of one parent families in families with children	12.2	13.7	14.8	18.5	20.9
Denmark					
Average number of persons per household	2.5	2.3	2.3	2.2	2.2
Share of families with children in all households	33.1	30.6	23.4	22.5	22.5
Share of one parent families in all households	4.5	5.2	4.2	4.2	4.1
Share of one parent families in families with children	18.9	20.4	18.0	18.6	18.3
Netherlands					
Average number of persons per household	2.8	2.6	2.5	2.4	2.3
Share of families with children in all households	49.3	45.4	41.6	38.2	36.2
Share of one parent families in all households	6.0	5.8	5.4	5.6	5.7
Share of one parent families in families with children	12.2	12.8	12.9	14.6	15.7

.. Data not available.
a) Because of differences in national definitions of households, a comparison of trends in household levels is more appropriate than a comparison of levels. The Australian data cover children aged 0-14, while the Dutch data cover all children living at home (including students over 18) as part of the household, which explains why the share of families with children in all households "appears" to be higher than in Australia. The Danish household definition counts all persons aged 18 as "his/her own family", even if they share dwellings with other students or live at home. Compared to the Netherlands this practice has a dampening effect on the number of families with children in Denmark, and *inter alia* an upward effect on the number of households without children and an upward effect on the total number of households (and a corresponding downward effect on average household size).
b) 1981 for the Netherlands.
c) 1986 and 1991 for Australia.
Source: Information supplied by national authorities and OECD (2002c).

children lived with both parents, down from 80% in 1980, and 15% lived in one-parent households, as against 11% in 1980.

Lone-parent families and family dissolution

Most lone-parent families result from family dissolution. Although definitional aspects hamper cross-country comparisons (Australia data concern legal separation of couples), the incidence of divorce seems higher in Australia than in the other two countries (Chart 2.5). The average duration of marriage in Australia at the time of divorce is around four years shorter (although this is also influenced by the difference between legal separations and divorce). In any case, trends in family dissolution differ: since 1980, divorce rates declined in Denmark while they increased in both Australia and the Netherlands, underlying the upward trend in the incidence of lone-parent families in these two countries.

Chart 2.5. **Divorce rates and mean duration of marriage**

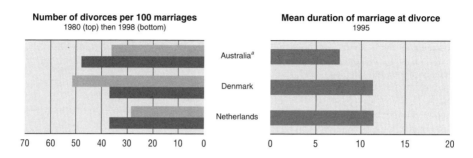

Number of divorces per 100 marriages
1980 (top) then 1998 (bottom)

Mean duration of marriage at divorce
1995

a)   Australia: median duration between marriage and final separation.
Source: ABS (2000 and 2001a); and EUROSTAT, New Cronos database, Theme 3.

The incidence of teenage motherhood is not considered a major problem in the three countries under review. In Australia, the teenage birth rate is 17 teenage birth per 1 000 women giving birth (ABS, 2001). Denmark and the Netherlands have teenage birth rates that are the lowest in the EU at 7 and 10 teenage births per 1 000 women giving birth, respectively. However, once teenage motherhood occurs in the Netherlands, the poverty risk is 80%, compared to 23% in Denmark (Berthoud and Robson, 2001), and being born to a teenage mother is found to increase the risk of impeding child development (Christoffersen, 2000). As shown below, lone-parent families have a high poverty risk compared to other families with children. But the situation faced by lone parents who have been married is likely to be better than for lone parents that have never married: they are likely to be older and have had more labour market experience. They are also more likely to have an ex-partner who has more than a minimum income, which usually increases the amount of child support they should receive.

2.3.5. Work and family decisions

Work and family decisions are made in the context of a broad set of interacting factors including opportunities and preferences, family formation, parenthood, caring and intergenerational care arrangements, education, and work and earning opportunities later in life, and retirement prospects (Nederlandse Gezinsraad, 2001). This is not a review of, for example, health and elderly care policies, education or retirement policies, but clearly such policies affect opportunities that influence "current" work and family decisions. Similarly, employment, gender equity, childcare and income policies impinge on the existing work and family life balance and thus affect both work and family life decisions, including family formation, parenthood, family dissolution.

In that context the broad story in terms of family developments is less positive (see above). Increasingly family formation is being deferred, if not postponed indefinitely until parents have received more education and when one or both members of a couple are more securely established in their careers. Some people may not have the number of children they would otherwise prefer, with implications for the age structure of the population, discussed above. Furthermore, family breakdown is more common than previously. Though it is possible to put a positive gloss on such statistics, as previously financial dependence and societal pressure led to couples remaining together despite unhappiness in the relationship, family dissolution often causes suffering. It would be surprising were such statistics entirely unrelated to the stresses of balancing work and family life.

The decline in fertility has caused concern, particularly in Australia, and has also been linked to insufficient support for families; work and social environments that do not foster gender equitable solutions in paid and unpaid work, and the absence of almost universal subsidised childcare, and income support during child-related leave (McDonald, 2000; Probert, 2001). Among the three countries under review Denmark has the most comprehensive leave and childcare system (Chapters 3 and 4). Since 1980, coverage of childcare of 0-2-years-olds has grown from 40 to 80%, while child-related leave was extended from 14 weeks to 20 weeks in 1984, and 24 weeks in 1985. Ever since, the total fertility rate has gone up, but only by 0.3 percentage points. Some nevertheless claim that this supports the notion that extensive family-friendly benefits support fertility (Knudsen, 1999). More strikingly, the Australian and Dutch total fertility rates do not show an increase during the 1990s, a period of economic growth which normally has a cyclically positive effect on fertility rates (Chart 2.6).

OECD (1999) suggested that child-rearing and paid work may be complementary, rather than alternative activities. Chart 2.6 shows how the two have varied over the past decades. In the period after 1985, Danish activity rates oscillate around 75 to 80%, the share of female full-time employment increases and so does the fertility rate. Since 1985, total fertility rates remain largely the same in Australia and the Netherlands as Australia experienced growth in both female full-time and part-time employment, which in the Netherlands was mainly part-time. This is not really evidence in favour of the hypothesis – many other changes have taken place in society over this period which might have influenced decisions about childbirth – but it does suggest that there is no intrinsic contradiction between women having children and achieving some of the labour market goals as well.

2.4. Labour market outcomes

Key labour market indicators show a general improvement of labour market conditions during the 1990s in Australia, Denmark and, especially the Netherlands,

41

Chart 2.6. **Female activity rates, share of female part-time employment and total fertility rate, 1970-2000**

Percentages

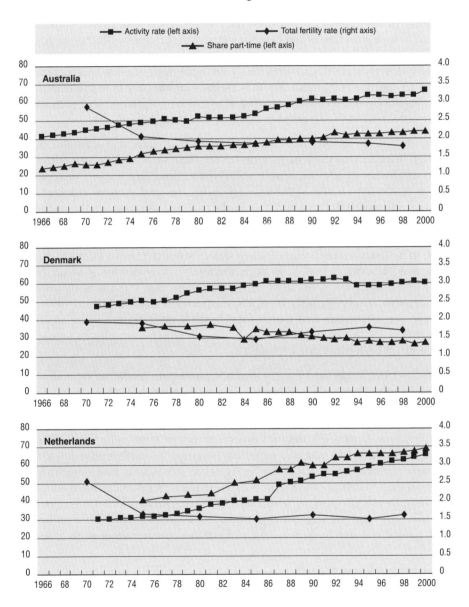

Source: ABS (2001) ; EUROSTAT, New Cronos Database, Theme 3; OECD (1993 and 2002d).

where unemployment fell by 5 percentage points and the employment rate increased by almost 12 percentage points (Table 2.5). By 2000, employment rates and activity rates in all three countries were above the OECD average, while unemployment rates were equal to or below the OECD average. Employment growth was predominantly concentrated in the services sector (OECD, 2000a), which facilitated an increase in the prevalence of female part-time work in both Australia and the Netherlands. The proportion of public sector employment in dependent employment (not including self-employment) is highest in Denmark where it accounts for one-third of employment: about twice as high as the share of public sector employment in Australia and the Netherlands.[2]

Table 2.5. **Key labour market indicators, 1990 and 2000**
Percentages

	Australia		Denmark		Netherlands		OECD	
	1990	2000	1990	2000	1990	2000	1990	2000
Activity rates (labour force over population 15-64)								
Men and women	73.0	73.8	82.4	80.0	66.2	74.9	69.5	70.1
Men	84.4	82.0	87.1	84.0	79.7	83.9	82.8	81.1
Women	61.5	65.5	77.6	75.9	52.4	65.7	57.3	61.3
Employment rate								
Men and women	67.9	69.1	75.4	76.4	61.1	72.9	65.2	63.6
Men	78.5	76.6	80.1	80.7	75.2	82.1	78.2	76.3
Women	57.1	61.6	70.6	72.1	46.7	63.4	53.3	57.1
Share of employment in:								
Industry and agriculture	31.7	26.7	33.1	30.2	30.6	25.1	..	..
Services	68.2	73.3	66.3	69.5	68.0	70.2	..	..
Public employment	19.1	16.4	32.6	32.9	15.0	12.8	..	..
Share part-time employment								
Men and women	22.6	26.2	19.2	15.7	28.2	32.1	14.3	15.3
Men	11.3	14.8	10.2	8.9	13.4	13.4	6.6	7.6
Women	38.5	40.7	29.6	23.5	52.5	57.2	25.0	25.7
Unemployment rate								
Men and women	7.0	6.3	8.5	4.5	7.7	2.7	6.0	6.3
Men	6.9	6.6	8.0	4.0	5.7	2.2	5.4	5.8
Women	7.2	5.9	9.0	5.0	10.9	3.5	8.1	7.8
Long-term unemployment (percentage of total unemployment)								
Men and women	21.6	27.9	29.9	20.0	49.3	32.7	30.9	31.4
Men	24.4	30.6	26.3	20.1	55.2	31.7	29.7	30.1
Women	17.8	24.0	32.0	20.0	44.6	33.4	32.3	33.0
Spending on active labour market programmes (percentage of GDP)	0.3	0.5	1.1	1.5	1.1	1.6	..	..

.. Data not available.
Source: OECD (2001f).

Part-time employment grew in Australia and the Netherlands, but fell in Denmark over the 1990s. Changing female labour force behaviour in both Australia and the Netherlands led to increased female labour force participation and a reduction in gender employment gaps. In Australia, gender gaps in employment and labour force participation were also reduced as male participation and employment rates declined. On the other hand, both male and female employment and activity rates increased in the Netherlands, but the rise in female employment rates was remarkable and not matched in other OECD countries: 17 percentage points in ten years.

2.4.1. *Changes in female labour force pattern and behaviour during the life course*

Most of the movement in labour market outcomes during the 1980s and 1990s is related to changes in female labour market behaviour, particularly in Australia and the Netherlands. In Denmark, employment rates for Danish female workers have been oscillating around 70% since the mid-1970s (female activity rates were already 47% in 1950 and 54% in 1970 (Knudsen, 1999). Employment rates for female prime age workers in Denmark have been persistently over 80% since the beginning of the 1980s (Chart 2.7). Employment rates of prime age female workers in Australia and the Netherlands have only recently reached about 70%. The increase of employment among female prime age workers in the Netherlands was strongest throughout the 1990s, whereas employment growth among female workers in Australia was most pronounced during the 1980s.

Age-related employment profiles show that employment rates of prime age male workers are above 80% in all three countries (Chart 2.8). Apparently, the presence of dependent children has little effect on the male labour force status. Available cohort data illustrate the changes in female employment over the life course. Although employment rates of younger female Danish workers are not low when compared internationally, they are when compared to female workers who are about 40 years of age. Younger Danish women are increasingly pursuing tertiary education (see below), and it thus appears that female employment rates in Denmark are highest when children are about 10-15 years of age. Dutch employment rates peak just before the average age around which women in the Netherlands have their first child (almost 29 years of age). By contrast, employment rates of Australian women who are likely to care for young children (30-34) are lower than for younger workers or women at age 40-44.

Available cohort data also illustrate that employment rates of Danish women have not changed dramatically over the last few decades (Chart 2.8) while in Australia and especially the Netherlands successive cohorts (after 1946-1950) generally have higher employment rates than their predecessors at the same age.

Changes in Australian female labour force behaviour have been compiled over a wide range of cohorts (Chart 2.9, and Young, 1990). On average women in older

Chart 2.7. **Female employment rate, by age group, 1983-2000**
Percentages

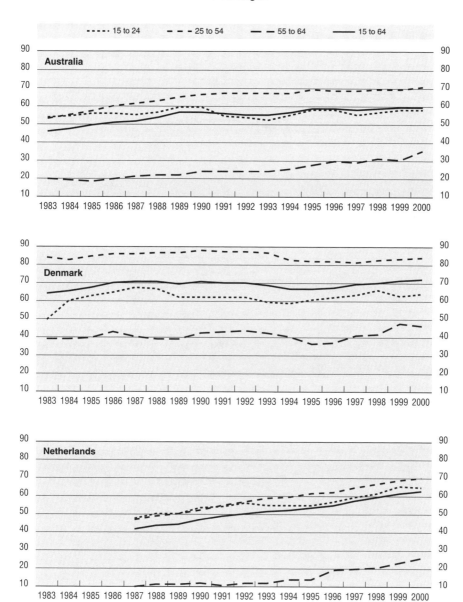

Chart 2.8. **Age-related employment profile of women and men**
Cross-cohort comparisons of employment rates by age*a*

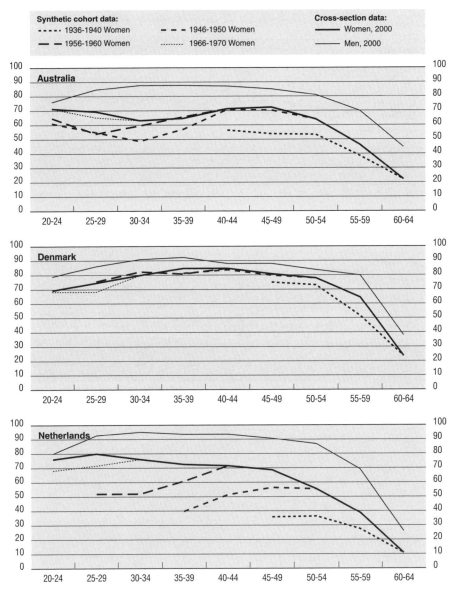

a) The chart combines cross-sectional data by age and gender for the year 2000 with "synthetic cohort" data for women belonging to selected age cohorts.

Source: OECD (2002d).

Chart 2.9. **Age-specific labour force participation rates of females in Australia**
Cohort experience

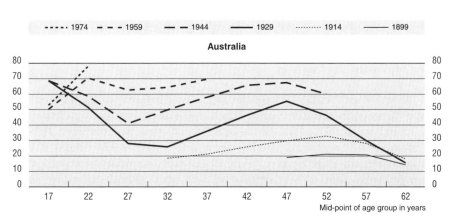

Source: Young (1990).

cohorts left school at an earlier age, and were also relatively young at the arrival of their first child than at present (nowadays 28 years). Women in older cohorts were thus more likely to be in low-paid jobs and had a limited chance to grow attached to a career path than women in more recent cohorts. These reasons contribute to lower female participation rates for older cohorts compared to later cohorts.

Notwithstanding the different levels and different degrees of variation, female Australian labour force participation still follows an M-shaped pattern over the life course. Participation rates increase with age until the age of marriage or the age at which the first child is born, upon which participation rates decline for the duration of the childrearing years. When the children have grown into adolescents, mothers return to the labour market to start to leave again in their early 50s, often initiated by the need to care for older family members (DFACS/DEWR, 2002). Rather than leaving at the time of marriage, later cohorts have tended to remain in paid work until the birth of the first child, while the tendency to leave on the birth of the first child has decreased. Hence, the dips in the Australian M-curve have become less pronounced.

2.4.2. The nature of employment and gender differences

Facilitated by a growth in the service sector, employer demand for flexible labour has led to a growth of forms of employment of limited duration, either in terms of contract duration, hours worked per week or both. Employers may prefer to use flexible employment arrangements to reduce labour costs, using labour when it is most needed, limiting labour hoarding and to reduce overall employment adjustment costs. On the other hand, flexible labour supply is fed, in part, by households' desire to work at hours that are compatible with caring obligations. Although overall gender employment gaps have narrowed, there are striking differences in the nature of the employment relationships that men and women have.

Full-time employment and long hours

In Denmark with its limited gender gap in employment rates, there is considerable difference in the number of hours that males and females usually work (Chart 2.10). Almost 95% of the prime age Danish male workers work 35 hours or more per week (the standard working week in Denmark is 37.5 hours). Australian prime age males work the longest hours: 70% of men in employment work 40 hours or more per week (and 25% of employed men work 50 hours or more; see ABS, 2001b), compared to 52% in the Netherlands and 42% in Denmark.

Of all prime-age female workers (25-54) 65% works 35 hours or more per week in Denmark, compared to 55% on Australia and only 30% in the Netherlands. But when Australian women work on a full-time basis, they work longer hours than in Denmark and the Netherlands: 35% of Australian women work 40 hours or more compared to 15% in the other two countries.

Part-time employment

Part-time employment, defined as less than 30 hours per week is sometimes an important tool for parents to combine their work and care obligations. Part-time employment predominantly concerns women: in 2001, women's share in part-time employment was about 69% in Australia and Denmark, and over 76% in the Netherlands (OECD, 2001f). Among female workers of all ages, part-time employment gained popularity in both Australia and the Netherlands during the 1980s and 1990s, and by 2000, 40% of female Australian workers and 55% of Dutch female workers were in part-time employment (Chart 2.11).[3] Denmark defies the international trend, and the incidence of female part-time employment actually fell from over 36% in 1983 to about 23% in 2000.[4]

Part-time employment among women of all ages has increased in Australia and the Netherlands. This seems to be concentrated at younger ages, when work is often combined with schooling. The incidence of part-time employment among female workers aged 25-54 seems relatively stable in these two countries, and has fallen sharply in Denmark (Chart 2.11). Part-time employment does *not* appear to be increasing in prevalence among women of childrearing age in the three countries under review.

Chart 2.10. **Incidence of hours worked**^{a} **among prime-age workers**
Percentages

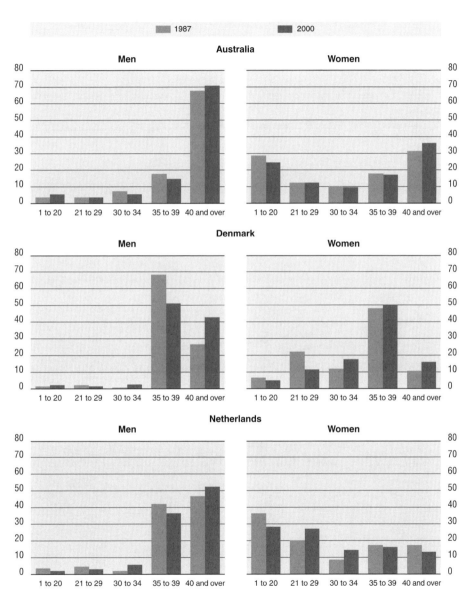

a) Usual weekly hours worked in Denmark and the Netherlands; actual hours in Australia.
Source: OECD database on the distribution of employed persons by usual weekly hour bands.

Chart 2.11. **Incidence of female part-time employment, all ages and 25-54, 1983-2000**

Percentage of total employment

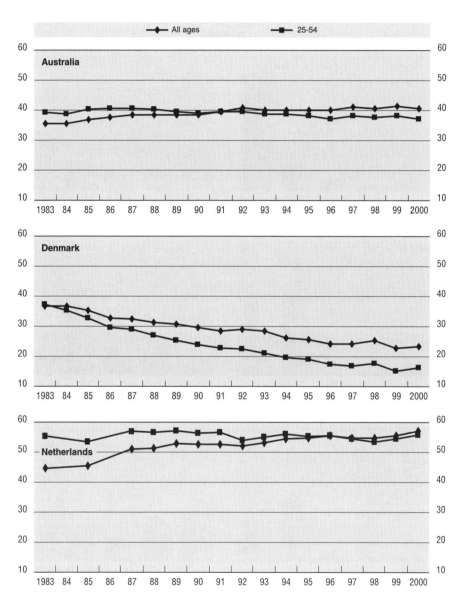

Source: OECD database on full-time/part-time employment.

Temporary work

Temporary work is another form of flexible labour that may help individuals and households to combine work with other activities. Temporary work includes various types of employment including working under a fixed-term contract, seasonal and casual work, and working under contract for a temporary work agency. Fixed, short-term labour contracts may suit workers when they are in education or transition to full labour market retirement. Parents with children may choose this form of employment, particularly as it facilitates supplementing household income when time allows it. On the other hand, this form of employment will be less conducive to parents when it concerns the main or only breadwinner in a family with children, as it raises concerns on job and income security and often attracts lower hourly wages than permanent employment. Over the years, temporary employment has grown slightly and now covers 16% of female employees in the Netherlands, while about 11% of female employees in Denmark work on a temporary basis (Table 2.6). Temporary employment in Australia (if defined in a similar way to that used in other countries) is no larger than 5%.

Casual work

One of the striking features of the Australian labour market is its high proportion, 27% in 2000, of "casual" employees (employees without paid holiday and sick-pay entitlements, which are "loaded", cashed into the hourly wage). In 2000, women accounted for 55% of casual employment, and two-thirds of part-time

Table 2.6. **Share of temporary employment in dependent employment**

Percentages

	1990	2000
Australia		
Men and women	..	4.7[a]
Denmark		
Men and women	10.8	10.2
Men	10.6	8.7
Women	11.0	11.7
Netherlands		
Men and women	7.6	13.8
Men	6.1	11.4
Women	10.2	16.9

a) 1998.

Source: OECD (2002d); Australia: Secretariat estimate based on information provided by the Australian Bureau of Statistics.

casual employment (ABS, 2001c). A considerable share of new jobs created during the 1990s concerned "casual" employment, while the number of full-time permanent jobs is approximately the same in 2000 compared to 1990. Casual employees often work for the same employer for a considerable period of time: just over half of casual employees worked for the same employer for over 12 months and 13% were with their employer for more than five years (ABS, 2000a).

Concentration of female employment in industrial sectors

Female employment is concentrated in certain sectors, in the three countries under review. In particular, the personal services (hotels, restaurants, recreation, domestic services) and social services (government, health and education) sectors have a high share of female employment. The financial and insurance sector (under producer services) and retail trade (under distributive services) also have high shares of female employment: ranging from 45 to 55% across countries (Table 2.7). Mining, construction, agriculture, manufacturing, electricity, gas and water supply are highly male dominated in terms of employment. Not surprisingly, occupational concentration is not unrelated to the sectoral patterns. Females are the predominant employees among service workers and clerks, but only make up 20% of the plant and machine operators.

Educational attainment

Across countries employment rates for both sexes improve with level of educational attainment. Gender employment gaps are smallest for workers with tertiary education (Table 2.8 and Box 2.1). The overall increase in female employment in the Netherlands mainly concerned medium to high-skilled female workers whose employment rates are almost on par with their Danish counterparts. By contrast, the employment rates of low-skilled female workers in the Netherlands are well below those in Australia and Denmark. More than in the other countries, single earnership in the Netherlands is strongly related to educational attainment. More than half of the married female workers with relatively low education attainment levels live in single earner households, while this is only 10% for the high-skilled female workers (Keuzenkamp *et al.*, 2000).

2.4.3. Mothers in employment

While Danish employment rates have been around 70% over the last 10-15 years, female employment rates in Australia and the Netherlands have been increasing rapidly to just over 60%, with a large part of employment growth being of a part-time nature (Box 2.2). Employment rates for mothers with very young children in Australia increased from 29% in 1985 to 45% in 2000 (see annex at the

Table 2.7. **Female employment shares by sector, 1998**

Percentages

	Total	Agriculture, hunting and forestry	Mining and quarrying	Manufac- turing	Electricity, gas and water supply	Construc- tion	Producer services[a]	of which sub-sector Financial services	Distributive services[a]	of which sub- sector Retail trade	Personal services[a]	Social services[a]
Australia	43.4	31.0	9.6	26.0	17.0	13.6	46.5	57.0	42.6	55.9	47.7	64.8
Denmark	46.1	22.2	..	31.3	20.6	9.5	44.7	50.6	36.5	46.4	58.6	70.9
Netherlands	41.1	28.2	14.5	22.0	14.8	7.9	40.8	45.0	37.9	52.3	56.9	59.9
OECD[b]	42.7	29.3	13.0	29.5	17.7	7.9	45.3	51.4	39.8	51.8	56.8	63.2

.. Not available.

a) The sector **Producer services** includes the following sub-sectors: Business and professional, Financial services, Insurance services and Real estate; **Distributive services**: Retail trade, Wholesale trade, Transportation and Communication; **Personal services**: Hotels and restaurants, Recreation and amusement, Domestic services, Other personal services; and the **Social services** sector includes: Government proper, Health services, Education and Miscellaneous.

b) Average of 24 OECD countries: Australia, Austria, Belgium, Canada, the Czech Republic, Denmark, Finland, France, Germany, Greece, Hungary, Ireland, Italy, Luxembourg, Mexico, the Netherlands, New Zealand, Norway, Portugal, Spain, Sweden, Switzerland, the United Kingdom and the United States.

Source: OECD (2002d).

Table 2.8. **Employment rates by level of educational attainment and gender, 1999**

Percentages

	Both sexes			Men			Women		
	Less than upper secondary education	Upper secondary education	Tertiary education	Less than upper secondary education	Upper secondary education	Tertiary education	Less than upper secondary education	Upper secondary education	Tertiary education
Australia	59.1	76.2	82.0	72.1	84.0	88.7	49.9	62.9	75.7
Denmark	61.7	80.7	87.9	69.5	84.8	90.5	55.6	75.8	85.3
Netherlands	56.8	78.3	87.2	75.4	86.6	90.8	41.8	69.2	82.5
OECD[a]	64.0	77.0	85.1	79.6	86.1	91.2	50.8	67.3	78.4

a) Average of 29 OECD countries ; excludes the Slovak Republic only

Source: OECD (2001h).

Box 2.1.   **Educational attainment and literacy of the population**

Denmark appears to have the most educated population of the three countries with about 80% of the working-age population having at least secondary education, compared to 65% in the Netherlands and 58% in Australia (see table
below). Gender gaps in educational attainment for the overall working age population exist in all three countries, but are strongly related to gender differentials
among the older population. Educational attainment, in terms of formal qualifications, has increased over time, with both men and women aged over 55 having a
lower rate of tertiary qualification or at least secondary education than subsequent generations. Nevertheless, gender gaps persist for younger age groups in
the population with at least secondary education in Australia (see table below).
In Denmark, there is no longer a gender gap in educational attainment for those
younger than 45, while in the Netherlands educational attainment is similar
across the genders for people below 35 years of age.

Table Box 2.1.   **Population with at least secondary education
and tertiary education by age group and gender, 1999[a]**

Percentages

		25-64	25-34	34-44	45-54	55-64
				At least secondary		
Australia	Male	65	70	66	64	54
	Female	50	61	52	46	33
				At least tertiary		
	Male	26	26	27	28	19
	Female	27	32	31	27	15
				At least secondary		
Denmark	Male	83	88	80	84	75
	Female	76	87	79	74	58
				At least tertiary		
	Male	26	28	25	28	21
	Female	27	29	33	26	17
				At least secondary		
Netherlands[a]	Male	69	73	70	68	61
	Female	60	75	65	51	39
				At least tertiary		
	Male	27	28	29	29	22
	Female	21	27	23	18	12

a)   1998 for the Netherlands.
Source: OECD (2000b and 2001h).

Box 2.1. **Educational attainment and literacy of the population** (*cont.*)

Tertiary education rates are similar for the working age population in the three countries concerned except for female tertiary education rates in the Netherlands, although the younger generation of Dutch women is rapidly catching up. In Denmark and Australia, the rate of female tertiary qualification is actually above the male tertiary education rate for those aged under 45: particularly in Australia women with at least secondary education are more likely to pursue tertiary education than men. In all, gender gaps in education are closing in all three countries, while in terms of tertiary education successive cohorts of women in Australia and Denmark have achieved better educational attainment than men.

Literacy scores generated by the International Adult Literacy Survey (IALS) broadly confirm the view of skills and competencies of adult populations given by educational attainment levels for the three countries under review (OECD/ Statistics Canada, 2000). Literacy scores are highest in Denmark where at least 68% of the population has at least a moderate level of literacy), closely followed by the Netherlands (64%) while Australian literacy scores are somewhat lower at 55% (OECD, 2001e). As with educational attainment, gender gaps exist for the whole working age population, but are narrowing as literacy scores are highest among the younger age groups.

end of Chapter 2). Over the same period employment rates of mothers with children aged 3-6 increased from 47 to 63%. Since 1989, employment rates for mothers in the Netherlands with a child not yet 6 years of age doubled to 60% in 1999 (OECD, 2001f). In all three countries employment rates of all mothers with children (0-16) are somewhat above employment rates for all women of working age, but that merely reflects the relatively low participation rates of older women in all three countries.

Mothers in Denmark are most likely to be in full-time employment regardless of the age of the child (Table 2.9). In Australia 59% of all mothers with children works part-time, and the predominance of part-time employment in the Netherlands is even higher: the incidence of part-time employment is 85% and 90% for mothers with one and two children, compared to 53% for women without children (OECD, 2002d).

Among the Australian mothers with children aged 0-3 only one-third works full-time, while this is 40% amongst mothers with children aged 3-6.[5] It thus appears that maternal employment rates in Australia change with the age of the

Box 2.2. **Attitudes to mothers being in paid work**

The extent to which traditional gender roles persist, with women withdrawing from employment in order to care for children depends not only on the availability of feasible alternatives, but also on cultural attitudes. However, it is difficult to be precise on the role such attitudes play in driving outcomes in any one country. The International Social Survey Programme in 1994/95 includes a survey "Family and Gender Changing Roles II", covering over 20 countries, including the Netherlands and Australia (an earlier ISSP survey, conducted in 1988, covered the Netherlands, enabling changes in attitudes to be viewed over time). Although critical of the ISSP-methodology, Probert and Murphy (2001) also find that "a majority of Australians hold the view that young children should be cared for by their parents or grandparents".

Concerns exist in all countries about the effects on children of women being in the workforce. The 1994 survey showed that the Dutch were less concerned than the Australians about the ability of working mothers to establish a secure relationship with their children: 70% (up from 55% in 1988) as against 53% saw that a working mother could establish as secure a relationship with their child as a non-working mother. At the same time more Dutch people were of the view that "a pre-school child is likely to suffer if his or her mother works" than disagreed with this, but at 44%, less likely to agree with the statement than Australians (at 50%). When asked whether women with children under school age should work or not, only 4% of Australians thought that mothers should be in full-time employment, while 31% favoured part-time employment: two-thirds of Australians felt that mothers with young children should be at home in 1994/95. By comparison, 20% of the Dutch population favours full-time employment for women with young children, while female part-time work and staying at home score a response-rate of 40% each (Evans, 2000).

In Denmark, the appropriateness of women being in work with young children being in childcare was a contested issue in the 1950s (Borchorst, 1993), but most mothers are now in full-time employment. However, when Danish mothers are asked about the desirability of parental labour force attachment in families with children below 7 years of age, 80% of mothers indicates a preference for part-time work and part-time day care. Half of these mothers respond that fathers should work full-time, while the other half indicates a preference for the dual part-time earner model (Christensen, 2000). The actual work patterns of Danish mothers with young children do not match their preferences, as expressed in this survey.

These responses for Australia and the Netherlands suggest that in both countries a significant proportion of the population are opposed to mothers of young children being in work, with some indications that younger people have more liberal attitudes than older people.

Nevertheless, interpreting such survey results in terms of gender attitudes is difficult, in that they to a large extent generate a response conditioned by the circumstances, rather than underlying preferences. This issue has been explored by

---

Box 2.2.   **Attitudes to mothers being in paid work** (*cont.*)

trying to uncover preferences by considering employment behaviour of immigrants from different countries into one common labour market: the United States (Antecol, 2000). After controlling for exogenous variables (*e.g.* time of residency in the US) and other variables as educational attainment, the presence of children and their age, it was assumed than any underlying gender employment gap differences among immigrants reflect underlying preferences. It turned out that gender employment gaps in the US among immigrants from Australia, Denmark and the Netherlands are similar (ranging from 25.7 among Dutch immigrants to 28.5 among Danish immigrants), whereas gender employment gaps in the countries of origin are very different. Emigrants may not be typical of a country's population and this result does not invalidate the responses to attitudinal surveys, but it does show that they should be interpreted in their context.

---

youngest child in Australia. Indeed, evidence for Australia shows the importance of small changes in the age of the youngest child on maternal employment rates which in 1996 were about 25% for mothers with a child not yet one year of age, and 50% for mothers with a child aged 1-2 (McDonald, 1999). For women in couple relationships with two children, 22% of those with one infant worked at least one hour and this increased to 48% if the youngest child was 1-2 years. It appears that the age of children plays a major role in determining the nature of maternal employment in Australia.

Dropping out of the labour force around childbirth

Table 2.9 clearly shows that only a limited number of Danish mothers exit the labour force upon childbirth: employment rates for mothers with very young children in Denmark are only slightly below those of mothers with older children. Most Danish mothers are in full-time employment, but the incidence of part-time employment increases with the age of the child. In Australia, the maternal employment rates of mothers with the youngest child aged 0-3 are almost 20% below of mothers with the youngest child aged 3-6 (see below). This shows that a significant proportion of women leave the Australian labour force upon childbirth.

In the beginning of the 1980s, two out of three mothers stopped working upon childbirth in the Netherlands, and by the end of the 1990s this had reduced to one in four mothers (CBS, 2002). Available evidence for the Netherlands suggests that low-skilled mothers spent on average 13 months at home upon childbirth (Gustaffson *et al.*, 2002), and that these mothers are the most likely to be in single earner families.

Table 2.9. **Employment rates of women and mothers by age of the youngest child**

		Women[a]				Mothers with youngest child aged 0-16				Mothers with youngest child aged 0-3				Mothers with youngest child aged 3-6				Women 15-64
		All	Full-time	Part-time	On maternity leave	All	Full-time	Part-time	On maternity leave	All	Full-time	Part-time	On maternity leave	All	Full-time	Part-time	On maternity leave	All (from LFS national)
Australia	1980	41.8	27.0	14.8	..	44.3	19.0	25.3	..	29.0	11.1	17.9	..	47.8	21.3	26.5	..	48.0
	1985	42.5	26.8	15.6	..	54.5	22.8	31.6	..	42.4	14.4	27.9	..	62.8	26.4	36.3	..	49.4
	1990	48.8	29.1	19.7	..	56.0	23.5	32.5	..	44.7	15.8	28.9	..	64.1	26.1	37.9	..	57.1
	1995	50.0	28.5	21.5	..	56.7	22.8	33.6	0.4	45.0	15.0	30.0	..	63.5	25.1	38.4	..	58.9
	2000	51.6	28.8	22.6	0.2													62.8
Denmark	1985	68.3	38.3	30.0	..	..	..	..	..	..	..	..	..	..	..	..	..	68.3
	1990	71.6	44.1	27.5	..	..	..	..	..	..	..	..	..	..	..	..	..	71.6
	1995	67.1	43.3	23.8	..	..	..	..	..	..	..	..	..	..	..	..	..	67.2
	1999	71.8	47.5	24.3	..	76.5	65.4	4.7	6.4	71.4	49.0	2.4	20.0	77.8	72.2	4.2	1.4	72.0
Netherlands	1985	35.3	17.1	18.2	..	..	..	..	..	..	..	..	..	..	..	..	..	35.7
	1990	46.4	18.8	27.6	..	..	..	..	..	..	..	..	..	..	..	..	..	46.6
	1995	54.1	18.3	35.7	..	..	..	..	..	..	..	..	..	..	..	..	..	54.1
	1999	61.8	20.1	41.7	..	..	..	..	..	..	..	..	..	..	..	..	..	61.8

.. Data not available.

a) As national sources are used, results are slightly different from those reported in the OECD *Labour Force Statistics* (OCDE, 2001g). Australia: data for women and mothers with youngest child aged 0-16 are based on "person data". They are not directly comparable to data for mothers with youngest child aged 0-3 and 3-6 which are based on families data. Information for Denmark are derived from the Danish law model rather than from labour force statistics.

Source: Information provided by national authorities.

Mothers with medium levels of educational attainment are likely to work part-time, and mothers are very likely to remain in part-time employment throughout childhood. Highly-skilled female workers are the most likely to be in full-time employment in the Netherlands (Keuzenkamp *et al.*, 2000).

Comprehensive information on the intensity with which parental leave is being used in Australia is not available. A recent survey among workers in New South Wales, reports that 17.5% of female workers had less than 4 weeks of unpaid leave around childbirth, while 5% of female workers resigned because of the absence of (paid) maternity leave. Most women using parental leave thus do so for at least 4 weeks, but it is estimated that about 50% of the Australian female workers in employment during pregnancy do not return to employment within 18 months (Buchanan and Thorntwaite, 2001). In all three countries low-skilled female workers are most likely to withdraw from the labour market in the aftermath of childbirth.

Childcare and child-related leave

Maternal employment rates are, of course, affected by the prevalence of childcare facilities and leave arrangements. Of the three countries under review, participation in formal childcare for children aged 0-4 was highest in Denmark at 74% of all children in this age group (Table 2.10). Despite a recent increase (Box 2.3), Australia and the Netherlands have much lower participation rates in childcare for young children (22% and 17% respectively). In both these countries parents with young children make greater use of informal care arrangements, and public spending on childcare is relatively limited (Chapter 3).

Participation rates for pre-school children are high in all three countries, but highest in the Netherlands, at 98% or more, mainly because of school based

Table 2.10.   **Basic indicators on childcare and child-related leave, 2001**

	Australia	Denmark	Netherlands
Child participation rate in formal child care (0-3)[a]	31.0	64.0	17.0
Pre-school age participation rate[b]	66.0	91.0	98.0
Public spending on child care (per cent of GDP)	0.3	2.1	0.2
Maximum duration of leave around childbirth (months)	12.0[c]	12.0	4 + 6 months part-time[c]
Public spending on pay during leave (per cent of GDP)	..	0.5	0.2

a) Age 6 months to 2 for Denmark.
b) Pre-school age participation: for Australia the figures are for ages 3 and 4; for Denmark, 3-5; and for the Netherlands, 4 and 5.
c) 12 months parental leave in Australia and 6 months part-time parental leave in the Netherlands are generally unpaid.
Source: ABS (2000b) and national authorities.

Box 2.3. **Childcare and female labour supply**

In 1970, the proportion of 0 to 3-year-olds in formal childcare in Denmark was about 20% with female labour force participation rates of about 55%, and an incidence of female part-time employment around 35-40%. At present female labour force participation rates in Australia and the Netherlands are in-between 65 and 70%; the incidence of female part-time employment is 40% in Australia and close to 60% in the Netherlands, with childcare coverage of very young children at about 17-22%, often on a part-time basis. It thus appears that the Dutch and particularly the Australian female labour market situation are not dissimilar from the Danish one in 1970. The increase in Danish female employment rates before 1970, and the increase in female employment in Australia and the Netherlands since 1970 were established with the use of informal care arrangements, as it largely preceded the increase in formal care capacity (Chapter 3).

Chart Box 2.3. **Share of children enrolled in day care, Denmark**

Source: Danish Center for Demographic Research (1999).

Since 1970, Denmark expanded coverage of formal childcare for very young children (0 to 3) from 20 to about 70% (see chart above). This capacity expansion has facilitated an increase of the female labour force participation rates of about 20 percentage points, while a large share of female part-time employment became full-time. As female participation rates already exceed 65% in both Australia and the Netherlands, the employment gains of further increasing childcare capacity in these two countries should not be overestimated, although it is likely to contribute to a shift from part-time to full-time employment for female workers.

pre-school classes (Chapter 3). The use of full-time childcare facilities clearly con-tributes to the high full-time participation rates in Denmark. Use of childcare facili-ties in Australia and the Netherlands is more often on a part-time basis, and this also reflects on the nature of female employment in these two countries. Never-theless, while participation in pre-school is very high in the Netherlands as from the age of 4, mothers often remain in part-time employment.

In comparing maternal employment rates across countries, it should be rea-lised that mothers on child-related leave (Chapter 4) are counted as employed, whether they are in work or not. This is particularly important when comparing employment rates of mothers with very young children. Child-related leave bene-fits in Denmark are more generous than in Australia where maternity leave is often not paid, or the Netherlands where duration is considerably shorter (Table 2.10). Hence, the use of maternity/parental leave in Denmark is much higher than in the other two countries. Table 2.9 above showed that the employment rate of Danish mothers with very young children is 71%, but more than a quarter of these mothers are on paid leave. The proportion of Australian mothers with young children in employment who are on leave is very small. Hence, the difference between the in-work rate of mothers with young children between Australia (45%) and Denmark (52%) is much smaller than what employment rates may suggest.

Employment across households with children

Male participation rates seem hardly affected by the presence of children: they generally work full-time, and even more so when children are present in the family.[6] But in line with the variation of maternal employment rates there are striking cross-country differences in the allocation of paid work across families with children. Across all households with children, single earner couple house-holds remain the most common in the Netherlands (Table 2.11), although other patterns of employment are increasingly common. In Australia, and particularly in Denmark, couple families where both parents are in employment are much more common. In about one in six Australia households where children are present the parent(s) do not have a job, and, as in Denmark and the Netherlands, joblessness amongst households with children is mainly concentrated in lone-parent fami-lies (see below). Joblessness amongst couple families decreased during the 1990s in the Netherlands but increased in Denmark, where it nevertheless remains at a low level.

During the 1980s and the 1990s the proportion of single earner families amongst couple families with children declined sharply, in both Australia and the Netherlands (Table 2.12 and annex at the end of the chapter). Whereas the pro-portion of single earner couples with children increased somewhat in Denmark (this being related to the relatively low employment rate for young Danish women

Table 2.11.   **Households with children by employment status**

Percentages

	2 parents			1 parent		All households with children
	No one in employment	One in employment	Both in employment	Not in employment	In employment	
Australia						
1990	5.9	36.6	41.2	9.1	7.2	100.0
2000	5.9	28.6	44.6	11.0	9.9	100.0
Denmark						
1991	1.7	7.9	72.4	3.3	14.6	100.0
1999	3.1	11.6	66.9	5.2	13.3	100.0
Netherlands						
1990	6.9	54.6	25.2	8.8	4.5	100.0
2000	4.2	43.8	35.4	8.3	7.4	100.0

See Annex at the end of Chapter 2.
Source: National authorities.

Table 2.12.   **Couple families with children by employment status**

Percentages

	No one in employment	One in employment			Both in employment				Families with children
		Total	Full-time	Part-time	Total	2 full-time	1 full-time, 1 part-time	2 part-time	
Australia									
1985	7.4	48.1	46.3	1.8	44.5	17.6	26.1	0.7	100.0
1990	7.1	43.7	41.4	2.3	49.2	24.2	24.1	0.9	100.0
2000	7.5	36.2	32.4	3.8	56.3	21.7	32.9	1.7	100.0
Denmark									
1991	2.4	10.6	..	..	87.1	..	..	..	100.0
1999	5.3	17.5	..	..	75.2	..	..	..	100.0
Netherlands									
1990	8.0	63.0	..	..	29.0	..	..	..	100.0
2000	5.0	52.0	..	..	42.0	6.7	33.8	1.4	100.0

..   Data not available.
See Annex at the end of Chapter 2.
Source: National authorities.

compared to female workers aged 35-40, Charts 2.7 and 2.8). Nevertheless, single earner couples still make up half of all the couples with children in the Netherlands, while both parents are in work in two-thirds of Australian couple families with children, and 82% of Danish couple households with children.

As maternal employment mainly is full-time in Denmark (Table 2.12), dual earner couples in Denmark largely concern families where both parents work full-time. In 60% of Australian families with children one of the parents, usually the father, works full-time, while the mother works part-time. For the Netherlands this full-time/part-time model concerns about 80% of all dual earner couples and in one quarter of these families women work less than 12 hours (Keuzenkamp *et al.*, 2000). The dual part-time earner model is not a frequent "reconciliation" solution among parents in couple families with children (Table 2.13), but its desirability is making inroads in the Dutch policy debate (Bovenberg and Graafland, 2001).

In line with maternal employment trends, employment patterns within couple families vary with the age of the children. When the youngest child is under 4 years of age, single-earner families are the most prevalent in Australia, although the "1 + 0.5 worker solution" has gained in popularity over the years (annex at the end of the chapter). In Denmark, the incidence of single-earner families is higher for families with very young children, than for all families with children, but the difference is small. In both Australia and Denmark, the second-earner returns to work, or increases hours to full-time employment when the youngest child is of pre-school age.

Again, among potential dual earner couples , the "1 + 0.5 worker family" is the most popular in Australia. But because modern Australian mothers have a higher degree of labour force attachment than in the past and increase their labour supply when children grow up, the dual full-time earner model is now almost as popular as the single-earner solution among Australian couple families with children aged 3-6 (annex at the end of the chapter). Younger families in Australia are less likely to opt for the single-earner solution than their predecessors.

Time use by parents in couple families

In all three countries under review, men generally spend more time in paid work than women, even when both partners are working full-time. The gender gap in unpaid housework remains considerable in all three countries. Danish women in full-time work spend almost twice as much on caring activities as men, while women in part-time employment (more dominant than full-time employment among mothers with young children in both Australia and the Netherlands), spend almost three times as much on caring than their spouses. However, Table 2.13 suggests that men have somewhat increased their contribution to unpaid housework in recent years in all three countries. Nevertheless, mothers remain the main carers in couple families.

Time spent on caring for children decreases with the age of the child, but the gender gap in caring remains approximately the same: Australian women spend twice as much time on caring until the child is 15 (ABS, 2001a). A similar pattern

63

Table 2.13. **Average daily time spent by parents in couples with a child under 5 on childcare, unpaid and paid work**

	Men (average for all men)				Women in full-time (paid) work				Women in part-time (paid) work				Women mainly at home			
	Paid work	Childcare	Other unpaid	Total paid and unpaid time	Paid work	Childcare	Other unpaid	Total paid and unpaid	Paid work	Childcare	Other unpaid	Total paid and unpaid	Paid work	Childcare	Other unpaid	Total paid and unpaid
	Hours	Minutes	Hours	Hours	Hours	Minutes	Hours	Hours	Hours	Minutes	Hours	Hours	Hours	Minutes	Hours	Hours
Australia																
1987	6.7	0.8	1.8	9.3	3.5	2.5	3.8	9.8	2.7	2.6	4.4	9.7	0.1	3.7	5.1	8.9
1997	6.1	0.9	2.0	9.0	6.0	1.7	2.9	10.6	2.9	2.3	4.6	9.7	0.5	2.8	5.5	8.8
Denmark																
1987	7.2	0.5	1.9	9.5	5.4	0.9	3.1	9.4	4.1	0.7	4.1	8.9	0.6	1.5	5.4	7.5
2000	..	..	..	..	..	..	..	..	..	..	..	..	..	..	..	..
Netherlands																
1990	5.4	0.5	2.4	8.2	..	..	..	..	1.6	1.5	4.9	8.1	0.1	1.7	5.8	7.6
2000	6.0	0.6	2.2	8.8	..	..	..	..	2.4	1.7	4.7	8.8	0.5	1.9	5.3	7.7

Paid work includes working in a family enterprise (which explains why "housewives" report some paid work) and is averaged over the year, including weekends and paid leave (this explains why the figures may appear low).
Childcare is defined strictly, as to requiring parental physical involvements and includes for example, feeding, bathing and dressing children.
Other unpaid work is broadly defined and includes for example, travel to school with children, cooking, washing dishes, house cleaning, and shopping.
Source: OECD (2001f) and additional information provided by the Netherlands authorities.

can also be found among Dutch parents: mothers remain the main caregivers throughout childhood (Keuzenkamp *et al.*, 2000).

Raising children increases the time pressure on men and women. A quarter of Australian men and women in couple families without children feels pushed for time, while this concerns half the men and 60% of the women in couples with children. In Australia, there is a significant difference in the time pressures felt by working women and women not in paid employment, but there is little difference in the perceived time pressure between women in part-time or full-time employment (ABS, 2001a). In the Netherlands, response to time surveys indicate that parents without children spend about 90 hours per week on employment, housework, care and leisure, while this is close to 110 hours for parents in families with children aged 0-3 (Keuzenkamp *et al.*, 2000). Parents with young children seem to "find" more time than anybody else.

Lone-parent families and employment

Lone-parent families face particular issues related to balancing family and work, as they have no partner with whom they can share either the caring or the earning role. The poverty risk among lone-parent families is high, and particularly so for lone-parent families without work (see below). Lone parents in Denmark have a very high employment rate, with nearly three-quarters being in work, marginally higher than the participation rate of women generally. Nevertheless, since 1990 the employment rate of lone parents has gone down in Denmark by about 10 percentage points. In Australia and the Netherlands employment among lone parents has become more prevalent, but at about 47% the proportions of lone parents who work in Australia and the Netherlands remains well below general female employment rates in these two countries (Table 2.14).

Among lone-parent families, employment rates are lowest among lone parents with very young children. This is somewhat surprising for Denmark, as lone parents are not treated differently from other parents when it comes to activity testing and benefit receipt (Chapter 5). Moreover, childcare places are available from when the child is 6 months of age in 80% of municipalities, and from one year in the remainder. (Chapter 3). Nevertheless, it appears that lone parents are much more likely than other Danish mothers to withdraw from the labour market, at least on a temporary basis.

Unlike Denmark, however, the Netherlands has no activity testing on lone parents with very young children (up to 5), and a relatively low level of participation expectations on lone parents with school aged children, being more similar to Australia in this regard (Chapter 5). In Australia, lone parents are almost as likely to work part-time as full-time, and while part-time work may help them balance work and family and provides some level of independent income, there is concern about the extent to which work establishes independence from public support (Chapter 5).

65

Table 2.14. **Employment rates among single parents, by age of the youngest child**
Percentages of working age population

	1985	1990[a]	1995	2000[b]
Australia				
With children (all ages 0-14)				
Lone parents in employment	37.4	44.2	43.2	47.3
Full-time	13.2	18.4	20.3	24.4
Part-time	24.2	25.7	22.8	22.9
With young children aged 3 or under				
Lone parents in employment	25.2	31.0	26.8	30.2
Full-time	9.6	15.6	14.5	19.0
Part-time	15.5	15.4	12.4	11.2
With young children aged 3 to 6				
Lone parents in employment	38.4	49.4	53.7	53.2
Full-time	15.9	22.2	28.6	27.6
Part-time	22.5	27.1	25.1	25.6
Denmark				
With children (all ages 0-17)				
Lone parents in employment	..	81.4	72.9	71.9
With young children aged 3 or under				
Lone parents in employment	..	65.1	53.3	50.8
With young children aged 3 to 6				
Lone parents in employment	..	83.3	70.5	70.2
Netherlands				
With children (all ages 0-17)				
Lone parents in employment	..	34.0	..	47.0

a)   1991 for Denmark.
b)   1999 for Denmark and 1997 for the Netherlands.
Source: Informations supplied by national authorities.

2.4.4. *Female and male earnings*

Gender wage gap

The gender wage gap[7] is smallest in Australia and Denmark, and considerably larger in the Netherlands. Significant reductions in the non-managerial gender pay gap occurred in Australia during the 1970s as a result of national equal pay decisions: it closed further in the 1980s and remained relatively stable during the 1990s (DFACS/DEWR, 2002). In Denmark the gender wage gap has been fairly stable over the last three decades (Datta Gupta *et al.*, 2002), while it declined somewhat in the Netherlands during the 1990s (Arbeidsinspectie, 2000).

The difference between full-time male and female median earnings expressed as a percentage of male median full-time earnings is about 8% in Denmark, 10% in Australia and 13% in the Netherlands (Table 2.15). At mean earnings levels, the wage

Table 2.15.   **The gender wage gap,[a] basic indicators[b] in 1999[c]**

	Hourly earnings, full-time wage and salary employees				Hourly earnings, all wage and salary employees			
	Ratio of mean	Ratio of median	The gap at the bottom quintile[d]	The gap at the top quintile[d]	Ratio of mean	Ratio of median	The gap at the bottom quintile[d]	The gap at the top quintile[d]
Australia	91	92	96	87	89	90	96	85
Denmark	89	93	96	87	89	92	95	88
Netherlands	80	86	85	80	79	87	86	81
OECD[e]	84	86	86	85	84	85	86	84

a) Percentage ratio of female to male wage.
b) Persons aged 20 to 64 years except for Australia: 15 to 64 years.
c) Data refer to 1999 except for Australia: 2000.
d) Ratio between the upper earnings limits of, respectively, the female and male earnings distributions' quintiles.
e) Unweighted average for 19 OECD countries: Australia, Austria, Belgium, Canada, Denmark, Finland, France, Germany, Greece, Ireland, Italy, Netherlands, New Zealand, Portugal, Spain, Sweden, Switzerland, United Kingdom and the United States.
Source: OECD (2002d).

gap is larger: about 11% in Australia and Denmark and 21% in the Netherlands (OECD, 2002d). The gender gap in wages is largest in the Netherlands across the earnings distribution (Chart 2.12). At the bottom of the earnings distribution females earn more or less the same as men in Australia, which is related to the high proportion

Chart 2.12.   **Gender earnings ratio at each decile of the male earning distribution**
Hourly earnings for all wage and salary workers

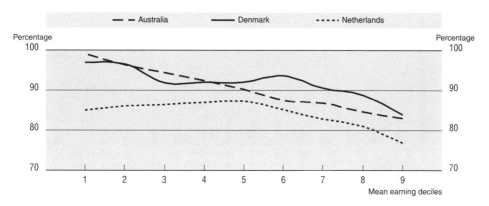

See notes to Table 2.15.
Source: OECD (2002d).

of women in casual employment. Moreover, in terms of hourly wage rates, women earn much the same whether they work full or part-time, while men in part-time earn less per hour than males in full-time employment (DFACS/DEWR, 2002).

Gender wage gaps remain considerable, especially in the Netherlands. To a certain extent these are related to female employment being concentrated in sectors (see above), where wage gains have been relatively limited. Also women are more likely to be in part-time employment, take child-related leave (Chapter 4), or withdraw from the labour force, and all these factors hamper female career progress, contributing to increasing wage differentials across the genders at higher earnings levels. Although methodological and data differences make a direct comparison of results impossible, national studies indicate that "unexplained" variation between male and female earnings is significant. For example, Reiman (2001) finds that unexplained differences account for 61% of the wage variation across male and female workers in Australia. Arbeidsinpectie (2000) finds that among business sector employees in the Netherlands the wage difference between male and female workers is 23%, while the unexplained wage difference is around 7%.

Ever since the 1960s and 1970s, female employment rates in Denmark have been persistently high at over 75%, while work and family reconciliation solutions in Australia and the Netherlands often involve mothers working part-time. These

Chart 2.13. **Distribution of couples where the male partner worked full-time by the ratio of female to male annual incomes from work, 1996**

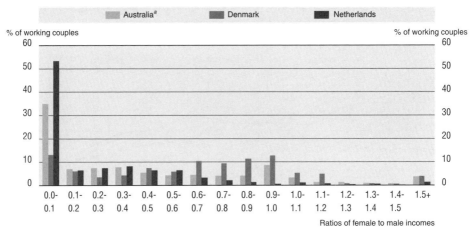

a) 1997-98 for Australia.
Source: European Community Household Panel (ECHP, wave 4); Australian 1997-98 Survey of Income and Housing Costs.

labour market outcomes and the gender wage difference, have their obvious effect on the gender distribution of annual earnings in household income. It is clear from Chart 2.13 that men contribute most to household earnings in all three countries. Considering all couple households wherein men work in the Netherlands, in half of the families the contribution of female earnings to total household income is less than 10%.[8] And there are very few households in the Netherlands where the contribution of female earnings is larger than 70% of what males contribute. In Denmark the situation is more egalitarian, with a large proportion of families in which women bring in from half to equal earnings into the household. In Denmark, in households where there are two earners on average women earn 70% of spousal earnings, while this is 44% for Australia and only 26% in the Netherlands. Although the Dutch model often refers to a "one-and-a-half earner" model, a "one-and a quarter" description seems more apt.

2.5. Income inequality, poverty and child poverty

Cross-country comparable information for OECD countries on trends in income inequality and poverty for the mid-1980s to the mid-1990s suggests Denmark has the flattest income distribution among OECD countries (Förster, 2000). The degree of income inequality in the Netherlands represents an "average" for continental western and northern European countries, while the degree of income inequality in Australia is comparable to that of the United Kingdom, but significantly less than in the United States (Förster, 2000). Both Australia and Denmark experienced a modest decrease in income inequality between the mid-1980s and the mid-1990s (Table 2.16). In both countries lower income groups experienced a

Table 2.16. **Evolution of income inequality**

	Levels		Absolute changes[b]			
	Gini coefficient[a]	P_{90}/P_{10} Decile ratio	Gini coefficient		P_{90}/P_{10} Decile ratio	
	Mid-1990s	Mid 90s	Mid-1970s to Mid-1980s	Mid-1980s to Mid-1990s	Mid-1970s to Mid-1980s	Mid-1980s to Mid-1990s
Australia	30.5	3.9	2.1	−0.7	0.2	−0.4
Denmark	21.7	2.7	..	−1.1	..	−0.2
Netherlands	25.5	3.2	0.7	2.1	0.1	0.4

.. Data not available for the mid-1970s.

a) The income distribution measure used here is the "Gini coefficient". This is a statistical measure that has a value of "0" if every person in the economy has the same amount of income, and "1" if one person had all the income, and everybody else had no income at all. Income has to be adjusted to take account of family size by assuming an equivalence scale of 0.5.

b) Absolute change is the difference in the value of the index.

Source: Förster (2000).

reduction of market income, but as a result from tax and transfer policies their disposable income nevertheless increased. By contrast, over the same period disposable income inequality in the Netherlands increased, as lower income groups in faced a reduction in disposable income.

Poverty rates in Denmark are generally well below those in Australia and the Netherlands. Child poverty rates are similar in Australia and the Netherlands at about 10%, with a substantially higher poverty risk for children in lone-parent families. Child poverty was reduced from the mid-1980s to the mid-1990s in Australia and Denmark but increased in the Netherlands. In fact, over that period, poverty rates fell in Denmark across all groups of the working age population, whereas they increased in the Netherlands. Table 2.17 shows that in Australia there was a significant decline in poverty rates among jobless households, and the overall group of working age households with children until the mid-1990s.

Jobless lone-parent families experienced substantially greater poverty rates in all three countries compared to lone parents in work, with Australia having the greatest differential – of nearly 33 percentage points, as against around 24 percentage points for both Denmark and the Netherlands. From the mid-1980s to the mid-1990s, poverty rates for lone-parent families in work were slightly higher than for all families with one worker, except in the Netherlands where they were substantially higher (17% as against 7.6%). Everywhere, households with two adults in employment experienced the lowest poverty rates.

As noted above, at 2.2% of GDP, Australia spends the greatest level of resources on cash payments to families with children while Denmark and the

Table 2.17.   **Poverty rates by selected family type and work attachment, mid-1980s to mid-1990s**

	Below age 18	Total working-age population			Total single parents		
			With children	Without children		Non working	Working
Australia, level 1994	10.9	8.5	9.4	7.1	26.9	42.1	9.3
change, 1984-1994	−4.6	−3.0	−4.0	0.4	−19.8	−37.9	2.0
Denmark, level 1994	3.4	3.8	2.6	5.3	16.2	34.2	10.0
change, 1983-1994	−1.2	−0.8	−1.1	−0.9	−4.5	−19.1	−3.2
Netherlands, level 1995	9.1	7.0	7.6	6.3	33.0	41.3	17.0
change, 1984-1995	5.8	3.6	4.6	2.2	18.5	25.4	6.9

Poverty rate: percentage of persons living in households with incomes below 50% of median adjusted disposable income of the entire population.
Source: Förster (2000).

Netherlands (despite universal family payments) spend considerably less. This shows that the Australian social benefit system is much more targeted on poor families with children (see Background Annex to the Review) than it is in the other two countries. In Denmark and the Netherlands the main source of redistribution of resources across households is *not* the social benefit system, but the high degree of progressivity in Danish and Dutch tax system through which these benefits are financed. Hence, the combination of redistribution through both the tax and the benefit system is what matters when considering the effectiveness of public policy in reducing poverty.

From 1985 to 1995, the poverty rates increased in the Netherlands across the population, both before the redistribution of resources through the tax/benefit system and after taxes and benefits were accounted for (Chart 2.14, Panel A). In 1995, post tax poverty rates are about one-third of pre-tax poverty rates, but the poverty reducing impact of the Dutch tax/benefit system had weakened since 1985. By contrast, and despite increased pre-tax poverty rates, post-tax poverty rates for the entire population in both Australia and Denmark were lower in 1995 than in 1985.

As noted above, child poverty rates are lowest in Denmark (about 3%), and about 10% in Australia and the Netherlands. But where in Denmark and Australia, child poverty rates are on par with those across the entire population, in the Netherlands child poverty rates are about 2 percentage points above poverty rates across the population (Chart 2.14, Panels A and B). In both Australia and Denmark tax/benefit systems reduced the pre-tax poverty rate among children by about 75%, compared to 50% in the Netherlands. Trends in the impact of tax/benefit systems on child poverty rates are rather similar to the impact on poverty rates for the entire population (the slope of the arrows in Chart 2.14, Panel B).

Lone-parent families are at a relatively high poverty risk and social policies substantially reduce poverty rates among this family group in all three countries under review (Chart 2.14, Panel C). Particularly, Australian tax/benefit policies became more effective in reducing poverty among lone parents from the mid-1980s to the mid-1990. But over this period, the poverty alleviating power of the Dutch tax benefit system declined. Whereas, pre-tax/transfer poverty rates among lone parents were actually lower in 1995 (70%) than in 1985 (80%), post-tax/transfer poverty rates increased form 15% to over 30%.

National studies evidence poverty trends since the mid-1990s, although this information is not fully comparable across countries. Information on poverty trends for Denmark from 1994 to 1998 suggest a decline in the incidence of poverty, but no obvious change in the distribution among families with and without children (Socialministeriet, 2001). A substantial decline in child poverty since the beginning of the 1980s in Australia is also found by Harding and Szukalska (2000),

Chart 2.14. **Poverty rates before and after accounting for taxes and transfers, specific population groups, mid-1980s and mid-1990s**

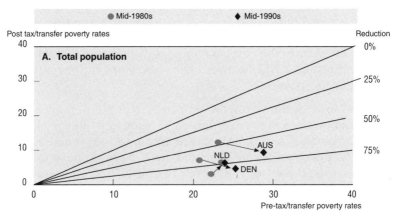

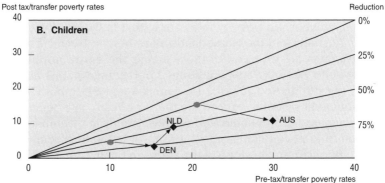

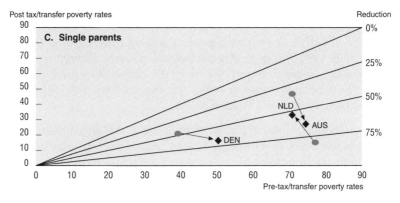

Source: Förster (2000).

however, child poverty rates remained fairly stable for the 1995-1998 period. Since, 1995 the incidence of poverty has declined across all income groups in the Netherlands, and particularly among those over 65, and households with children (SCP/CBS, 2001). Around 60% of children in low-income families live in single parent families, and while the number of single parent families is rising in the Netherlands (Table 2.4), the proportion of lone-parent families on low-income fell from 53 to 42% over the 1995-1999 period. This trend contributed to an over-all decline in child-poverty rates by about 10% since 1995 (Information provided by the Netherlands Ministry of Social Affairs and Employment).

2.6. Conclusions

Society has changed over the last 25 years, and to a large extent this is due to changing family formation. Fewer children are being born at a later age of the mother and the number of families with children is declining in Australia and the Netherlands while fertility rates have edged up since the mid-1980s in Denmark. Ever since the 1970s, female employment rates in Denmark have been persistently high at over 75%, while part-time employment has become less important. Over the last 20 years or so, female labour force participation has increased markedly in Australia and the Netherlands. But where overall gender employment gaps may have reduced, the nature of employment outcomes across the genders remains very different. Female employment is more likely to be part-time and temporary, and concentrated in certain sectors (e.g. health and social care services), and earnings differentials with male workers continue to exist. Educational attainment levels of female workers are still below those of men, but such differences are falling over time.

Childrearing certainly affects female employment patterns much more than male labour force behaviour. High childcare participation and comprehensive paid leave arrangement contribute to high full-time maternal employment rates in Denmark (Chapters 3 and 4). But work and family reconciliation solutions in Australia and the Netherlands often involve mothers working part-time. However, the evidence seems to suggest that a significant proportion of mothers with young children in Australia increase their hours worked when children grow up, while it seems that once part-time work has been taken up, it remains the labour force status for many women in the Netherlands.

These labour market outcomes have their obvious effect on the gender distribution of annual earnings in household income. Men contribute most to household income, even in Denmark with a relatively small gender gap in full-time employment, on average women earn 70% of spousal earnings, while this is 44% for Australia and only 26% in the Netherlands. Indeed, the popular "one-and-a-half earner" model in that country is really a "one-and a quarter" model in terms of household earnings.

Available evidence for all three countries suggests men have somewhat increased their contribution to unpaid housework in recent years, but that mothers, nevertheless remain the main caregiver to children. The increase in female participation has yet to translate into gender equity in all employment outcomes.

Being in employment reduces the risk of poverty, particularly for lone-parent families. Joblessness among lone parents is much higher in Australia and the Netherlands than in Denmark, and Chapter 5 discusses in detail the challenges that lone parents and public policy face in reducing their non-employment and poverty risk.

Annex to Chapter 2

Table 2A. **Employment by household with children**
AUSTRALIA
A. Households with children (all ages 0-14)

	2 parents						1 parent			All households
	No one in employment	One in employment		Both in employment			No one in employment	One in employment		
		FT	PT	2FT	1FT, 1PT	2 PT		FT	PT	
1985	6.3	39.9	1.6	15.2	22.6	0.6	8.6	1.8	3.3	100.0
1990	5.9	34.6	1.9	20.3	20.2	0.8	9.1	3.0	4.2	100.0
1995	6.9	26.2	2.7	17.6	26.9	1.2	10.5	3.8	4.2	100.0
2000	5.9	25.6	3.0	17.2	26.0	1.4	11.0	5.1	4.8	100.0

B. Households with youngest child 0-4 years of age

	2 parents						1 parent			All households
	No one in employment	One in employment		Both in employment			No one in employment	One in employment		
		FT	PT	2FT	1FT, 1PT	2 PT		FT	PT	
1985	5.4	50.9	1.2	8.2	15.9	0.5	13.3	1.7	2.8	100.0
1990	6.5	41.7	1.8	11.8	24.9	0.7	8.6	1.9	1.9	100.0
1995	7.6	35.1	2.9	12.2	25.3	1.0	11.7	2.3	2.0	100.0
2000	6.7	35.6	3.4	11.9	24.8	1.3	11.3	3.1	1.8	100.0

C. Households with children with youngest child aged 3 to 6

	2 parents						1 parent			All households
	No one in employment	One in employment		Both in employment			No one in employment	One in employment		
		FT	PT	2FT	1FT, 1PT	2 PT		FT	PT	
1985	4.0	26.0	1.6	13.8	19.3	0.5	21.4	5.5	7.8	100.0
1990	4.4	24.6	1.4	21.8	31.5	0.7	7.9	3.5	4.2	100.0
1995	6.3	20.1	2.5	19.3	29.4	1.6	9.6	5.9	5.2	100.0
2000	5.6	18.7	3.1	18.4	28.6	1.5	11.3	6.7	6.2	100.0

Note: PT = part-time, working under 35 hours per week ; FT = full-time, working 35 or more hours per week.
Source: Australian Bureau of Statistics.

Table 2A.　**Employment by household with children** (*cont.*)
DENMARK
A. Households with children (all ages 0-17)

	2 parents			1 parent		All households
	No one in employment	One in employment	Both in employment	Not in employment	In employment	
1991	1.7	7.9	72.4	3.3	14.6	100.0
1995	2.8	12.0	66.5	5.1	13.7	100.0
1999	3.1	11.6	66.9	5.2	13.3	100.0

B. Households with youngest child under 3 years of age

	2 parents			1 parent		All households
	No one in employment	One in employment	Both in employment	Not in employment	In employment	
1991	2.1	9.4	77.4	3.9	7.2	100.0
1995	4.4	18.9	65.5	5.2	5.9	100.0
1999	4.7	17.5	67.5	5.0	5.2	100.0

C. Households with children with youngest child aged 3 to 6

	2 parents			1 parent		All households
	No one in employment	One in employment	Both in employment	Not in employment	In employment	
1991	2.0	7.5	72.5	3.0	15.0	100.0
1995	2.3	10.5	66.3	6.2	14.8	100.0
1999	2.6	10.1	68.6	5.6	13.1	100.0

Source:　Information derived from the Socialministeriet "Danish and Law model" rather than from labour force statistics.

Chart 2.13 in the text showed the distribution of the female/male earnings ratio in households with children. Strictly speaking that information is not entirely representative as it is based on available data of all couple families in which men work. A more comprehensive picture is obtained when the income data also cover all couples families where the female is the only earner.

Both measures are presented in Chart 2A. It shows that the female to male earning ratios are slightly lower across the board, but the overall picture is not substantially different: men contribute most to household earnings.

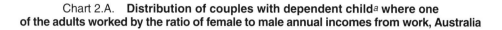

Chart 2.A.   **Distribution of couples with dependent child*a* where one
of the adults worked by the ratio of female to male annual incomes from work, Australia**

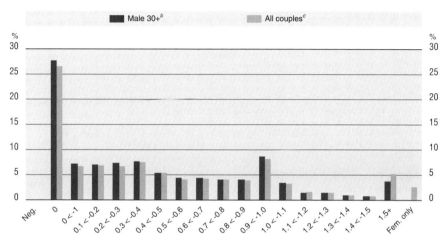

Ratios of female to male incomes

a) Dependent child: aged 15 years or under or full-time students under 25 years.
b) This column represents the data which appears to be most compatible with the data for Denmark and the Netherlands. It shows: Male partner working 30 or more hours per week. Ratio of female earned annual income to male earned annual income. (Earnings from Wage and Salary or Own Business.) Excludes households where one partner records a negative income, or the male records nil net income.
c) This column includes all households where one of the partners work – and hence includes households with a non-working male partner. It identifies households where women are the only partner with earned income. These are identified as "Fem. only".
Source: 1997-98 Survey of Income and Housing Costs in Australia.

Notes

1. At their first birthday 91% of all Australian children lived with both their parents, by the age of 15 this proportion had decline to 77%.
2. A significant part of the teachers – about 3% of the labour force (OECD, 2001e) – in both Australia and the Netherlands are in independent private schools that are financed by the State.
3. In Australia and the Netherlands, about a quarter of all female workers work less than 20 hours per week.
4. The incidence of female part-time employment in Denmark according to national definitions (self-assessment) was around 45% during the 1970s.
5. The employment rate of Australian mothers with the youngest child aged 3-6 is 9 percentage points above that of all Australian mothers and has been for the last ten years, while in 1985 the gap was only 3 percentage points (see annex at the end of Chapter 2).
6. The incidence of part-time work among men with children is lower than for men without children in both Australia and the Netherlands (OECD, 2001d).
7. The gender wage gap is measured using the percentage ratio of female to male earnings; the closer this ratio is to 1, the smaller the Gender wage gap.
8. Of course it would be more appropriate to capture all working couples including those where women are the only breadwinner, but as Chart 2A in the annex of Chapter 2 shows for Australia this does not generate a substantially different picture.

Chapter 3

Availability and Affordability of Good Quality Childcare

This chapter looks at how public policy has influenced the availability of quality affordable childcare which enables parents to balance work and family.

Mothers no longer automatically withdraw from the labour force to look after the children. Danish mothers largely stay in the labour force as facilitated by the comprehensive child-related leave benefits. Temporary withdrawal from the labour force is more common in Australia and the Netherlands, but more and more mothers remain in the labour force through adjusting their hours of paid work. Thus, the traditional pattern of maternal care at home is increasingly being abandoned meaning that mothers and fathers who work choose to look after care needs through childcare services. Indeed, the availability of affordable quality childcare is critical in facilitating that choice.

For parents to trust their young child to the care of others is not a decision taken lightly. Some parents will always prefer parental care to non-parental out-of-home care – whether formal or informal. But it is essential that parents who wish to maintain their labour force attachment are comfortable with both the quality of the childcare available, as well as its price. In Australia and the Netherlands informal care plays a very significant role. It is obviously cheaper, and parents may be more comfortable using a relative, friend and/or neighbour. Quality considerations point to another driver behind the use of (formal) childcare facilities: that of early childhood development, which has seen growth in early childhood services as part of improving child outcomes, especially in Denmark. While not driven by family/work reconciliation objectives, this is not fundamentally incompatible with them either.

Government policies influence both quality and price. The use of formal childcare has increased in all three countries, in different ways, resulting in different patterns of childcare participation. Denmark has very high formal childcare coverage for children from a very early age, and while parents have a choice as to whether they use childcare, widespread usage has become the norm. Public expenditure on childcare is high compared to the other two countries. Public childcare expenditure is widely considered as "an investment in the future", contributing to better outcomes across a range of factors, including child development, educational achievement, gender equality and future labour supply. In Australia too, childcare expenditure is seen to contribute to future family and community functioning as well as meeting immediate care needs, while in the Netherlands public spending (and that of employers) is largely related to labour market considerations. Both Australia and the Netherlands have increasing rates of participation in formal childcare, but with different types of provision, different levels of utilisation and different organisation and funding methods. Given this, the debate about childcare is also different in each country. In Denmark, the focus is now largely on quality issues. This is also a factor in the Australian policy debate, but there remain issues of capacity, especially in out-of-school-hours-care. In the Netherlands, where employers play a major role, issues revolve around capacity and the parental choice in care facilities; quality has been less of a focus. However, quality assurance through the re-introduction of centrally determined quality standards and inspection procedures is one of the pillars of proposals for new childcare legislation.

3.1. Childcare: what are the policy objectives?

3.1.1. *Promoting gender equity, female labour force participation and increased labour supply*

The pattern of childcare use depends in part on what people want childcare for. In Denmark, childcare developed to support the labour market aspirations of women, and the promotion of gender equity (Socialministeriet, 2000). In Australia, the growth in childcare services in the 1970s arose from demands by women for the right to seek and remain in employment (Press and Hayes, 2000). Paid work aspirations by women are associated with increased participation in advanced education. They can also be motivated by income needs or aspirations of the family. Either way, these aspirations sit well alongside employers' preferences to have access to a wider labour pool. Government involvement in Australia in recent years has explicitly directed more resources to childcare where it is used to support employment attachment. In the Netherlands childcare was – until the early 1990s – an issue between employers wanting to increase labour supply, and employees wanting childcare while they work. The government has increased its role in recent years. Childcare services were developed through collaboration between employers and unions, as part of the industrial agreements (VWS and OC&W, 2000). Labour demand has increased pressures on women to return to the workforce more quickly after childbirth. In fact, concerns on labour supply are a significant factor in all three countries under review, reinforcing strong gender equity goals, where they exist. The Danish strategy is to have strong labour market participation by women, with a comprehensive childcare provision building on parental and child-minding leave which is often available within the first year after birth. The aim is that childcare is available for all children from age 6 months,[1] although capacity constraints exists in some places, notably Copenhagen. In general, parents thus have a choice: return to work when the child is 6 months; alternatively, one of them (usually the mother) can stay at home to provide parental care for about one year as facilitated by paid leave arrangements (Chapter 4). In Australia and the Netherlands the approach is to provide formal childcare where parents choose to use it, but because of capacity constraints this is not the norm in the Netherlands.

3.1.2. *Supporting labour market attachment for those receiving income support*

Childcare has also been used to facilitate the labour market reintegration of working-aged beneficiaries with young children. The re-activation costs can mean extra expenditure in the short term; however, the case for such policies rests on their long-term impacts. Australia, through its Jobs, Education and Training (JET) programme provides additional resources – by way of childcare matching services and free care – for job seekers needing childcare, while caseworkers involved in the newly established Transition to Work programme sometimes extend their job-matching role to include care-matching (Chapter 5). In addition, the 2001 Australians Working Together package provided an increase in resources for childcare to aid labour market reintegration.[2] The Netherlands has a specific central government programme (KOA) funding the purchase of childcare places for lone parents and other beneficiary families with work-related childcare needs. However, specific funding of childcare for welfare recipients is not a feature in Denmark, given more comprehensive childcare coverage and the expectation that women will be in work.

3.1.3. *Promoting child development and strengthening families*

Many parents using childcare in Australia believe that it will benefit their child, with 44% citing this as the main reason for using childcare in a recent survey (AIHW, 2001). This points to the case of childcare in promoting child development objectives. In addition recent funding increases have been part of the "Stronger Families and Communities" initiative,[3] indicating a community objective for childcare. Over a quarter of Dutch parents report that they use childcare primarily because it is good for the child. (Commissie Dagarrangementen, 2002.) With regard to child development both Australia and the Netherlands have education sector based pre-schooling available for "older" school children not yet of school age. In Denmark, these years are not considered to be part of formal education, so there is no explicit childcare curriculum, although guidelines relating to child development are under discussion. However, the Danes put the greatest emphasis on the child development aspects of childcare, and this is reflected in the legislated objectives for childcare (the Social Services Act): learning, social development

81

and care. These are deemed to be of equal weight. Childcare is seen to contribute to children developing "independence and autonomy". A recent survey showed most mothers believe that their young children should be in childcare, even if they themselves are not working (Christensen, 2000) and indeed this is now the norm with debate being more around the age at which a young child will benefit from childcare (6 month or 12 months or other) rather than whether childcare is good for the child.[4] In all three countries childcare is seen as way to enhance child development, to enhance school readiness and later educational and life out-comes, augmenting the learning and development done at home (VWS and OC&W, 2000; Socialministeriet, 2000; Press and Hayes, 2000).

3.1.4. Helping priority groups

All three countries provide childcare places for child welfare purposes (where there are specific care, neglect or abuse concerns). In fact, one of the most effec-tive aspects of the Danish system is its social role. High coverage of formal care facilities, contacts with social workers also employed by local government and in conjunction with the system of health visitors towards all children until they are 18, facilitates early identification and intervention of children with specific care needs and/or in neglect situations. In these situations childcare costs can be met fully where this is considered appropriate or where parents would not otherwise agree to the children attending childcare.

In Australia, the federal government has identified priority groups for childcare to be: families with special needs, those requiring childcare in order to engage in employment or training, and services for Aboriginal and Torres Strait Islanders (AIHW, 2001). However, it is up to each childcare centre to manage its intake, and priority does not equate to waiting list management. In the Netherlands local gov-ernment can purchase childcare places for groups with particular needs, such for immigrant children, to assist with their integration and that of their parents. How-ever, such funding is limited to families where there is no parent at home. There is also specific funding to buy childcare in order to promote employment reintegration (as noted above). In Denmark, priority is generally given to those families who have been waiting longest for childcare, irrespective of employment status or family type, however, children about whom there are specific social or developmental concern (such as with immigrant integration and in some cases the parental employment) can be placed at the head of the waiting list.

3.2. Different types of childcare

Childcare services can be grouped into four broad categories:[5]

- Group care in centres that are sometimes organised within the education sector (centre-based care);

Box 3.1. **Different types of formal childcare services**

Australia (Mandatory school age: 6 years)

Centre-based Day Care: group care in a centre, primarily for children from birth to school age. These can be publicly run (*e.g.* in some municipalities in Victoria) but are mainly private, both commercial and non-profit institutions.

Family Day Care: mainly for those not of school age (can be used up to age 12), provided by registered caregivers. Local co-ordination units oversee the placement of children, and recruitment of caregivers.

Early Education Services: kindergartens and pre-schools for 4-6-years-olds. Operate in term time. Part of the State level education sector, non-compulsory. Can be provided in childcare centres, if so funded by education authorities.

Out-of School Hours Care: before and after school care and school holiday care, run akin to centre-based care.

Occasional Care: often irregular hours centre-based care. Often used at short notice, such as when a job-seeking parent is called to a job interview, or for short-term needs, such as attendance at a short duration training course.

Australia also has *In-Home Care* for families in difficult circumstances and who do not have access to mainstream services, and other flexible childcare arrangements such as *mobile care* in unusual circumstances. *Playgroups* are also available, providing activities for families, where children are usually accompanied by a parent or carer.

Denmark (Mandatory school age: 7)

Local government and self-governing day care institutions: these are centre based and include:

- *Crèches*: for children from 6 months up to 3 years;
- *Kindergartens*: for older children aged 3 up to and including 6 years; and
- *Age integrated institutions*: covering all age groups.

School leisure time facilities (SFO): for young school children after school, often in the school grounds.

Pool scheme institutions: private schemes in agreement with a municipality, attracting a per child subsidy. Initiators can be businesses (for employees' children), housing societies, boards of independent schools, etc. Private firms can operate these schemes but not take any profit from childcare services.

Family Day Care: mainly for children 6 months to 3 years. Child minders are engaged and supervised by the municipality and supported by centres for childminders, where they meet (weekly for a half/full day) in larger groups.

83

Box 3.1.   **Different types of formal childcare services** (*cont.*)

The Netherlands (Mandatory school age: 5)

Child Day Care centres: from age 6 weeks to 4 years provided by private (commercial and non-profit) institutions.

Family Day Care: child minder services mediated through an official day-care agency (1.3% of 0-4 children attend).

Play Groups: for 2-3-year-olds, these are groups where children play with friends. Most children using Play Group attend 2-3 sessions of between 2.5 and 4 hours a week.

The *Primary School Kindergarten*: from 4 years until starting primary school, on primary school grounds, these are part of the education system: maximum 5.5 hours a day.

Out-of-School Hours-Care: for young school aged children, often in association with childcare.

- Child minders based in their own home looking after one or more children (family day care);
- In-home care provided by a carer who is not a family member but frequently lives with the family (nannies); and
- Informal care provided by relatives, friends and neighbours.

Public policies often concern the first two of these. Nevertheless, there is considerable variety in type of provision (centre-based care, home-based care, playschools, kindergartens, etc.) and the age at which children can access the different types of formal childcare (Box 3.1 summarises the provisions in the three countries under review).

Informal care usually lies outside of any official framework – as does the use of nannies – and rarely attracts public funding.[6] Informal care is less available now than in earlier years because of lifestyle changes – not only are more mothers working, but so too are more grandmothers. In addition, more families now live further from wider family networks of support. Nevertheless, informal care remains an important aspect of family/work reconciliation strategies (see below).

3.3. The importance and nature of childcare use in the three countries under review

3.3.1. Participation and overall capacity

A simple count of the number of children in formal childcare gives some indication of the extent to which families are using services to augment what might a generation ago have been a completely informal or family activity. Of the three countries in this study, Denmark has the highest usage of formal childcare for younger children with nearly two out of three very young children in childcare. Australia and the Netherlands[7] both have much lower levels of participation for this age group. For "older" children not yet of school age the comparison is complicated by differences in the compulsory schooling age.[8] Not only is the compulsory schooling age in the Netherlands low (5 years), but the vast majority of children aged 4 also attends school [since the 1980s pre-school (4-6) and primary schools (6 onwards) have been integrated]. Thus participation rates in the Netherlands are high from age 4 onwards, with Denmark also having high participation levels, while participation in Australia is moderate (see Table 3.1).

However, determining the level of participation is more complex than a simple numbers count, given the considerable variation in the amount of time children spend in childcare services in each country. Table 3.1 shows that in Denmark most children use childcare full-time (between 7 and 8 hours a day). In Australia only a round 9% use care for more than 35 hours a week, with the bulk using between 5 and 19 hours care a week. The Netherlands also sees most children in childcare part-time. Thus, participation numbers mask considerable differences in capacity since the use of formal childcare in Australia and the Netherlands is much more on a part-time basis than in Denmark.

In Denmark, the expansion of formal childcare took place in the 1960s and 1970s (see Chart Box 2.3). In 1950 about 25% of all children younger than 2 years old attended formal childcare, while by 1980 this had grown to 38% (Rostgaard and Fridberg, 1998). The high participation and capacity levels continued to increase throughout the 1990s. Long-day childcare capacity in Australia increased fourfold in the 1990s,[9] with growth in family day somewhat smaller. In the Netherlands, childcare capacity increased from 22 000 places in 1990 to about 126 000 in 2001 (VWS and OC&W, 2000).

3.3.2. Centre-based and home-based care

Centre-based care accounts for most of the formal care provisions in all three countries. Family day care services (care in the home of the carer) plays a significant role in Australia, where it accounts for just under a quarter of formal care for

Table 3.1. **Importance and nature of childcare services: key indicators**

	Australia (1999)	Denmark (1999)	Netherlands (1997)
Participation rate % of children in formal pre-school childcare by age	0-3: 31% 4 *plus*: 47% 4 years: 73% 5 years: 21%	½-2: 64% 3-5: 91%	0-3: 17% 4 years: 98% 5 years: 99%
Average annual growth rate in pre-school aged participation	0-11 year olds: 7.3% pa (1991-2000) (excludes pre-school)	0-2: 0.8% pa (1989-1999) 3-5: 1.7% pa	0-3: 32.5% pa (1989-1997) 4-7: 13.8% (excludes pre-school)
% of children using out-of-school hours care	5-11 years: 8.2%	6-9 years: 81%	4-13 years: 2.9% (1999)
Informal care	42% of under 6s (26% only use informal care)	Low reliance as primary out-of-home care	Over 50% use informal care
Capacity rates Number of places as % of total children in age group	**2000** Under 6s 16.8%	na	**2001** Under 4s: 13.3% 4 and 5 years: 98.5%
Number of out-of-school places	44 400 179 800		na 31 000
Indicators of part time/ full time usage for pre-school aged children	Mainly part time: 0-5 hours: 13% 5- 9 hours: 25% 10-19 hours: 38% 20-34 hours: 16% 35+ hours: 9%	Predominantly full-time: only 3% enrolled in part time care in 1998	Mainly part time: Approx. 2 children in childcare for each place offered in 1997. Most children use childcare 3-4 days a week.
Type of service (2001): For under 4 year olds	19% FDC, 64% centre based (of which 73% commercial private, reminder non-profit):	(under 3s) ⅔rd FDC, ⅓rd centre based; 70% of centre based care is municipal, as is most FDC.	Mainly centre based Predominantly private sector. Playgroups often use municipal premises.
For 4 years to school age	7% FDC; 29% childcare centres; 65% pre-school (education sector)	(3 years to school age) Mainly centre based – None education sector	Mainly pre-school (education sector)
Public expenditure (2001) Public childcare (including pre-school) expenditure as per cent of GDP	0.2%	2.1%	0.24%

pa: per annum.
Source: Australia: ABS (1999 and 2000b); AIHW (2001); DFACS (1999) and supplementary communications; Denmark: Socialministeriet (2000); Netherlands: OECD (1999a) and VWS and OC&W (2000).

under 3-year-olds and 10% for 3 and 4-year-olds (ABS, 2000b). In Denmark, home-based care supervised by municipalities represents around two-thirds of child-care used by children aged under 3, after which age its use declines in favour of centre-based care (Socialministeriet, 2000). By contrast, in the Netherlands only around 10 500 children (per annum about 200 000 children are born in the Netherlands) use family day care services, reflecting preferences to use centre-based care, or not use formal care at all.

In both Australia and the Netherlands centre-based care is split between those places which are part of the "care" sector and those which are part of the "education sector" – that is funded and overseen by education authorities. In Australia about 14% of all children aged 0-4 were in an education sector place – known as either "pre-school" or kindergarten. This represents about 36% of children in for-mal childcare and mainly covered those aged 3 to school age. In the Netherlands the equivalent services account for almost all the childcare participation of those aged 4 and 5. Such services mirror primary school (and in fact many are part of pri-mary schools) following term times and being part day rather than full day facili-ties. Many of the children attending education-based centres also use other forms of formal childcare in other hours. Denmark has no equivalent education sector-based care.

3.3.3. Informal care

Informal care is important particularly in Australia and the Netherlands, where formal childcare capacity is limited. In the Netherlands, more than half of the dual earner families used informal care arrangements while about 30% of these families used formal care arrangements (Keuzenkamp *et al.*, 2000). In Australia, 26% of chil-dren under 6 are cared for through informal care arrangements only, with 42% having some informal care – higher than the number using any formal childcare (38%). Grandparents provide most of the informal care and the bulk (61%) use it for less than ten hours a week (ABS, 2000b). Informal care plays a lesser role in Denmark, but in all countries, it plays a role in augmenting formal care even when this is used.

3.3.4. Public and private provision

The type of organisation providing care varies as well across the countries, with local government provision predominating in Denmark at around 70%, and the non-profit sector – the co-called "self-governing facilities" providing 30% of centre-based childcare places (Box 3.2). These are typically operated by a group of parents in a local area, but they can also be operated by businesses (to provide childcare for employees), housing associations and the like. Direct government provision is much more limited in the Netherlands, where municipalities organis-ing childcare subsidies sometimes run such centres themselves or otherwise

Box 3.2. **Public or private provision of childcare?**

Local government in Denmark is the main provider of childcare, while provision in both Australia and the Netherlands is mainly private. In Denmark the predominant view is that public provision of services, with local authority management and overview by parental boards is most likely to ensure both capacity and quality (see below). Danes generally deem it to be unacceptable to make a profit out of caring for children. Hence, commercial centres play a very limited role in Denmark and the constraints imposed on such providers are tight. They are not permitted to make a profit from the childcare service itself (*i.e.* by increasing fees), with their return coming from a management fee and any profit they make on additional services provided – such as laundry services. In effect, the private providers operate as private sector managers of publicly owned facilities, rather than being free to set up a service where they assess there to be a market demand. Results so far have been mixed, with a marginal increase in supply on the one hand, but concerns about quality and viability on the other. It is likely that the tight constraints that have been imposed will continue to mean that private sector involvement in childcare provision will be barely viable.

In Australia and the Netherlands childcare provision is mainly operated privately. To some extent this is because the role of municipalities in Australia is traditionally limited, and an infrastructure for locally-provided public childcare simply does not exist in many places, although there are exceptions, most notably in the State of Victoria. In the Netherlands the role of municipalities is traditionally larger and they do play an important role in that they allocate subsidies from central government to their own centres or non-profit centres.

Moreover, in both Australia and the Netherlands there is resistance to a heavy burden of childcare costs on the public budget in a matter that is largely considered a subject of parental discretion. Private provision is geared towards serving customer demand (see below) and may also be conducive to introduce innovative practices in service provision. There is an important time dimension to this, in that when the demand for childcare emerged a quick response was needed for which expanding private provision was deemed more suitable rather than exploding public budgets and tax-rates. Indeed, private sector involvement has enabled a significant growth in supply in both countries and representing around 90% of the growth in places between 1991 and 2000 in Australia (Purcell, 2001). Further, in Australia, the policy tradition has been to provide a public subsidy at a level that draws out a larger total investment in childcare from the private purse. In the Netherlands almost all of the growth has also been in private sector provision, in part through privatisation of services, with municipalities purchasing places in services they previously owned. Thus, the private sector plays a major and growing role in childcare provision in the Netherlands, as it does with regard to other "care markets" (*e.g.* care for the elderly and disabled). Such enterprises often do not (or are legally not permitted) pay out profits to investors or other stakeholders, but re-allocate the operating surplus towards the entrepreneurial core activity. In that sense, childcare providers can be regarded as "non-profit organisations" (Bovenberg and Gradus, 2001).

Box 3.2.   **Public or private provision of childcare?** *(cont.)*

In addition, and in sharp contrast to the other two countries under review, Dutch policy is that employers should equally share in the cost of childcare with parents and the government. Although, employer involvement does not preclude public provision, it certainly makes private provision more likely.

Private provision is associated with recent reform towards funding consumers (see below), rather than providers, and allowing clients to choose the service that best meets their needs and preferences (Press and Hayes, 2000). In that context, public policies financially supporting parents stimulate supply and provide equity for parents using private sector services. This is sometimes seen as representing a shift from childcare as a service, to being a business (*op. cit.*). In Australia the development of an innovative quality assurance system is part of a response to address such concerns (see Section 3.5).

---

subsidies non-profit organisation. But about three-quarters of childcare provision is operated through the commercial private sector. Direct government provision exists in Australia, but is very limited (*e.g.* some municipal centres mainly in the State of Victoria). 98 or 99% of all centres are run privately: almost three-quarters on a commercial basis, the remaining centres are community-based.[10]

3.3.5. *Public expenditure on childcare*

Given the considerable differences in formal childcare capacity in the three countries under review, it is not surprising public spending on formal childcare is far higher in Denmark, at 2.1% of GDP than in both Australia and the Netherlands (Table 3.1). With the introduction of government's Stimulative Measures Programme, public spending on childcare increased to 0.1% of GDP in 2001 in the Netherlands. Together with expenditure through the education sector on pre-schooling, public expenditure on childcare across both education and social sectors is around 0.24% of GDP. The increase in childcare capacity in Australia during the 1990s was related to an increase in public spending on formal day care increased from 0.06% in 1990 to 0.2% of GDP in 1999 (DFACS, 1999; ABS, 1999; and OECD, 2001h). As in the Netherlands, Australia also funds some early childhood services through its education sector, but on a much smaller scale – at nearly 20% of the level of social services expenditure.

This pattern is reflected in the average public expenditure per child under school age using childcare in each country. Including education funded pre-school

---

services but excluding school aged services, Denmark spends approximately $US6 300 per child per annum, four times as much as the Netherlands at $US1 500. Australia spends more than the Netherlands but still far less than $US2 200. The cost differences in part reflect the high incidence of full-time childcare in Denmark, as against part-time childcare in the other two countries, as discussed above.

3.4. The cost of childcare

The choice between a parent looking after a child at home by withdrawing from the labour market, using formal or informal childcare, or a mix, is strongly influenced by the cost of childcare services. Table 3.2 shows the variation in average annual cost of full-time care for day care services and for family day care services in the three countries. The information has to be interpreted carefully, because of regional cost differences, differences in classification and variability of costs for late hours care, but one thing is clear: formal childcare does not come cheap.

The cost of a childcare place in a centre appears lowest in Australia: about US$PPP7 000 compared to about twice as much in Denmark and the Netherlands. However, the gap is not that large in reality. The number of children per staff-member largely determines the cost of a centre-based childcare place. This staff ratio is highest for care for very young children. Childcare centres in Australia cover both 0 to 3-years-olds and larger groups (3-5). A rough estimate on the weighted average for care for 0-3-year-olds and the kindergarten population leads to a cost of about US$PPP9 000 in Denmark, compared to US$PPP7 000 for a comparable service in Australia. Staff-to-child ratios in childcare centres in the Netherlands are relatively high (spending does not cover pre-schools) contributing to the relatively high childcare costs in that country.

Table 3.2. **Average annual costs of childcare**
in US$PPP

	Australia (2001)	Denmark (2000)	Netherlands (2001)
Centre-based care (in US$PPP)	6 945.8	14 214.5	12 206.9
Child-to-staff ratio	5:1 (0-2 years)	3:1	4:1 to 6:1
	8: 1 (2-3 years)		
	10:1 (4-5 years)		
Kindergarten (in US$PPP)	..	6 592.0	..
Child-to-staff ratio		6:1	
Family day care (in US$PPP)	6 388.7	8 822.7	..
Child-to-staff ratio		3:1	

For Denmark, Crèche is centre-based care for 6 months to 2 year olds, kindergarten is for 3-year-olds to school age.
.. Data not available.
Source: National authorities.

Staff thus are an important determinant in childcare costs. Staff in Australia is relatively lowly paid at around two-thirds of the average earnings level, whilst salaries for assistants vary considerably, but at a much lower level. Qualified staff aspire to the salaries of pre-school teachers where those salaries are higher. Public childcare staff in Denmark have higher wages – childcare assistants get around two-thirds of average earnings, pedagogues averaging 85% of average earnings, centre managers around average earnings level. In the Netherlands salaries are similar to those in Australia, with assistants getting around 50% if average earnings and group leaders two-thirds of average earnings [OECD Secretariat calculations based on information in Press and Hayes (2000), Socialministeriet (2000) and VWS and OC&W (2000)]. Of course, staff-to-child ratios and the remuneration of staff not just affect the overall cost, but also the quality of service, an issue returned to below.

Another factor that contributes to the relatively high childcare cost in the Netherlands is the limited use of home-based (but regulated) family day care. Such services, widely used in Australia and Denmark, have lower cost structures for staff and for space. Family day care in Denmark is considerably cheaper than centre-based care, although staff-to-child ratios are similar. In any case, few households – especially low-income households, could afford to pay the full costs of a childcare place. But of course, in reality they are not asked to. Costs are shared between parents and central government in Australia and between parents and local government in Denmark. In the Netherlands, employers also pick up a substantial share of costs. In Australia, some employers pick up costs and may access fringe benefit tax exemptions for this.

3.4.1. *Financing of childcare*

The method of funding for childcare varies considerably across the three countries. In the Netherlands financing of childcare is shared across parents, employers and the government. Basically parents who are in employment will get a subsidy from their employer towards the cost of childcare. Those who do not get an employer subsidy (see below) can get a subsidy funded by local government. Some parents will meet the total cost themselves. In Denmark and Australia employers play a very limited funding role, with financing largely shared between parents and local or central government respectively. The public funding methods vary considerably across the countries as well. While all have income-related assistance towards the parents share of costs, this is managed in different ways. Both Denmark and the Netherlands have direct operational funding to childcare providers, whilst this plays a very minor role in Australia.[11] Financing flows also show the number of actors involved in the area, pointing to possible policy coherence issues.

Denmark has the simplest public financing system. Local government funds childcare services out of local taxes, and from other municipal funding, which

Chart 3.1. **Childcare funding flows: Denmark**

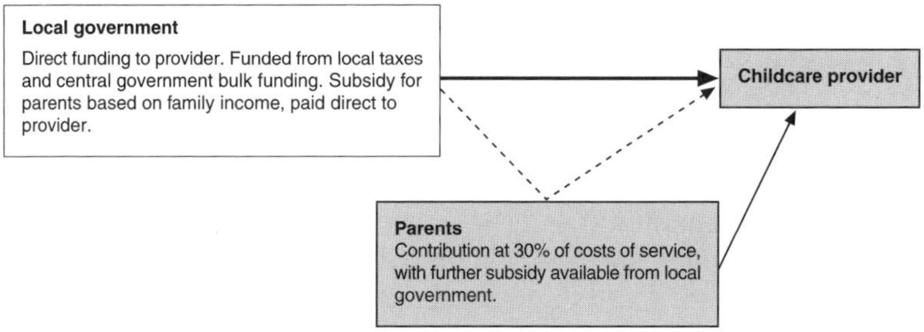

Local government
Direct funding to provider. Funded from local taxes
and central government bulk funding. Subsidy for
parents based on family income, paid direct to
provider.

Childcare provider

Parents
Contribution at 30% of costs of service,
with further subsidy available from local
government.

Source: Danish authorities.

includes bulk funding from the central government. Each local government can
determine how much it each spends on childcare. The parental contribution is set
at a share of costs (a maximum of 30% – discussed below in the section on user
subsidies) with the balance being paid directly to the provider (as shown in
Chart 3.1). Staff of local family departments manage both centre-based and home-
based care in their area, and work with social and health workers if necessary to
intervene in cases where child development may be at risk.

Australia differs from both Denmark and the Netherlands in that both Federal
and State level governments are involved in financing childcare, but the vast bulk
of public funding is from the former. Pre-school services are funded by State and
Territory education departments. Most of the public funding for other formal childcare is by way of the user subsidy, financed though general taxation, taking
account of family circumstances and are paid directly to providers chosen by parents. There are small amounts of operational or other programme expenditure –
some from the States – also paid directly to providers (see Chart 3.2). The compli-
cating factor in Australia is that while most pre-schools are based in school settings, some childcare centres also receive funding for pre-school services for
covering children that are 4 years of age or in the year prior to attending school. In
Australia even though there are three layers of government involved, funding
flows operate reasonably well, however parents can have difficulty finding available places, especially in some localities (see below).

Childcare in the Netherlands has the most complicated set of public funding
arrangements (Chart 3.3). Places in pre-schools are funded from the central government directly (through the Ministry of Education) and are free to the user. For
childcare in other than pre-schools one central government department (VWS)

Chart 3.2.   **Childcare funding flows: Australia**

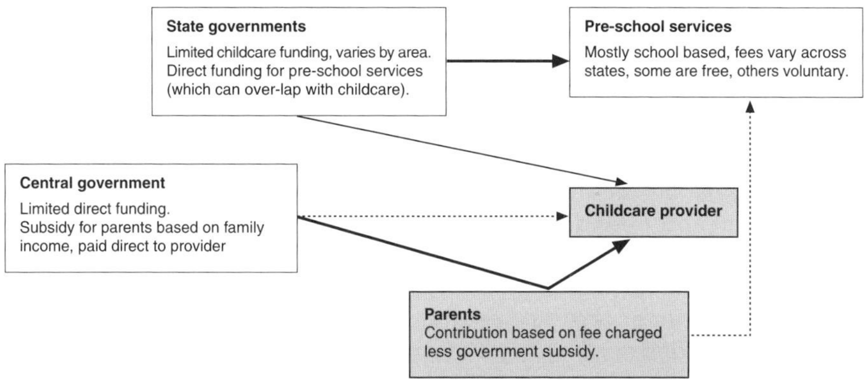

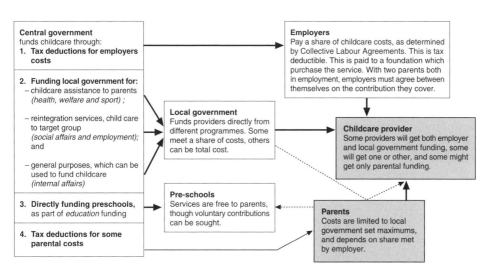

State governments
Limited childcare funding, varies by area.
Direct funding for pre-school services
(which can over-lap with childcare).

Pre-school services
Mostly school based, fees vary across
states, some are free, others voluntary.

Central government
Limited direct funding.
Subsidy for parents based on family
income, paid direct to provider

Childcare provider

Parents
Contribution based on fee charged
less government subsidy.

Source: Australian authorities

Chart 3.3.   **Childcare funding flows: the Netherlands**

Central government
funds childcare through:
1. **Tax deductions for employers
   costs**

2. **Funding local government for:**
   – childcare assistance to parents
   (health, welfare and sport) ;

   – reintegration services, child care
   to target group
   (social affairs and employment);
   and

   – general purposes, which can be
   used to fund childcare
   (internal affairs)

3. **Directly funding preschools,**
   as part of *education* funding

4. **Tax deductions for some
   parental costs**

Employers
Pay a share of childcare costs, as determined
by Collective Labour Agreements. This is tax
deductible. This is paid to a foundation which
purchase the service. With two parents both
in employment, employers must agree between
themselves on the contribution they cover.

Local government
Funds providers directly from
different programmes. Some
meet a share of costs, others
can be total cost.

Childcare provider
Some providers will get both employer
and local government funding, some
will get one or other, and some might
get only parental funding.

Pre-schools
Services are free to parents,
though voluntary contributions
can be sought.

Parents
Costs are limited to local
government set maximums,
and depends on share met
by employer.

Source: Netherlands authorities.

allocates resources for some specific groups – such as refugees (often directly to the provider) and childcare support in general, while another department (Social Affairs), allocates subsidies for lone parents (the KOA programme)[12] and employment integration. These two ministries cover 75% of the *public* contribution towards childcare costs. The remaining 25% of the *public* contribution comes from untied general municipal funding (the "Municipality fund") from the Ministry of Internal Affairs. With this central funding, the municipality finances childcare providers to supply a certain number of childcare places. This process is obviously administratively cumbersome (accounting rules are different for the different central government grants) and bound to involve administrative waste. The complex funding streams are also exposed to the risk of cost shifting. They also make it difficult to be certain of how much public money is actually being spent on childcare services at any point in time. The Dutch system is further complicated by its reliance on employer-provided support for childcare.

3.4.2. Employer funding of childcare in the Netherlands

The role of employers in financing (and in the organisation) of (non-education sector) centre-based childcare[13] for employees in the Netherlands has no parallel in Denmark[14] or Australia. This arises from a time when the government was reluctant to be involved. Employers faced a labour shortage and moved, together with unions, to encourage women to remain in work, by addressing childcare needs. They do this by including a contribution towards the cost of childcare for employees in industrial agreements (CAOs). The contribution is usually a proportion of the payroll and often goes to a childcare foundation established by employers and unions to purchase childcare places from private providers.[15] A typical contribution would be equivalent to 0.1 to 0.5% of the payroll.[16] This type of involvement by employers raises issues about driving up labour costs, though if the expenditure is effective in increasing aggregate labour supply, there may be some offsetting downward pressure on wage rates.

Since the early 1990s, the government has become more heavily involved, with funding to local government to assist parents without employer subsidies and to increase capacity within the childcare sector. However, it still strongly promotes the notion of tripartite funding of childcare. Currently about 65% of industrial agreements include childcare provisions. The government would like this to be higher – around 90%. All employers covered by a particular labour agreement share costs, except larger enterprises that sometimes choose to have their own system. Because costs are shared within rather than across industries, an agreement on childcare costs is likely to be more expensive for an employer in a female dominated industry, rather than a male dominated one, as for example in the health sector. In the past, employers only contributed to childcare costs of female workers, but now, employers no longer make this distinction, so that employers of both parents (and different industries) contribute towards childcare costs. In practical terms many employers also collect the parents share (where they are employees) by withholding it from their pay (and reducing their social security contributions up to 20%), and passing it on to the childcare provider.

As would be expected, the actual share of costs met by employers has increased as the number of agreements providing for childcare has grown over time. In 1989 employers met 7% of childcare costs. By 1996 this had increased to 25% – and it has remained around this level since then. The government finances around a third of the costs (through funding described above) and parents pick up the remaining costs: 42% (OECD, 1999a).

In order to give employers incentives to provide childcare support, Dutch employers can deduct 30% of the costs of employee childcare from taxes and social security contributions levied on wages. In Australia the costs of childcare provided by an employer to their employees, where the childcare is located at the workplace, are deductible for fringe benefit tax purpose. This usually operates as part of a salary sacrifice scheme, where by the employee exchanges salary if the employer pays childcare costs. However, such tax support is relatively small, and moreover parents cannot use Child Care Benefit (see below) towards these childcare costs. This is one reason why employer-provided care is not widespread in Australia. In Denmark there are no tax deductions available for the use of private day care.

3.4.3. Public financing and parental choice

Operational subsidies or user subsidies?

All three countries use public subsidies to reduce the childcare costs parents face – either from central government (Australia), or from local government (Denmark and the Netherlands). In Denmark, local government funds childcare, mainly through direct provision and by funding self-governing institutions. The local government decides what it is prepared to spend on childcare, and funds the services directly. Parents are then required to pay a share (up to 30% to 33%)[17] of the costs. In the Netherlands, there is also direct funding from local government, to purchase childcare places for parents who do not receive an employer contribution. Again, parents are required to pay towards the costs.

The Danish situation thus largely involves financing of providers. However, Denmark does have a "free-choice scheme" where parents can be funded to use FDC they arrange themselves. The grant which is available is at a level set by the municipality but must not exceed 70% of the parents' documented costs, and the maximum is a sum equivalent to 85% of the net costs relating to the cheapest place in a day care facility for the relevant age group. In other words, the scheme cannot cost the municipality more than having a child in a public service, and is capped at a lower rate. The scheme was introduced for the same reason underlying Australian reform: to provide choice to parents in face of capacity constraints in the public sector. However it represents only a very small element of childcare provision.

In addition, the Danish government has recently announced that it will introduce an option where municipalities can allow parents to receive the subsidy themselves to look after their children at home. Municipalities will not be required to make this option available. This scheme will operate in the same way as the "free choice" scheme, except that the subsidy that parents would have received if they had their child in childcare will be payable to them. The payment is available for up to a year[18] at any time before the child starts school. It is contingent on the child not being in childcare, and on one of the parents not being in employment (and not being on paid leave from employment) so that they can look after the child. The scheme will probably become available from mid-2002.

In Australia, the federal government provided direct subsidies to community-based childcare providers until 1997. At that stage the direct operational funding to providers was largely withdrawn, to provide greater equity as for-profit services did not receive this funding. The emphasis moved to funding parents towards the cost of childcare fees, in order to give more choice to parents (Box 3.3). While there was criticism at the time of the change, this was largely related to the fact that there was a reduction in the level of total public funding for childcare at the same time. Public expenditure on childcare fell by 6% between 1996/97 and 1998/99. Utilisation of long day care fell over that period and a number of services closed. In the State of Queensland, 57 services closed in the late 1990s while 96 out of 350 services closed in the State of Western Australia, where there was also a withdrawal of state government funding. Subsequent increases in funding[19] through the introduction of childacre benefit have shown a significant increase in the utilisation of services.

3.4.4. User subsidies

There are user subsidies in each of the three countries, and these operate in different ways. In Australia the user subsidy is through the income targeted Child Care Benefit which follows a legislated formula. The market determines the price. In Denmark, central legislation sets the maximum share of childcare costs parents can be charged, and there is also fee relief for low-income families. In the Netherlands local government is responsible for setting policy on fees relief. There is a set of guidelines[20] prepared by the Ministry of Health, Welfare and Sport (VWS) in conjunction with the Union of Municipalities (VNG), but municipalities can vary from these. As in Australia, there is no maximum cost that providers can charge. However there is a maximum cost that the VWS will subsidise. Should municipalities seek to buy childcare places that cost more than this maximum, they lose the Ministry funding for that place. Details of how the user subsidies operate are shown in Table 3.3.

Box 3.3. **Reform of childcare funding in the Netherlands: providing greater choice**

Having only 17% of 0 to 3-year-olds in childcare in the Netherlands reflects a choice from many parents to care for their children at home. However, for many, that choice is severely constrained by very limited childcare capacity. Even though there has been marked growth in recent years, as a result of specific funding to increase supply, there remains only enough places for around 13% of under 4-years-olds (see Table 3.1). The limited capacity constrains the real choice open to mothers. The proposed new Dutch childcare support programme, that continues with the goal of extending affordable childcare, is broadly along the Australian model: providing *choice* to parents. Hence, like the Australian reform some years ago, financial support will be redirected from providers to parents with the aim to increase parental choice in terms of provision, rather than being unsure of being able to obtain a place in a subsidised (municipal) centre.

In line with recommendations of social partners, the explicit objectives of Dutch childcare reform are to "stimulate the operation of market forces" so that "childcare providers will have to respond to parent's wishes" (VWS, 2001). The stipulations contained in the Childcare Basic Provision Bill are expected to come into force in 2004 and will change how childcare (including out-of-school hours care) is funded and overseen. The notion of tripartite funding is retained, with the continuing expectation that employers will contribute the childcare costs. However, funding to local government to purchase childcare places will be redirected to users, via the Tax Department. Parents will receive a payment based on their income and on the costs of care used, and employers are expected to pay their part to parents directly, so that it follows the parental choice. Parents will be able to direct their funding to any licensed centre, rather than only being able to use services subsidised by the municipality or selected by their employer. Where there is no employer contribution (either because there is no childcare provision in the labour agreement or because the parent is not in employment) the state will pay an additional allowance.

The proposed new funding arrangements will affect how childcare is funded for most working parents. The projected reform will partly simplify the present multitude of financing streams. In future, the main public funding streams will directly go to parents (via the tax system), rather than involving different ministries and about 500 local governments. Moreover, all workers will have access to this benefit rather than only those covered by collective agreements that include employer-provided childcare support (about 60% of all workers). However, local government will still be funded to provide childcare of special target groups, with the likes of the KOA funding for childcare for lone parents remaining unchanged.

At the same time the government is including national quality standards into the childcare legislation, with the Bill being based on the principle that "childcare provisions contribute to the healthy development of the child in a safe environment" (VWS, 2001).

Table 3.3. **Public subsidy to parents for childcare costs**

	Australia (2001)	Denmark (2001)	Netherlands
Nature of subsidy	*Childcare Benefit*: eligibility based on individual family income; paid to service providers in order to reduce fees charged.	Regulated fees and fees relief for low income families.	Recommended maximum parental contribution.
Maximum fee	No maximum fees. Maximum benefit payments are: – A$ 129 per week for 1st child in approved care for 50 hours a week[a] or – A$ 21.70 for children in 50 hours registered care[a] a week (FDC) for families with incomes under A$ 29 857, or who are on income support. There is a minimum entitlement A$ 21.70 a week for families with income over A$ 85 653 (for one child, with higher amounts for multiple children).	Maximum parental fees are set in relation to the childcare operating costs for long day care (LDC) and family day care (FDC). No maximum for SFOs. Municipalities cannot charge parents more than 30% of the costs, except where they guarantee places for those from 6 months to school age, when the fee can be to up to 33%.	Maximum recommended payment for five days childcare per week is NLG 1 100 per month where family income is NLG 5 154 per month or more.
Minimum parental payment	None. Special Child Care Benefit can cover the full fee in special circumstances such as a child at risk, or where a family is in financial hardship. Need reviewed after 13 weeks. Administered by Centrelink.	Fees can be rebated totally for parents whose incomes does not exceed DKK 116 901 per annum where they have one child. Parents with incomes between this amount at DKK 362 701 a year receive a reduction in their fees.	Minimum recommended parental contribution is NLG 101 per month for five days childcare a week, where the family income is 1 683 or less.
	Subsidy depends on actual number of hours used.	Parents pay according to whether the care is full time or part time, however little part time care is available. There is only an indirect relationship between the amount of care used and the fee charged.	Parents can buy care in half-day sessions. Charges relate to how much care is used.

Table 3.3. **Public subsidy to parents for childcare costs** (*cont.*)

	Australia (2001)	Denmark (2001)	Netherlands
Multiple children	Payment is per child in care, on the following basis (maximum per week): 1 child: A$ 129.00; 2 children: A$ 269.64; 3 children: A$ 420.86; plus an additional A$ 129.00 + A$ 11.29 for each further child. In addition, the CCB income test taper rates increase for extra children.	For two or more children there is a further rebate of 50% of the fees on the cheapest care used. The low-income threshold for further fees relief is increased for each additional child.	Fees for subsequent children are a proportion of the fee for the first child (usually 33%).

a) Approved care includes long day care, family day care, some occasional care and some in-home care; Registered care is when a person pays grandparents, relatives, friends or nannies for childcare, and some private pre-schools and kindergartens.
Source: National authorities; Press and Hayes (2000); Socialministeriet (2000); VWS and OC&W (2000).

The user subsidies also apply to out-of-school-hours care. In Australia, the childcare benefit can be used for this purpose, while in the Netherlands these services are being included in CAO agreements, and are covered in the guideline on parental contributions for services. In Denmark outside-school-hours care (OSH) can be provided in schools settings or in childcare settings. The former attracts no maximum co-payment limit, but is about 37% on average.

In Australia, the number of hours of available subsidy depends on whether the childcare is required for labour market reasons or not. If there is no labour market reason, the maximum number of hours of subsidised care is 20 per week; otherwise it is 50 hours per week. This recognises that a main objective of the subsidy is to facilitate employment, but that there are also other objectives such as child development. Neither Denmark nor the Netherlands has such a distinction.

3.4.5. *Cross subsidisation*

In each of the three countries, the user payments vary with income, the rank of the child, but not with the age of the child. In Denmark, as discussed above, municipalities set fees in relation to costs, but they are able to charge parents the same fee for childcare, regardless of whether care was provided through a home-based facility or a centre-based facility by reducing the fee for the most expensive childcare service. In the Netherlands the guidelines and in Australia the childcare benefit do not differentiate by age for children under compulsory school age. However, the underlying cost structure is different from the fee structure. In Australian childcare centres (in line with regulations) the number of staff attending under 3-year-olds is about twice the number of staff caring for children in the age group 3 to 5. As staff wages constitute about 80 to 90 % of all costs of childcare centres, providers need to cross subsidise from the older age group to the younger age group. Most centres do this by having fewer places for under 3-year-olds than for older children. In the Netherlands, cross-subsidisation is less of an issue as staff ratios vary from 4:1 to 6:1 and childcare is expensive, especially in unsubsidised centres (see below).

3.4.6. *Costs after subsidies*

Affordability of childcare is an issue in all three countries. In Denmark parental fees (co-payments) were reduced from 35 to 30% of the costs of a childcare place in 1991, when a "sibling reduction" was also introduced reducing the parental childcare fee for a second (or subsequent) child by 50%. These two measures contributed to increased childcare participation in the 1990s (Table 3.1 and Chart Box 2.3, Chapter 2). In September 1999, 35% (up from 25% in 1990) of Australian women of working age who cited childcare as the main reason they were not looking for work put this down to non-affordability at that time (ACOSS, 2001). The other main reasons were a preference for parental care (54%) and quality and availability factors (7%), down from 25% in 1990, pointing to a significant improvement in capacity and quality (see below).

With the introduction of the Child Care Benefit on 1 July 2000 (replacing the previous provisions (Childcare Assistance and Childcare Rebate) maximum payments to parents with one child in formal care increased by approximately 7% (Costello, 1998). The CCB maximum rate would cover about 75% or the average costs of childcare. Expenditure on child assistance increased by about 25% (Whiteford, 2001). Calculations by the Department of Family and Community Services show that with the introduction of the CCB childcare costs have fallen across all family types and all service types. For example, for a couple with average earnings using 40 hours of private centre-based care, gap fees (which are gross fees less government assistance) represented about 10.4% of the disposable income in 1998; in 2000 this had fallen to 98.3%.

In the Netherlands, overall capacity remains constrained, the expansion of public childcare spending during the 1980s increased the number of subsidised care places, but private sector places play a major role and these are expensive (see below).

In Denmark, it is estimated that about one third of parents get their fees reduced by the income targeted assistance, on top of the effect of the fees cap of 30% of costs. At average earnings a family only has to pay around 72% of the fee charged. The result is that even though costs of care in Denmark are relatively high, the costs to parents are moderate. In Australia, fees assistance – even though income targeted – is available to a large proportion of parents with a higher threshold for maximum assistance than either Denmark or the Netherlands

(Table 3.4, Panel A). Australia also has a cut-out at more that twice the average earnings level for full-time care. The user subsidies have a significant impact on the affordability of childcare in the three countries. In shows that in the Netherlands and Australia low-income people have to spend 5.7 to 8.0% of the income on childcare, if they use full-time care. In Denmark, costs can be totally removed for families with an income below 40% at average earnings, although this is unlikely to occur frequently given the flat earnings distribution in Denmark. The assistance with costs (either by way of fees relief or maximum charges, or both) assists families further up the income range as well, especially in Denmark and Australia.

The cost of a second child in childcare are reduced in both Denmark and the Netherlands through explicit sibling support (50% fee reduction in Denmark, while the recommended fee for the second child being one-third of the first in the Netherlands). The discounts available for multiple children helps constrain the

Table 3.4. **Parental contribution as share of income for full-time childcare, 2001**

Panel A: Thresholds for fees relief

	Threshold: maximum relief to households with annual incomes under:	Threshold as % of gross APW	Parental fee as share of net income at threshold	
			1 child	2 children
Australia	A$ 29 857	69%	7.8%	14.5%
Denmark	DKK 116 901	40%	0%	0%
Netherlands	NLG 20 196	31%	5.7%	10.3%

Panel B: For one child families

	Income	Parental fee as share of net income at threshold		
		Australia	Denmark	Netherlands
Lone parent 1 child	⅔ APW	7.8	10.3	20.3
Lone parent 1 child	1 APW	9.9	15.5	25.9
Couple, 2 earners, 1 child	1⅔ APW	11.4	12.7	17.1

Panel C: For two child families

	Income	Parental fee as share of net income at threshold		
		Australia	Denmark	Netherlands
Lone parent 2 children	⅔ APW	12.3	12.4	25.7
Lone parent 2 children	1 APW	15.9	20.1	33.1
Couple, 2 earners, 2 children	1⅔ APW	18.1	28.3	22.1

Assumes full-time centre-based care. Australia, costs used are average costs for private day care centres, in Denmark, creche costs. Couple calculations assume two earners, one at APW and one at ⅔ APW. Calculations uses fees relief formula applicable in Denmark, CCB formula in Australia and VWS guidelines for parental contributions – these are used by the majority of municipalities but only apply to services which municipalities fund.
Source: OECD Secretariat estimation.

cost for families, however, in Denmark and the Netherlands it represents a further form of cross-subsidisation, and distances the cost from the number of hours of care used. In Australia, childcare benefit includes an additional subsidy, the multiple child rate, which reduces the cost of childcare where the second and subsequent children enter care.

In general, it appears that childcare costs are not a major deterrent for its use in Australia – given enhancements in public funding from July 2000 – and Denmark, especially where there is only one child in care, while costs are considerably higher in the Netherlands (Table 3.4, Panels B and C). More importantly the recommended guidelines concern the fees charged by the majority of subsidised municipal centres, *not* all private commercial centres. Fees charged by these centres can be considerably higher (1.5 to 2 times as high), and the recommended sibling reduction is not always embedded in the fee structure. Although parents using these centres can under certain conditions claim additional tax relief,[21] the cost of childcare for the parents that using these centres (at least in part because of limited subsidised childcare supply) is very high (Box 3.4 and Chapter 5).

Box 3.4. **Formal childcare costs and the incentive to work for second earners in the Netherlands**

Table 3.5 illustrates the critical role that childcare costs play in determining the incentives for a second adult in a household to enter work in the Netherlands. Panel A suggests that if the second earner earns the minimum wage and purchases five days of childcare in the unsubsidised sector, this will cost 84% of all the increase in after-tax earnings. At average earnings, the gain in income is even smaller. There is, in other words, virtually no immediate financial incentive for a second earner to work. The fact that earning more gives less return requires some explanation. Two effects are of relevance. First, even in the unsubsidised sector, childcare providers relate their charges to family income. Second, the *absolute* gain in income after childcare costs still is larger the greater is the income level. Note that if the second earner needs purchase only two days childcare, the net gains from working become higher.

Getting a subsidised childcare place makes a huge difference to the incentive for a second earner to work in the Netherlands. Even so, as shown in Panel B, around half the net earnings of the second earner go on childcare. Panels C and D show that having a second child needing care significantly reduces the return to work (though does not eliminate it if a subsidised, local authority childcare place could be found).

Table 3.5. **Childcare costs as a percentage of after-tax earnings of a second earner in a couple in the Netherlands**

Situation	2 days childcare	5 days childcare
Panel A. 1 child in unsubsidised care		
Minimum wage	65	84
Average wage	70	91
Panel B. 1 child in subsidised care		
Minimum wage	24	40
Average wage	41	59
Panel C. 2 children in unsubsidised care		
Minimum wage	126	161
Average wage	132	170
Panel D. 2 children in subsidised care		
Minimum wage	31	52
Average wage	54	77

Note: Childcare costs for children aged under 4.
Source: NYFER (1999).

While costs of formal childcare, even after public subsidy are high, Dobbelsteen *et al.* (2000) suggest that this has only had a limited effect on maternal labour force participation in the Netherlands. If mothers participate in employment they are much more likely to do so part-time. They suggest that it is plausible that the high costs of childcare have the effect of turning parents from high cost formal care to cheaper informal care, rather than leading to non-participation in the labour market.

3.5. Quality

3.5.1. *Parental preferences*

The choice of whether a parent stays at home to care for his/her child or children is influenced by social attitudes towards childcare (Chapter 2), and these are shaped by the debate about whether a child does better in care or at home. In 1999 54% of Australian women of working age citing childcare as the main reason they were not looking for work said that they preferred to look after the child at home (for other than financial reasons)[22]. In other words, neither unavailability or quality of childcare were the primary issues, indeed only 2.2% said quality was the main issue (ACOSS, 2001). In the Netherlands, there is no hard evidence on preferences, though concern over the variability of quality from one municipality to another does appear to have an influence (Trouw, 2001). In Denmark a citizens survey carried out in 2000 by Gallup Institute (for the government) respondents identified the educational content as being of crucial importance in both the school and the child services sectors. Satisfaction for kindergartens rated as 4.17 out of

103|

5 and day care scored 4.37 out of 5, suggesting a high level of satisfaction with childcare services. (Finansministeriet, 2000).

3.5.2. What is quality and how is it assured?

The use of childcare is also influenced by how parents perceive the quality of care being carried out. The concept of quality childcare reflects particular social and cultural contexts and changes over time, however, Kamerman (2001) suggests that there is a consensus emerging about the important dimensions of quality, which she lists as being: staff-to-child ratios; group size; facility size; staff qualifications and training; staff salaries and turn over. OECD work on the issue (2001i), also includes levels of investment; co-ordinated policy and regulatory frameworks; efficient and co-ordinated management structures; pedagogical frameworks and other guide-lines; and regular systems for monitoring. The debate about the impact of time spent in childcare (and the effect of both parents working) is live in all countries, as it is further afield. Box 3.5 looks at the issues involved in this emerging area.

In both Australia and Denmark there has been more of a focus on quality aspects of childcare than in the Netherlands, where capacity is still the main concern. In all countries local or state authorities licence childcare centres for health and safety purposes.[23] But more than safety standards, quality concerns about the standard of care and the nature of care-time activities have come to the fore. In both Denmark and the Netherlands, central government legislation assigns the responsibility for childcare standards to local government. In the former this has been the case since local government took over responsibility for childcare in 1973, however it only dates from 1997 in the Netherlands.[24] There, childcare providers have to meet these requirements in order to obtain a license which is a prerequisite to receiving tax benefits (VWS and OC&W, 2000). Interestingly, both European countries also have aspects of quality set down in the labour agreements of the staff who work in those centres. In contrast to this highly decentra-lised approach, Australia now has centrally determined procedures for approving which childcare services are eligible to receive Child Care Benefit payments. In addition, State and Territory governments are also involved in the regulation of childcare (Press and Hayes, 2000).[25] This is discussed in more detail in the next section. In both Australia and the Netherlands, the regulation of pre-schools rests with the education sector. In Australia, this is State level, while in the Dutch system, schools are autonomous, though are required to adhere to a range of national legislation, and are subject to supervision by the Education Inspectorate.

3.5.3. The Netherlands: central guidelines

In the Netherlands, there is a considerable degree of self-regulation within the childcare sector, with it developing voluntary quality standards aligned with

Box 3.5. **Child development**

There is consensus that the first years of life are critical for cognitive, physical, social and emotional development. (OECD, 1999b). Questions of how participation in childcare programmes and how parental work patterns impact on child development in these years concern parents, professionals, researchers and policy makes. These are issues about which there is considerable debate and often strong opinions. Any conclusions and usually heavily qualified and there is an understandable reluctance to generalise results from one country to another. Even so, it is useful to take a brief look at some of the issues involved.

In Australia, the Centre for Community Child Health (CCCH, 2000) describes a transactional model of child development looking at the interplay between the biological factors within a child and the caretaking environment. The model suggests "that developmental outcomes are the end result of a complex transaction between intrinsic or within child factors (*e.g.* such as genes, central nervous system development, temperament) and environmental factors (*e.g.* parenting style, amount of stimulation, socio-economic status)". Certain biological factors can be regarded as risk factors that create vulnerability (rather than poor outcomes per se) that can be increased or reduced by environmental factors.

The quality of the caretaking environment is influenced by: characteristics of the parents; socio-economic determinants; level of stress and support experienced by the family; the level and intensity of early learning experiences the child has; parenting style and family functioning; and parental mental health.

CCCH have reviewed a range of studies looking at the various risk factors and at interventions* influencing child outcomes, and while cautioning the application of results of overseas studies to an Australian setting, posit a number of general conclusions. They draw on Boocock's reviews (1995) of childcare in the United States and Sweden to conclude that: *a*) participation in a pre-school has benefits in terms of cognitive development and school success, and that this is more positive for children from low income families; and *b*) maternal employment and participation in regulated and high quality childcare, during infancy appears not to be harmful and may yield benefits for children. The key to positive results from out-of-home care for children revolve around services being of sufficient quality.

The results of the one Australian based study included in the CCCH review – the Australian Early Childhood Development study, carried out in the early 1970s – were consistent with the general conclusions, finding that aspects of the home environment affect social and emotional development *as much or more* than experiences in childcare.

Russell and Bowman (2000) reviewed literature on the effect of parental employment on families and children, concluding that there appears to be general agreement that there are no significant developmental problems for children of employed mothers. They cite research by Broom (1998) concluding that early

---

* The interventions examined included pre-school and childcare as well as child health surveillance, home visiting, parent education and programmes for children with developmental delay or disability.

Box 3.5. **Child development** (*cont.*)

employment for mothers can lead to less stress and in turn greater sensitivity towards their young babies. However they also note that workplace variables impact directly on job satisfaction, tensions and mood, that these impact on parenting behaviours, and in turn on children's behaviour (Stewart and Barling, 1996). Consistent with the conclusions of the CCCH literature review, Russell andBowman conclude that studies show that the quality of childcare is the most critical factor in determining whether childcare has positive outcomes or not.

Harrison and Ungerer (2000), in an Australian longitudinal study, looked at developmental outcomes and the use of non-parental care from birth to six. They found that childcare contributed to positive child development outcomes. Formal care produced better outcomes than informal care in terms of factors such as relationships with peers at pre-school, and independence, task focus and having fewer learning difficulties at school age.

Christoffersen (2000*a*, 2000*b* and 2000c) concludes from Danish research, that long hours of work by parents, and long hours in care, are less relevant than parental job satisfaction in determining whether long work hours impair or enhance child outcomes. He suggests that high stress levels in work are likely to be passed on to children resulting in the likes of higher levels of child anxiety or more conflict or lower levels of confidence etc. He also found that children of unemployed parents were more likely to suffer from such adverse indicators than children who spent long hours in childcare where parents work long hours. Children on long-term unemployed parents are particularly vulnerable, for example:

- half of children living in families with long-term unemployed parents experience break-up of the family, twice as high as for their peers; and
- 7% of children from families enduring long-term unemployment have experienced suicide or attempted suicide of one parent (3-4 times the rate of children of parents in employment).

These effects are reduced, but not eliminated by controlling for parental education, and other social circumstances.

According to the Nederlandse Gezinsraad (2001), 5-15% of children from the 120 000 families with long-term low incomes are "at risk" of poor developmental outcomes, a vastly higher percentage than nearly any other way of looking at households (for lone parents, for example, it is only 1-2% of children at risk).

In short, some research suggests that young people who participate in quality early childhood education and care are likely to develop better reasoning and problem solving skills; to be more co-operative to develop greater self-esteem, even though some of the direct gains such as in IQ rating for age appear to fade. Child development is influenced by the type of care children are exposed to – in the home and outside of the home. Quality childcare can enhance good parenting. Unemployment – and in particular long-term unemployment – can impact on child development. The extent to child development is influenced by childcare or by the incidence of parental employment or unemployment, the questions of how much quality childcare deliver benefits to children, and the optimal age for starting childcare are all questions of keen interest when looking balancing work and family, and are areas for on-going consideration.

Table 3.6. **Aspects of quality in the Netherlands**

Current association of Dutch municipalities "Model Law" on quality:	Proposed national framework: factors foreshadowed for inclusion
– Maximum groups size – Child-staff ratios – Housing – Hygiene – Safety – Use of certified playing materials – Training requirements of staff – Parent involvement.	– Personnel and financial management – Professional development – Quality of premises – Well-being of child – Pedagogy – Parental involvement – Complaints procedures

Source: OECD (1999a) and communications with national authorities.

international ISO standards.[26] They also have a set of model standards, which have been developed in conjunction with the Association of Dutch Municipalities, which 75% of municipalities have accepted (VWS and OC&W, 2000). The current guidelines are largely focussed on minimum standards in terms of safety and capacity, rather than development (Table 3.6). Even though the Netherlands has moved recently to decentralise quality standards, this looks as if it will be short lived. The Childcare Basic Provision Bill currently under discussion (see above) will lay down detailed quality standards, which providers will have to meet. The focus in the proposed guidelines shifts away from basic care towards development and has already drawn criticism from employers as to unnecessarily increase costs of childcare (VNO/NCW, 2001). Municipal health authorities will be responsible for supervising the quality of childcare. The proposed new childcare legislation has fuelled discussion on how to successfully procure quality childcare as well as a research programme into the effects of childcare on young children.

3.5.4. Denmark: *the role of parents*

There are no detailed centrally set quality guidelines in Denmark. Central legislation establishes requirements that local governments are responsible for, in order to ensure that children are supported "in the acquisition and development of social and general skills". The legislation states that, among other things, day care should facilitate experiences and activities likely to stimulate the imagination, creativity and linguistic skills of the child. However, with its emphasis on decentralised responsibility for quality, the Danish model has two interesting features. More so than in the Netherlands municipalities collaborate on quality issues and involve central government officials and unions representatives in their projects. Through such joint projects, such as a project on the development of

Table 3.7. **Denmark: aspects of quality in the Lyngby-Taarbaek Community**

Components of the Plan for Family Day Care in the Lyngby-Taarbaek Commune. The following are headings from the 2001 plan developed to guide the delivery of family day care services:

Principles for the children:
- Individual concern
- Care in a nice environment
- Early identification of social problems
- That the children have knowledge of certain things (like clothing, scissors, etc.)
- Creating self esteem
- Socialisation: how to behave with other children

Principles for the parents and carers:
- Close co-operation between parents and carers
- Creating a nice work environment for the carer
- Staff development (through training)

Source: Lyngby-Taarbaek Commune.

child competencies and staff competencies, local authorities are able to improve their quality standards (VWS and OC&W, 2000).

But the most remarkable feature about the Danish model is the parental role. Denmark has, since 1993, placed increasing emphasis on parental input and oversight in improving quality. Since then childcare has been overseen by parent boards (as well as by municipal authorities), which define principles for the care work carried out in the service within the framework of the legislation. The parent boards are elected and have some decision-making powers related to setting principles for activities in the centre and for budget management. They also have recommendatory powers related to staffing issues. The boards play a major part in setting the annual plans for the childcare services, which are the main mechanism for ensuring quality, and are submitted to the local authority funding the service. Municipal pedagogical advisers guided staff and parents in developing plans and in determining their own quality monitoring processes. An example of the components of a plan for Family Day Care in the Lyngby-Taarbaek Commune (Table 3.7) shows the similarity across the principles identified in the Australian quality systems (see below). Involving parents is a positive feature of the system, with strong ownership of the systems they help create, but without any external benchmarking, the system leaves local professionals in a very powerful position, relative to parents.

3.5.5. The Australian way: quality systems and licensing

The Australia Commonwealth government has developed quality assurance systems for both long-day care centres and for family day care, and has tied the ability for childcare providers to receive funding through the Child Care Benefit (and its predecessors) to satisfactory participation in the Quality Assurance system (Box 3.6). However, this development followed rather than preceded the rapid growth in private sector involvement in childcare from 1990. The Quality Improvement and Accreditation System (QIAS) for day care centres was introduced in 1994, while the Family Day Care Quality Assurance (FDCQA) system for family day care services, has only been in place since July 2001. Both are administered by the National Childcare Accreditation Council (NCAC) – a federally funded

---

Box 3.6. **Australia's Quality Assurance (QA) systems**

The National Childcare Accreditation Council in Australia was established to administer the Quality Improvement and Accreditation System (QIAS) for day care centres (introduced 1994, revised for 2002) and the Family Day Care Quality Assurance (FDCQA) system for family day care services (2001). Federal funding for providers, by way of being eligible to receive the childcare benefit is tied to these schemes. Both the QIAS and the FDCQA follow a five-step process which service providers must go through in order to become and remain accredited:

- *Step One*: Registration – services are required to pay a registration and annual fee.
- *Step Two*: Self-Study and Continuing Improvement – each service is required to carry out a self-study and develop a Continuing Improvement Plan on a cyclical basis, submitting a report to the NCAC every 2.5 years. Parents, staff and management are involved in preparing the self-reviews.
- *Step Three*: Validation – a peer validator visits the day care centre or family day care scheme, and prepares a validation report based on observations and a review of documentation. The report is submitted to NCAC.
- *Step Four*: Moderation – validators' ratings are moderated to ensure that assessments are consistent on a national basis. And
- *Step Five*: Accreditation Decision – the NCAC decides on accreditation and advised to the service providers. There are appeal procedures and centres that fail are required to submit another self-study report six months from the date of the NCAC decision.

Integral to the quality assurance systems are the sets of factors against which assessments are made. For long day care (LDC) there are ten "quality areas" and 35 principles sitting under these. For FDC there are six "quality elements" with 32 principles. It is against these areas, elements and principles that service providers assess themselves, and are gauged by the peer reviewers and moderators. Accreditation requires a satisfactory or higher rating on all quality areas/elements. Documentation sets out quality indicators for each factor.

agency accountable to the Commonwealth minister responsible for childcare. Work is currently underway to develop a similar system for outside school-hours care services.

The quality areas for LDC and quality elements for FDC are:

Quality area for long day care (LDC)	Quality element for family dar care (FDC)
1 Relationship with children	1 Interactions
2 Respect for children	2 Physical environment
3 Partnerships with families	3 Children's experiences, learning and development
4 Staff interactions	4 Health, hygiene, nutrition, safety and wellbeing
5 Planning and evaluation	5 Carers and co-ordination unit staff
6 Learning and development	6 Management and administration
7 Protective care	
8 Health	
9 Safety	
10 Managing to support quality	

Source: NCAC (2001 and 2001a).

While the system for FDC is very new, both the QIAS and the FDCQA appear to provide a comprehensive way of ensuring quality care. The QIAS has been well supported, partly because of the dual focus on improvement as well as accreditation. The innovative use of *peer review* (rather than a centralised inspectorate) and the emphasis on quality improvement rather than minimum standards are particularly noteworthy. The test for these systems relates to whether the standards can actually be properly enforced while there remains a waiting list for childcare places. To date only a handful of centres have in fact been temporarily disqualified from receiving childcare benefit.

In addition to the federal quality systems, each Australian State or Territory Government can regulate to licence childcare services. Not all States and Territories have chosen to do so, but those that do appear to look at many of the same things the federal systems take into account. For example, in the State of Queensland licensing of centres involves looking at physical facilities, the types of programmes offered, the number of staff with qualifications, the size of groups and the mix of ages of children, the fitness of and propriety of providers and staff (with police checks being required), and health and safety issues. Re-licensing is required every two years. The State of Queensland intends to revise its state legislation so as to improve the interactions. While central government considers that the dual systems are complementary, on the face of it, the result involves a considerable duplication of compliance activity required of service providers that could be avoided.

Furthermore, in the State of Victoria, childcare centres are eligible to receive funding from the State education authority in respect of the pre-school children in their care. This requires service providers to deal with yet another set of compliance rules.

3.5.6. *Staff issues for quality childcare*

Quality childcare relies on having the right number and mix of staff. The child-to-staff ratios, staff qualifications and training, salaries and the staff turnover have all been identified as key factors (Kamerman, 2001). These are issues in each of the three countries reviewed. In both the Netherlands and Australia childcare workers (as opposed to pre-school) tend to have lower levels of training and lower remuneration than those in the education sector. And those working in FDC are likely to have lower levels of education and training than those working in centre-based care (Table 3.8). In each country there are challenges in attracting and retaining suitably qualified people, given lower pay and status accorded work with young children (OECD, 2001i).

Day care centres in Denmark use highly trained pedagogues, who are on a par with schoolteachers in terms of training and salary. The Netherlands also requires day care centre staff who are leaders to have a middle or higher professional education. In all countries, qualified day care centre staff are assisted by unqualified or less qualified staff, who are lower paid. In Australia, these assistants can be casual employees. This can be because of shortages of trained staff, but also as part of a way of minimising costs. The use of casual staff gives rise to concerns about staff turnover and therefore continuity for children. Danish FDC co-ordinators are also usually qualified pedagogues. They select family day care workers who then attend induction training, with the opportunity for regular in-service training. In Australia, staff training requirements vary according to jurisdiction and service type. In some states, there is an explicit link between qualifications and

Table 3.8. **Qualifications required to work in childcare**

	Main type of staff	Initial training
Australia	Pre-school teacher	3-4 years university
	Childcare centre worker	2 years post-18 – 4 years university
	Family day carer	No qualification
Denmark	Pedagogue in LDC and as FDC Co-ordinator	3.5 years vocational higher education
	Assistant and FDC carer	No qualification
Netherlands	Pre-basic school	4 years vocational higher education
	Child care	3-4 years tertiary (non university) qualification
	Family day care	No qualification

Source: OECD (2001i).

the number of children the staff member can supervise.[27] FDC carers are not required to have a specific qualification, however individual schemes may require carers to undertake orientation training and may offer in service training. As in the Netherlands, pre-school teachers are required to hold a teaching qualification. In both Australia[28] and the Netherlands there remain concerns that workers with young children have low status rather than being seen as professions educators or caregivers. While there is in-service training available in each country, the ability to work in the sector unqualified clearly contributes to this image enduring.

Child-to-staff ratios are the highest in Australia for the younger age group, and higher in the Netherlands for the older age group (Table 3.2). Staff ratios are governed by state-level regulation in Australia. In both Denmark and the Netherlands, rules governing child-to-staff ratios in centre-based care, are determined locally. In the latter national requirements are found in collective labour agreements, as a way of ensuring employment conditions, rather than as a way of maintaining quality of service for the children. There are also rules governing group sizes, according to the age of the children – the maximum size for a group of 0-1-year-olds is 12 children, while the maximum group size for 4-12-year-olds is 20. In Denmark, ratios for family day care are regulated centrally – family day carer can have a maximum of five children – the average is between three and four.

There are particular recruitment and retention issues with rural and remote services in Australia, and with services for economically deprived areas in the Netherlands. There are either actual or anticipated shortages in trained staff in all three countries with the growth in services in recent years. If these shortages are not addressed they are likely to result in a greater share of care being provided by untrained staff – resulting in a reduction in quality, or in a shortage of care places – both of which will have adverse consequences for families.

Of course quality of provision must be balanced with cost and affordability (see above). There are tensions. For example, the higher the staff ratios, the less effective the interaction between children and carers. On the other hand, the lower the staff ratio (and the higher the ratio of qualified staff to all staff) the greater the costs of provision and the greater the number of households that will not be able to afford the price of childcare.

3.6. Childcare constraints

Childcare capacity in all three countries seems constrained, but in different ways. Survey data for Australia indicate there is some additional demand for childcare, for about 9% of children under 5, either through increased hours or new participants (ABS, 2000b). The survey suggests a significant drop in "unmet demand" between 1993 and 1999 (Table 3.9).

Table 3.9. **Indicators of extra care wanted by parents**

	Australia		
	Age	Numbers wanting more care	As % of children
Additional formal care required 1993	0-4	279 200	22%
	5-11	210 100	12%
Additional formal care required 1999	0-4	114 100	9%
	5-11	87 000	5%

	Denmark (2000)		Netherlands (1997)	
	0-2 year-olds	3-5 year-olds	0-3 year-olds	4-7 year-olds
Waiting lists 1993/94	10 775	5 440	51 896	8 466
Waiting lists (latest data)	4 037	1 223	32 237	5 562

Source: Australia: ABS (2000b); Denmark: Socialministeriet (2000); Netherlands: OECD (1999), VWS and OC&W (2000).

No comparable information is available for Denmark or the Netherlands, but waiting lists give some indication of the number of places being sought. In Denmark, the waiting list problem (at less that 1% of all children aged between 6 months and 9 years) is largely concentrated in a few municipalities (*e.g.* Copenhagen), especially where there is difficulty in getting suitable accommodation (for both centre-based and home-based care) and labour supply shortages in the childcare sector. Nevertheless, the data in Table 3.9 represent a small proportion of the numbers already in childcare. By contrast, in the Netherlands, though waiting lists have reduced, the numbers still continue to equate to a large share of the places available (25% for 0-3-year-olds and 21% for 4 to 7-year-olds). A recent survey indicated that 26% of parents with children not yet of school age faced a waiting period of over ten months (Commissie Dagarrangementen, 2002). This information confirms the finding that childcare in the Netherlands at current prices is not affordable for many, and that for many others who can afford the costs, capacity is too limited. Where childcare services are free – the education-based provisions – their utilisation is very high.

If childcare is generally affordable in Denmark and Australia – because of public funding, and there is a demand for more care, as demonstrated by waiting lists and by surveys of parents –, why is there not more supply? In Denmark, the question is only relevant to some areas where waiting lists are relatively long, and these are often urban areas where suitable facilities are either limited or very expensive to develop.

In all three countries constraints on increasing capacity relate to finding or developing suitable facilities, meeting licensing requirements, and recruiting suit-   113 able staff. Given that Australia appears to have largely addressed affordability issues, and cultivated a market for childcare, why has further supply not emerged? In part, this is related to the planning controls which apply to family day care and OSH care places (see below). There is a national planning system to identify where additional places can and should be established. The system is designed to target new growth to areas of greatest need. In each state a Planning Advisory Committee, with federal, state and local government representatives, uses this data to recommend areas where additional places should be allocated. A similar mechanism used to operate for centre-based care for a period.[29] This planning constrains supply by directing where growth can occur. It will act as a brake of FDC provision in some areas, but does not explain why there are shortages in some services.

The fact that the childcare benefit is paid at the same rate for young children as it is for older children could influence where the market seeks to expand. Services for younger children are more expensive to run because they have higher staff ratios. Thus, providers have to balance the number of places they provide across the age groups to ensure overall profitability. While they could differentiate their fees according to costs by charging more for younger children, this would make those services more costly for parents, given the flat rate CCB, and therefore reduce demand.

These factors do not explain why the use of childcare in Australia is so much lower than in Denmark. The issues associated with licensing and planning approvals must be seen as timing issues rather than fundamental constraints. The level of satisfaction with childcare services has improved, and affordability has also improved. However, throughout the 1990s, while capacity expanded very significantly, parental preferences to care for children at home remained reasonably constant. As noted above, in 1999 just over half of mothers who were not in employment and not looking for employment because of child related reasons stated that it was their preference to look after their children at home. This is not much different than in 1990 (where the figure was just under half) (ACOSS, 2001). In Denmark, the expectation is that children will be in childcare from a relatively young age, and a very large amount of public funding ensures this is possible. That same expectation has not evolved in Australia – nor for that matter in the Netherlands. In Australia and especially in the Netherlands, it is probable that the demand for childcare services would rise if the price to the user were reduced further. However at this stage it is unlikely that it would quickly rise to the levels observed in Denmark without a change in how parents prefer to care for their children in the early years.

3.6.1. Full-time and part-time care

As noted earlier in this chapter, in Denmark the bulk of childcare is used on a full-time basis, while both Australia and the Netherlands mainly use childcare on a part-time basis. Given the high rate of female labour force participation in

Denmark, the predominance of full-time childcare is not surprising, and similarly, it would be expected that part-time care would be more significant in the other two countries. In all three countries the childcare systems in theory offer people the choice of full-time or part-time care. However, there are constraints on how real that choice is.

In Denmark, the number of part-time places available has reduced in recent years. This is said to be because of a lack of demand on one hand and because there is no financial advantage – and there may even be a disadvantage in having to deal with more children, requiring more administration – for the same level of income – for local governments in offering part-time care. Further, the charging regime is not always that sensitive to the number of hours of care actually used, especially – where there is more than one child per family in childcare – because of the multiple child discounts. While multiple child discounts help with afford-ability, together with the lack of flexibility for parents wanting less than full-time care, parental contribution does not match well with the actual hours of care used. This means that in some municipalities parents buy more care than they need or use. The general policy framework allows municipalities to offer greater flexibility than is the general practice. The lack of match between fee and usage has been recognised by some municipalities, which are working on options for greater align-ment. Allowing more flexibility in hours of care available and amount of care that can be bought, together with a closer alignment of fee charged and actual use would both enhance efficiency in supply and in utilisation (OECD, 2002e; Social-ministeriet, 2000; and communications with Association of Local Authorities).

In the Netherlands it is possible to buy childcare in blocks of a half-day and full-day blocks. While full day full-time care is possible, its costs are prohibitive for most families (see above). In Australia, childcare can be purchase on a by-the-hour basis for family day care, so there is a fit between use and cost. However, for centre-based care is only available on a half-day session basis, so anyone wanting less than this will have to pay for more care than they need. There are also other constraints: it can be difficult for centres to change part-time places into full-time places if the parent needs extra hours unless that centre has unused capacity. In addition, the fact that much of the childcare work is part-time feeds into the issue of attracting professional staff, and improving the image of childcare as a career option. Australia recognises that there are extra costs in providing part-time care, and that fees are therefore likely to be higher than for full-time care by adding a "part-time" loading onto the Child Care Benefit that is payable.

3.6.2. *Opening hours*

Increase diversity in work-hours means that childcare services will be called on over a range of times as well. In Denmark, childcare service hours are governed by the local authority, which can leave the opening hours for the parents' board to determine. Different facilities can have different opening hours – with some opening early and others closing later to fit the increased variability on work hours. However, in practice, fewer services have been opening beyond 5 pm. In 1989 32% of services opened beyond 5 pm, but this had reduced to 24% by 1994 and 17% by 1998 (DA – Employers Confederation) in part because of budgetary constraints and industrial agreements with staff. This is an issue of concern for both employers and parents, who struggle to work full-time then make their way to the childcare service to collect their child. In both the Netherlands and Australia centres determine their own hours, depending on user demand, staff ability, and costs. In Australia they are required to be open at least 8 hours a day, 5 days a week, 48 weeks a year. As in Denmark, there is an issue with the cost of and availability of care services for those requiring extended hours services, particularly nigh-time services. This impacts particularly on parents who are employed in shift work industries, including nursing. In 2000 the government in Australia announced additional funding of A$ 65.4 million over four years to fund 7 700 home care places, aimed at addressing the needs of those engaged in shift work or non standard hours work. The programme will also assist parents with sick children and those in rural and remote areas who have problems finding suitable childcare services (DFACS/ DEWR, 2002).

Australian statistics (2000) show that 13% of women with children aged under 12 worked shift work, while 11% work on weekends.[30] While shift work is less common in the Netherlands, night-time work is more common – with 15% of women with children working at night. Many of these parents will arrange informal care, or will work while the other parent is at home with the children. The demand for formal care in these work times is likely to become increasingly important with increasing flexibility for hours in the workplace. This will increase the pressure on services to be more responsive (information provided by national authorities). The costs are likely to be higher for care in these situations, in order to attract staff to work at non-standard hours, and because of the relatively small numbers wanting care in any one location.

In terms of facilitating work parents have to work in with the hours of care they can obtain. They also have to allow for the time required getting children from home to care, and their own travel time to work. In all countries, most parents prefer to have the care located close to their home rather than close to their employment. Having more than one child of childcare age, or one child in childcare with another in school adds to the logistical challenge. Moves to make childcare hours more flexible in Australia, as well as the emphasis on increasing supply will address problems caused by rigidity in available hours of service.

Box 3.7. **Childcare and family friendly issues for indigenous Australians**

The family friendly policy issues for Aboriginal and Torres Strait Islander people are quite different from those facing the general Australian population, reflecting their different demographic, socio-economic and geographic characteristics (see Table Box 3.7). The Indigenous population comprised about 2.1% of the total population in 1996, but had nearly twice the annual growth rate at 2.3%. Mothers tend to be younger, as does the whole population, but life expectancy is shorter (ABS, 1999a). Households tend to be bigger (on average by one person) and there is a stronger emphasis of kinship links.

Table Box 3.7. **Statistics on the Aboriginal and Torres Strait Islander Population in Australia**

	Aboriginal and Torres Strait Islander population	Total Australian population
Number of babies per woman, 2000	2.2	1.7
Average age of mother at birth, 2000	24.5 years	29.8 years
Share of population under 25, 2000	60%	34.6%
Education participation at 15, 1996	73%	91.5%
Labour force participation rate, 2000	52.9%	64%
Unemployment rate, 2000	17.6%	6.6%
90% of population concentrated, 1996	25% of the continent	2.6% of continent

Source: ABS (1999a, 2000c and 2000d) and *www.workplace.gov.au*.

Aboriginal and Torres Strait Islander people have lower school participation and labour force participation rates and are more likely to be unemployed. They are also more likely to live in remote and rural areas where labour markets are extremely limited and transport and access to public services are major issues. Indigenous people have much lower incomes – with a median of 65.1% of the Australian median in 1996, with over half of all Indigenous families with children had incomes of 80-100% of the poverty line (Butler, 2000).

For Aboriginal and Torres Strait Islander people balancing work and family focuses largely around promoting economic and community development so as to address social disadvantage. Targeted programmes augment general childcare for this population. Multifunctional Aboriginal Children's Services provide care and education in remote populations specifically for Aboriginal and Torres Strait

---

Box 3.7. **Childcare and family friendly issues
for indigenous Australians** (*cont.*)

Islander children 0-12.* Multifunctional centres can also look at child health and nutrition. Although Indigenous people prefer to use informal care (AIHW, 2001), research has found that in Indigenous communities with multi-purpose childcare centres, children are more confident learners and are better prepared for school (Butler, 2000). One such a multifunctional centre is the Coolabaroo centre in Western Australia. Established to provide childcare while parents train, it offers more than just childcare. It also undertakes advocacy work for a community strug- gling to address serious problems, including poverty, drug dependency and vio- lence. Funding comes from federal and state programmes including childcare benefit and the JET scheme.

In terms of accessing public services, Centrelink is seeking to improve access to income support through its Indigenous Servicing Strategy. It involves strength- ening both Centrelink's capacity and that of the community, by working with the community so that they know what is available, and can have input into developing different delivery approaches.

Facilitating participation in education and employment are also major parts of the approach to addressing the needs of indigenous people. The Community Development Employment Projects (CDEP), is a very significant employment pro- gramme, run by the Aboriginal and Torres Strait Islander Commission. If this pro- gramme did not exist the unemployment rate amongst Indigenous people would be around 40% (Butler, 2000). There is also an Indigenous Employment Strategy involv- ing wage programmes such as assistance to employers, training programmes and cadetships for indigenous undergraduates. Under Australians Working Together, the government aims build on the existing CDEP organisations to take on the role of Indigenous Employment Centres, to provide intensive job assistance.

---

* In addition to Multifunctional Children's Services and Mobile Children's Services for the general population in rural areas.

3.7. Childcare-school-work time interface

When in school parents do not have to look after their children. Primary school hours on the curriculum are longer in Australia than anywhere else in the OECD at 996 hours per year. On a yearly basis, primary school hours in the Netherlands amount to 930 hours, but in Denmark only to 644 hours (OECD, 2001h). From this perspective, school hours *potentially* pose the biggest problem to Danish parents – but this is not the case, given high coverage of out-of-hours care services (see below). In practice, Dutch parents face the biggest headache in work, and school-hours, because they are so unpredictable.

During the 1980s, the Netherlands had an excess supply of teachers, and teachers were given extra holidays (the so-called ADV-dagen or "labourduration-shortening" in Dutch) while generous early-retirement packages were also made available. Nowadays, there is a shortage of teachers in the Netherlands, but the 14.5 ADV days still exist on top of the 55 scheduled holidays for primary school teachers in the Netherlands. Combined with higher than average sickness absenteeism rates (CBS, 2001b), it is not surprising that schools find it difficult to provide the planned number of hours. In the absence of replacement teachers, they regularly close for a day (often half a day for older children) at short notice, leaving parents to juggle for quick solutions to care for their children. In the school year 2000-2001, 35% of the schools had to send their children home because of teacher shortages (van Langen and Hulsen, 2001), and this proportion exceeded 50% in inner city schools.

3.7.1. Out-of-school hours care

In both Australia and the Netherlands pre-school care, which is part of the education sector, open during school hours. This starts between 8.30 and 8.45 am in the Netherlands and lasting 5.5 hours, and starts at 9 am in Australia, lasting up to 6 hours. Both are available five days a week, but are limited to term time. Danish schools operate for 20 to 25 hours a week. For all countries school hours mean the pre-children require other arrangements from the early afternoon. It also means that for many pre-school and school children require care before school as well. This is increasingly met through the use of out-of-school-care services (OSH), which are most developed in Denmark. In the Netherlands, 63% of working parents with school aged children responded in a recent survey that they had problems with the start time of schooling and the start time for work. At the same time, a massive 87% wanted some flexibility around the hours of care services (Commissie Dagarrangementen, 2002).

In Denmark, four out of five children participate in OSH care (up from three out of five in the mid-1990s), while Australia, with 145 000 children using out-of-school-hours care services is very low at 6.8%.[31] In the Netherlands the proportion of children using these services is even lower, at 2.9% reflecting that the development of services is very much in its infancy (information provided by national authorities). In Australia additional out-of-school hours care was rated as the single largest childcare service need, with demand for places for two children for every five already using out-of-school services (ABS, 2000b). In the Netherlands 39% of parents faced a waiting period of over ten months for out-of-school care services (Commissie Dagarrangementen, 2002).

In all three countries out-of-school-hours care is considered part of childcare services rather than education services, although in Denmark these services are often run

119|

in conjunction with primary schools. The school leisure time facilities (SFO) which is the largest OSH service, are located at schools and come under the management of the school principal. As with day care facilities for children not yet of school age, they have parent boards.[32] They are funded through municipal education and culture budgets. Parent contributions are expected, however, unlike childcare, there is no maximum contribution. Even so on average parents cover only 37% of costs. In the Netherlands, funding of OSH mirrors that of childcare, with an increasing number of CAOs extending their childcare provisions to cover services for school aged children. The guidelines for parental charges suggests that OSH fees be 50% or 66% of fees for childcare, depending on the hours of service. In both countries quality is regulated in the same way as for services for younger children. In Australia, Child Care Benefit is available to assist with costs, though the maximum payment for this age group is 85% of that for younger children. Quality standards are being developed along the lines of the QIAS outlined above, and the location of services is governed on the same basis as Family Day Care (i.e. regional planning committees approve where services can be established, in order to encourage supply in areas of need).

3.7.2. Issues for families accessing other services

There is a further dimension to the logistics of managing work and family, and that relates to the opening hours of shops and services. In all countries under review there has been a trend towards long opening hours in the retail sector. It is possible for families to do their necessary shopping in the evening or on weekends where they choose. However there has not been the same liberalisation of service hours in a number of professions or indeed in the area of public services. This means that it can be necessary for parents to take time off work in order to sort out applications for family assistance and the like. In Australia, Centrelink is looking to extend the hours of services provided. It has also made a lot of use of telephone-based transactions as a way of relieving time pressure on working parents. However, the Netherlands has been the broadest ranging in looking at the "daily routine" which families must manage. The Dutch government set up a project in 1998, "Dagindeling", in collaboration with the business sector, trade unions and others to look at the issues facing people in managing their daily lives. The project has identified the interface problems in the education sector as being particularly significant. One of the areas being explored in the project is the issue of co-location of public services which would make it easier for those with young children (among others) to use the services that are available. This ranges from the likes of libraries to health and social services (Box 3.8).

3.8. Conclusions

While childcare is used as a vehicle to advance a number of objectives it emerged in each of the three countries primarily in order to support employment

---

Box 3.8. **Other social services**

Childcare is a major element of social service provision, but there is also a broad range of other social services relevant to families with children that are available in all three countries. The bulk is provided at a sub-national level. In Australia, states and territories are involved in welfare service funding and provision, and there is also some local government involvement in some areas. In the Netherlands local government funds most social services, although there are also central government initiatives from time to time. For example, in 2000, the Ministry of Justice undertook a campaign to raise awareness about violence within the home. Central government is also involved in services for asylum seekers and in adoption services.

In Denmark, local authorities are responsible for ensuring the growth and development of children and young people, and use a range of services to assist in this task, such as counselling support for parents. Counties also play a role in social services where it makes sense to provide specialist services over a larger population base and in residential services where children are removed from the parental home for welfare reasons.

While traditionally social services have been a state level responsibility in Australia, recently the federal government has become involved in promoting a discussion about the family and the community, and in funding, in a limited way, a number of initiatives aimed at strengthening the family. In 2000, the government announced funding of A$ 240 million over four years for a Stronger Families and Communities Strategy, which promotes an early intervention and prevention approach to various problems. The strategy has three priority areas: early childhood and the needs of families with young children; strengthening marriage and family relationships and balancing work and family. While it is a strategy aimed at the family, it seeks to do so by promoting workforce attachment, and sits along side the government's Australian's Working Together initiative. There is a lot of language around encouraging partnership and the aim is clearly to engage a wider range of sectors in discussion of and action in social issues than has usually been the case in Australia. Funding is directed under headings including "Potential Leadership in Local Communities" and "Local Solutions to Local Problems". There are also more concrete items, with funding towards providing flexible choice in childcare (DFACS, 2000). Challenges to the Strengthening Families and Communities Strategy include monitoring the impact and ensuring that those most in need receive the help. However, there can be little doubt that a range of the issues related to balancing family and work are beyond the direct influence of governments, and an approach which sees a wider range of groups contributing to the discussion must be seen as a good thing.

---

participation by women. Indeed, it is a very significant factor in shaping the labour market choices which families with young children have. Even with similar historical driving factors, approaches to childcare in the three countries differ significantly. Parental choice about whether or not to use childcare is constrained by costs and by availability. However the nature of those constraints differs markedly across the countries. In Denmark 68% of 1 year old children use childcare – most of it full-time – and the system aims to provide places for children from the age of 6 months where parents want this. The Danes spend the most on childcare to ensure both supply and affordability, seeing it as very important in terms of child development. In Australia and the Netherlands parental choice is constrained by lower formal childcare capacity. Neither country has the same expectations in terms of child development, but both have increased public funding on childcare in recent years but spending levels remain significantly lower than in Denmark.

Quality is critical if parents are going to be willing to use childcare, and is more of a focus in Denmark and Australia than in the Netherlands. Parent involvement in Denmark is important, and quality is required by law, but with no benchmarking across municipalities and the system relies heavily on local childcare professionals (within the childcare services and within the municipal administrations). The Australian quality assurance systems offer a model here with the use of peer reviews being an innovative way of monitoring quality which could be of value to both Denmark and the Netherlands. That country's quality systems help support a very large and successful involvement by the private sector in providing care services, although to some extent it operates more through persuasion than rigorous enforcement. However, the system of licensing of services and accreditation for funding purposes, with the former operated at State level and the latter by the Commonwealth results in some duplication and higher compliance costs for providers than is necessary. The issue of quality is linked to that of child development. The emerging consensus is that childcare is not harmful to children, and can be beneficial, provided the care is of appropriate quality. How much childcare a child requires in order to get the child development gains ascribed to quality formal childcare is unclear.

The Netherlands could look to further use of FDC, as a lower cost way of increasing supply. It has a complicated funding set up, but the changes intended for 2004 will address some of this and at the same time give more power to parents in the choice of care. While the nature of childcare will depend on the employment preferences in each country, the virtual absence of part-time childcare in Denmark limits the choices open to parents. Denmark needs to look at how to ensure that charges are more sensitive to actual hours of care used and that more municipalities and parents are aware of and can actually utilise the flexibility which is available. Greater private sector involvement is unlikely to occur unless the regulations governing their entry into the market sector are liberalised.

In all countries the cost of childcare provision is high – particularly so in Denmark. However transfers bring the cost down for users to a level that is likely to be affordable for most in Denmark and in Australia, with special provisions to reduce the cost even further for the very poor, through policies on maximum parental contributions and through fees relief. The net costs in the Netherlands after fee relief are relatively high, and particularly when considering that access to subsidised care is restricted and fees in private commercial centres can be significantly above the recommended guidelines. This and the limited capacity are likely to be the main constraints facing most parents in choosing part-time rather than full-time care. This cost constraint does not exist for most Australians. However, the participation levels remain relatively low, reflecting the continuation of a strong preference among many to care for young children at home. The normative expectations that childcare is an important element of child development which have developed in Denmark do not hold in either Australia or the Netherlands.

There is no differentiation between subsidies in any of the three countries, to recognise the higher cost structures for very young children, which might explain in part the lower participation rate in care for children under the age of 3 in Australia and the Netherlands. The level of co-payment or parental contribution to the costs of care is critical to both affordability of care: the lower the co-payment, the more likely people are to choose childcare over parental care. However, as labour supply is affected by many factors it is much more difficult to tie an increase in labour supply to changes in the fee structure. For example, the reduction of parental co-payments in 1991 in Denmark led to a greater use of childcare. But at the same time female employment rates declined from 1991 until 1995 to increase thereafter.

The availability of care services for young children outside of standard work hours is an issue in all countries, and – if labour market trends towards less standard employment arrangements and hours continues, this will become an increasing challenge over time. The issues of rigidities in services relates to the school aged population as well, as the demands for out-of-hours-care are likely to increase. Parents in the Netherlands face the additional problem of uncertainty in compulsory school hours, making it virtually impossible for parents to plan very far ahead. Current policies and practice in this area are particularly "family unfriendly". At the same time the Netherlands has been exploring a wide range of issues related to balancing work and life, which could offer potential solutions to some of this problems arising from the lack co-ordination of services around children.

Notes

1. Municipalities are required to have places for children when they are 12 months of age, and are encouraged to have places available from age 6 months. If they can provide a place from that age they are able to ask for a higher parental contribution (at 33% of costs as opposed to 30% of costs) across all services.

2. From 1 July 2001, the Australians Working Together package provides funding for additional outside school hours care services, particularly for high need areas such as rural and regional areas, as well as increasing the value of fee relief to low income families and those with special childcare needs.

3. In 2001, the Prime Minister and the Minister for Family and Community Services announced funding of A$ 65.4 million over four years to provide greater flexibility and choice in childcare especially aimed to meet the needs of shift workers, families working outside standard business hours, those with sick children and families living in rural and regional areas, as part of the Stronger Families and Communities Strategy (DFACS, 2000b). In home childcare by a trained worker, and subsidies to private centres in rural areas are among the approaches being used.

4. The views on child development and the role of women may be less comfortable for "New Danes" – recent migrants –, but at the same time it is considered important for the integration of both the child and the adults.

5. Specialist residential care can be seen as a fifth category. Such care has been provided for welfare purposes, either providing care, protection and control for children and young people under the guardianship of the state, or for reasons related to health or disability. The use of residential care has been declining in many countries with an emphasis on keeping children within their own family and with a move away from institutional care. This raise particular work/family balance issues that lie beyond the scope of the current study.

6. In Australia, informal carers can become registered and parents are then eligible for a minimum level of financial assistance through Child Care Benefit.

7. Approximately 52% of Dutch 2-3 year olds attend a playgroup for a couple of hours per week (OECD, 1999).

8. The compulsory school age for children is 5 years in the Netherlands (though children can remain in an early year "pre-school" cycle until age 6); 6 years in Australia and in Denmark it is reasonably high at age 7.

9. While there was an overall growth in participation in childcare of 19% (including pre-school), there was a relatively higher growth in the childcare sector per se, with a fall in the number of children attending pre-school in the education sector, of 13% (ABS, 2000b).

10. Community-based childcare facilities have been long established in Australia, reflecting the community impetus behind the growth in childcare in the 1970s. Their share of

provision has declined in relative terms with the growth in commercial services in recent years.

11. Some minor commonwealth operational funding programmes still exist in Australia, where there is a need that user funding is unlikely to meet. For example, the Supplementary Services Programme assists programme development, the Special Needs Subsidy Scheme (SNSS) helps with children who have high on-going support needs, particularly those with disabilities through funding for additional staff and there is limited funding for in-service training. Operational subsidies are also available to multifunctional Aboriginal services and multifunctional services, some occasional care centres, and for the co-ordination units for family day care services and time limited funding for services in disadvantaged areas. State and Territory governments also finance pre-school services through direct funding of providers, in line with the funding methods used in the education sector.

12. In the Netherlands, municipalities have discretion in using their share from the "Municipality fund" for childcare purposes and to decide how much of the reintegration funding will go to childcare. However they have no discretion over funding from the KOA programme. There are risks that where new funding for specific groups is introduced, such as KOA, expenditure on those groups formerly coming from discretionary funding, will simply be reduced offsetting the new funding. This means that the initiative may succeed in ensuring a minimum amount of resources to that group across the country, however it does not mean that there will necessarily be a net increase in expenditure on childcare.

13. Typically, employer-supported care does *not* cover family-day care. Private family-day care (as in "gastoudergezinnen") does exist in the Netherlands, but is not regulated. Thus, employers could not possibly verify claims that children are in such care (or in care of, for example, grandparents), whereas such care is often cheaper and preferred by many parents.

14. In Denmark private and public enterprises may establish enterprise-based facilities to help their employees. The children of employers will be entitled to some or all the places in the facility. Enterprise-based facilities may be established either as independent self-governed day care facilities or as a pool scheme day care based on an agreement with the local government and subject to ordinary funding. The enterprise may provide additional funding as well.

15. There is variation in the models that employers use (Arbeidsinpectie, 2001). The fee structure as above is popular, but some employers cap their expenditure at a certain level. Contributing to variation in the level of childcare support for parents across industries. It is also possible that new parents (or new employees) applying for funds find that the employer budget is already exhausted, meaning that they will have to wait until the new year (or until employee drops out of the scheme) before they receive support.

16. Such agreements originally covered services for children aged 0-4 years. They are now being extended to cover out-of-school care for children up to age 12. As the age range is extended, the payroll fee will increase.

17. Municipalities can reduce the parental contribution in order to equalise fees for different childcare services. Fees can also be varied according to the age of children, to reflect that different costs apply to different age groups.

18. The payment is available for a minimum of 8 weeks and a maximum of 12 months. The period of home-based care has to be continuous – the payment can not be taken in

125|

parts. There is a maximum level of payment that will be made- that is equal to the daily cash benefit, and a maximum number of three children whose subsidies can be taken this way at any one time.

19. Current expenditure is now at A$ 1.36 billion (2000-2001). The government spent A$ 4.7 billion in the four years 1997-2001 which is a 36% increase from the previous four year period. For the year 2001-2002, the projected expenditure rises to A$ 1.52 billion (Communications with DFACS).

20. These are also be used by some employers in determining the level of subsidy they will provide under CAOs.

21. Childcare costs for children under 13 are deductible from personal income tax, where the contribution exceeds the recommended guidelines. The childcare has to be licensed and there is a maximum deduction is NLG19 393 (Ministerie van Financien, 2001).

22. In the same survey at the start of the 1990s 47% of the 194 000 women of working age citing childcare as the main reason for not looking for work, did so because they preferred to look after the child at home (ACOSS, 2001).

23. Zoetermeer, a local authority in the Netherlands, has hygiene and safety standards where the summary extends to 17 headings and 143 criteria.

24. The Temporary Decree on Quality Regulations for Childcare (1996) expired in 2001. They covered the responsibilities of municipalities to regulate child health and safety, staff ratios for services, room size and out door play space, sleeping room requirements for babies, regulations related to child minders, parental influence on facilities and complaints procedures. They also required parent centres to inform parents of pedagogical policies, but did not cover child development per se.

25. In Australia, LDC is regulated in all States and Territories, while FDC is regulated in some States and the ACT. OSHC is regulated in the Australian Capital Territory with some other States moving towards regulation. Several states are also engaged in developing, reviewing or implementing early childhood curricula (South Australia, Queensland, Western Australia, NSW, ACT).

26. ISO standards are standards registered with the International Standards Organisation – a non-governmental organisation established in 1947 with an aim to promote the development of standardisation and related activities across the world. Participation is voluntary.

27. For example, in the ACT, staff have to hold at least an associate diploma certificate if they are to supervision children. This requires two years of study and allows a person to supervise up to 18 children. A full early childhood certificate taking four years of study, allows supervision of up to 33 children.

28. In Australia, the Commonwealth Child Care Advisory Council's report "Child Care: Beyond 2001" noted that these factors contributed to the low self esteem of people working in childcare services and the report highlighted an urgent need to address status and standing issues.

29. However, the legislation remains in place enabling this to be re-established should the need arise.

30. The percentage of men with children aged under 12 working shift work or on weekends was higher that the percentage of women in Australia in 2000.

31. The Australians Working Together package announced in 2001 reserved funding for an additional 5 300 places at the cost of A$ 16 million over four years.

32. This is the same board which oversees the school at which the SFO is located.

Chapter 4

Leave from Work to Care for Very Young Children

This chapter discusses how different leave arrangements available to working parents caring for very young children operate, what they costs and what they achieve in terms of equity and efficiency.

Such leave benefits are of great value to parents with very young children, but can only have a limited effect on the reconciliation solutions parents find when children are older (Chapters 5 and 6).[1] Nevertheless, leave arrangements upon childbirth are or have recently been a major policy issue in all three countries under review. In Australia and Denmark, policy debate has concerned the design of income support provisions during parental leave periods. In the Netherlands, the discussion has centred on leave arrangements for all workers with care-responsibilities.

This chapter outlines the different nature of leave arrangements in some key respects (detailed information on programmes can be found in the Background Annex to the review): possible leave trajectories; the use of leave by men and women; and expenditure on leave benefits. The remainder of the chapter outlines the various (related) reasons (labour supply, poverty and smoothing family incomes, gender equity) that underlie the provision of paid leave, and discusses the efficiency and equity effects in the context of current Australian and Danish debates on the payment of income support during leave.

4.1. Key-elements of child-related leave arrangements across countries

To get an overview of the different national systems, it is simplest to describe the basic trajectories of leave, and this is done in a stylised way in Chart 4.1. This is not supposed to outline all the options available to a two-adult family, as these ultimately depend on whether the mother uses all options available to her and whether the man is prepared to take some of the leave to which he is entitled. Also, *low-income* families have access to other income support benefits that are not specifically tied to leave arrangements. These important qualifications to the basic story illustrated in Chart 4.1 are discussed in more detail below, while the various access criteria that must be satisfied in order to qualify for leave and accompanying income support are discussed in the Background Annex to the Review.

127|

Chart 4.1. **What leave can a mother take? A stylised representation**

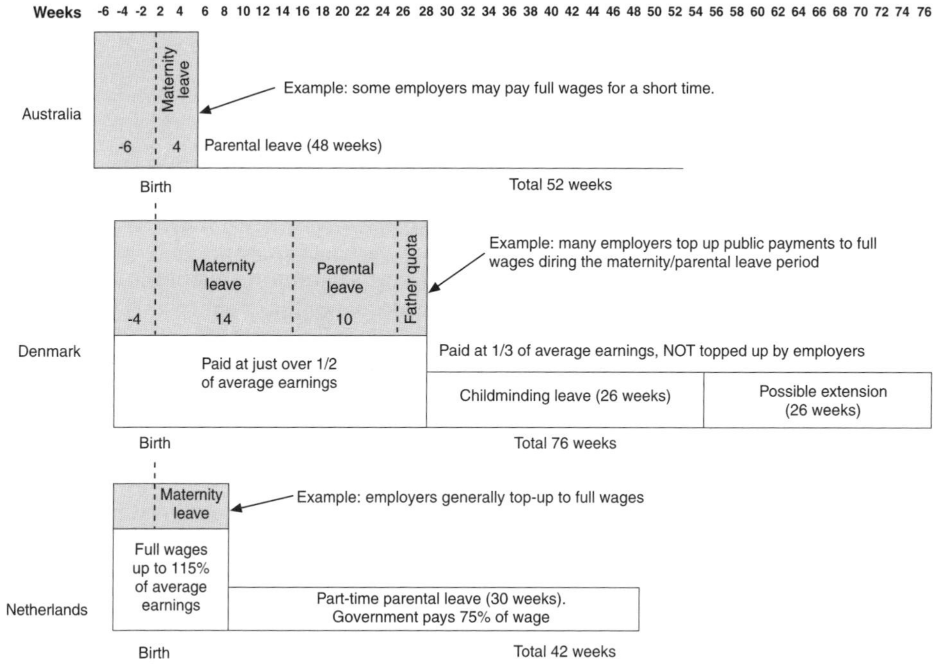

Weeks -6 -4 -2 2 4   6 8 10 12 14 16 18 20 22 24 26 28 30 32 34 36 38 40 42 44 46 48 50 52 54 56 58 60 62 64 66 68 70 72 74 76

Australia

Maternity leave

Example: some employers may pay full wages for a short time.

-6   4   Parental leave (48 weeks)

Birth   Total 52 weeks

Denmark

Maternity leave   Parental leave   Father quota

-4   14   10

Example: many employers top up public payments to full wages diring the maternity/parental leave period

Paid at just over 1/2 of average earnings

Paid at 1/3 of average earnings, NOT topped up by employers

Childminding leave (26 weeks)   Possible extension (26 weeks)

Birth   Total 76 weeks

Netherlands

Maternity leave   Example: employers generally top-up to full wages

Full wages up to 115% of average earnings

Part-time parental leave (30 weeks). Government pays 75% of wage

Birth   Total 42 weeks

Source: National authorities. See also Background Annex to the review.

In Australia, the statutory right is to 52 weeks of unpaid leave, starting from childbirth. Some employees are paid by their employer for some of that leave – for example, by agreement through workplace bargaining and this concerns many public sector employees (Chart 4.1 shows four weeks, though this is only an example). Up to six weeks leave before the expected birth date may also be available. Although the large majority of employees do not receive pay from their employer while on maternity/parental leave, *Family Tax Benefit*(B) is paid to most single earner households and this benefit is worth 6% of average earnings, and an income-tested lump-sum payment: the *Maternity Allowance* (see Background Annex to the review for programme rules). The government has announced plans to allow families to reclaim some of their tax payments made in previous years when they have children (see below).

In Denmark, a mother is entitled to 18 weeks maternity leave (of which four weeks are before the expected birth date). The mother is also entitled to a flat rate payment during this period (at a level which is about 55% of average wages), but under collective agreements many employers top the payment up to the wage level. Thereafter, there are ten weeks of parental leave, with the same flat-rate payment (and where, again, collective agreements often lead to employers top-ping-up the payment). After the ten weeks of parental leave that are accessible to both parents, there is a two week period that can only be used by fathers on a "use it or lose it" basis. Thereafter, childminding leave of 26 weeks is possible, with a flat rate of payment which is lower than that given to those on maternity and parental leave (about ⅓ of average wages). Under collective agreements, this may be extended by a further 26 weeks, but employers do not make payments during childminding leave. As described below, legislation has been passed to change this system.

In the Dutch system, there are 16 weeks maternity leave, with wage payments made by the government up to a bit over the average wage rate in the economy. Thereafter, legislation only allows for leave being taken part-time on an unpaid basis (see below). In a typical case, a mother would go back to work, but for 6 months would be entitled to work only half the hours she did before childbirth. Under some collective agreements (e.g. in the public sector), she would neverthe-less be paid 75% of her previous wage.

Around childbirth, fathers are individually entitled to leave periods of limited duration: a week unpaid leave in Australia, two weeks paternity leave and two days leave in the Netherlands[2] In 2001, fathers in Denmark could also use an addi-tional two weeks of leave (the so-called "father quota"), but this has been removed.

As they are individual entitlements, the Dutch parental leave and the Danish childminding leave both allow for simultaneous use of leave by both partners. Except for the first week of parental leave entitlement is family-based in Australia. For example, fathers in Denmark could take up to 26 weeks of childminding leave simultaneous to the mother being on maternity leave. Similarly, Dutch parents in two-adult families have the opportunity to take leave simultaneously, by working on a part-time basis while caring for their child(ren) during a 6-month period.

4.1.1. *Usage of leave*

Usage of leave provisions is highest in Denmark. The proportion of women in employment who are on maternity/parental leave at any point in time is about 3% and 1.7% in the Netherlands; considerably higher than in Australia (Table 4.1). The employment rate of mothers with young children is similar to the ratio of mothers that take paid maternity/parental leave in both Denmark and the Netherlands (it is lower in Australia, indicating that a significant group of mothers leaves the labour force on childbirth, Chapter 2). At 37 000, the number of mothers using

129|

Table 4.1. **Female employment rates and use of maternity/parental leave, 1999-2000**

	Australia (2000)[a]	Denmark (1999)	Netherlands (1999)
Female employment rate	61.6	71.6	61.3
Employment rate of mothers with young children[b]	45.0	71.4	60.4
Number of women taking paid maternity leave during a year relative to the number of all births	..	73.0	62.5
Proportion of women counted as employees on maternity/parental leave	0.3	3.0	1.7

.. data not available.
a) Data on parental leave include carer's leave.
b) Under 3 years old for Australia and Denmark; under 6 years-old for the Netherlands.
Source: ABS (2001d); OECD (2001g); and OECD Secretariat calculations based on information supplied by national authorities.

parental leave in the Netherlands is significantly lower than the number of mothers that use maternity leave – about 125 000. This is so because of the relatively strict eligibility criteria (employees have to work for an employer for at least 12 months, while maternity leave is open to all females including self-employed workers), and because parental leave is often unpaid.[3] In 2000 only about 10 000 mothers of very young children used childminding leave in Denmark (compared to 80 000 women who used parental leave). The limited take-up is related to both the low level of income support during Childminding leave, and the availability of childcare places in many municipalities when the child is 6 months old (Chapter 3).

Men may be entitled to leave, but they take little advantage of it. Most Australian and Dutch men take just a few days leave around childbirth. Most Danish fathers use the two-week paternity leave period, and in about 20% of cases the father cares for children during the 25th–26th week (the "father quota" period). Outside of this period, Danish men are as unlikely to take leave as men in the other two countries.

4.1.2. *Spending on paid leave*

In Australia, paid leave is more likely to be provided by the larger enterprises, and in those sectors (financial services, public sector) that have a large proportion of well-qualified women among their workforce. Estimates on the availability of paid maternity leave on overage range from 15 to 23% in private sector workplaces with more than 20 employees (Morehead *et al.*, 1997; WFU, 1999), but information on overall employer spending is not available.

In Denmark, public spending on income support during leave amounts to over 0.5% of GDP (Table 4.2). Public income support during maternity/parental

Table 4.2.   **Public spending on maternity and parental leaves**
Percentages of GDP

Denmark	
Maternity, paternity and parental leave benefits	0.36
Childminding leave benefits	0.13
Netherlands[a]	
Maternity leave	0.21

a) In 2001, the Dutch government awarded tax advantages worth about 11 million Euros to employers who provided
     paid parental leave to their employees.
Source: National authorities.

leave is topped up to full wages for about 80% of the workers, and its value is about 0.2% of GDP.[4] Public spending on maternity pay amounts to 0.2% of GDP in the Netherlands and in view of its high level, Dutch employers only have to pay top-ups to female high-earners.

4.2. Equity and efficiency in the provision of leave

Some period of recovery after childbirth (and repose beforehand) is medically desirable,[5] but beyond that there are wider societal concerns to do with labour supply, gender equity, income support and child development that influence policy. There may also be a case for some period of paid leave if it reduces demand on otherwise hard-pressed and highly subsidised childcare systems (Chapter 3). All these factors impinge on policy intervention towards leave arrangements, but policy needs careful balancing against other uses of public funds that may be more effective in achieving the relevant policy goals.

4.2.1. The business case

There is a business case for employers introducing paid leave to the extent that it improves motivation of the workforce, increases retention rates of employees, and/or attract new staff (Chapter 6). Some employers, especially public ones, may also grant leave benefits because of a perceived social obligation towards the community. Costs consist of three items: the production lost due to worker absence; continued (partial) payment of wage to the absent employee during the leave period; and the cost associated with hiring and employing workers replacing the absent employee. As employment adjustment costs increase with skill levels, employers face stronger incentives to provide leave benefits to high-skilled employees, for which it is difficult and costly to find replacement workers. Also employers have less incentives to provide leave benefits to their workers in times of labour market slack when replacements workers can be found with relative ease.

In the absence of legislation extending the accessibility of leave and wage payments to all workers, their distribution among the workforce would be very unequal.

This "business case" has not been strong enough to lead to extensive provision of maternity pay in Australia. In the other two countries, employers are not expected to pay full pay during leave as there are public benefits, but they often do top-up these payments. Again, coverage of top-ups is not universal, and private sector employers in the Netherlands hardly ever pay parental leave.

4.2.2. Labour demand and supply

As shown above, when parental leave is unpaid, the effective duration and take-up of leave are considerably lower than in the case of paid leave. However, take-up rates do not provide a good indication of the replacement cost to employers, as they do not capture female workers who withdraw from the labour force upon childbirth. And while their number is limited in Denmark, about 50% of the Australian female workers in employment during pregnancy do not return to employment within 18 months upon childbirth (Chapter 2). Both the use of (paid and unpaid) leave and (temporary) labour force withdrawal incur replacement costs on employers, while the need to find replacement workers will increase the demand for labour. In terms of replacement costs paid leave arrangements a priori do not generate different demand for "replacement" labour than unpaid leave or labour force withdrawal.

But apart from associated replacement costs and the loss of production due to worker absence, paid leave is different from unpaid leave and labour force withdrawal, in that it incurs additional employer costs either through increasing the burden of taxation including social contributions, or direct continued wage payments. Paid leave increases hourly labour costs which will have a negative effect on the quantity of labour demand. That said, the increase of the effective hourly wage rate could attract additional labour supply, which, in turn, will exert downward pressure on wages. The effects of paid leave arrangements on employment outcomes are uncertain.

The Danish leave system has contributed to consistently high female employment rates over the last 25 years. In the Australian and to a lesser extent the Dutch system current generosity of benefits is at a much lower base. In such a situation extending generosity of child-related leave benefits, and thus female returns to work and labour force attachment, could increase female labour supply. However, as employment rates of young females (without children) in both counties are already high (Chapter 2), it is unlikely that this effect will be very strong.

4.2.3. Public income support

In all three countries, governments provide income support to sustain income levels of families with children. Averting poverty during childcare is an objective in all three countries, and benefit systems are in place to cope with this (Chapter 2 and the Background Annex to the review). Paid leave also helps redistribute household income from periods when it was high to when it is low. This is one of the traditional functions of social insurance systems, and it is no surprise to find some such paid leave schemes in the Netherlands, where insurance is publicly operated and Denmark where it is union-managed, but not in Australia where this tradition never took root, and the tax/benefit system provides income-tested social support financed out of general tax revenue.

4.2.3.1. *Denmark*: Paid leave in a comprehensive formal care system

The current Danish child-related leave system is the most generous of the three countries, and is being extended. Recent reform does not affect paternity and maternity leave, but the family-based entitlement to parental leave of ten weeks has been individualised and extended to 40-46 weeks at the existing rate of public income support.[6] However, entitlement to pay during this period will remain family-based, so only one of the parents will be able to receive income support during the full leave period (parents can take leave at the same time, but overall payments cannot exceed the amount paid to one parent who takes leave for the maximum period). Childminding leave will be abolished, however,[7] so the maximum length of leave (which only a limited number of mothers take) will be reduced. However, assuming that employers top-up benefits for this longer period of *parental* leave, most female workers in employment will be tempted to take around 60 weeks of leave upon childbirth.

Both the abolition of childminding leave and the extension of the parental leave period reflect perceived weaknesses in the current system. As childminding leave can extend the leave period significantly there is a possibility that some mothers are caught in a "leave trap" when siblings are borne within a year to 18 months. It becomes possible to spend a significant amount of time outside of employment; especially when leave is combined with some period of unemployment benefit. Abolishing childminding leave reduces the chances of falling into the leave trap.

The logic of the extension of paid parental leave is further explained by the difficulty which some local governments in Denmark have had in providing childcare places for all children from the age of 6 months (Chapter 3). Under the existing system, substantial continued wage payments stop after 6 months, but if a childcare place cannot be found, one parent (the mother, usually) is forced to remain caring for the child for a further few months on reduced income until a childcare place comes available. The extension of leave will remove the hiatus in income, and leave the majority of women who choose to return to their previous employer having a continuous earnings stream.

133

Other new government proposals allow (not mandate) local governments to pay the equivalent of childcare subsidies to parents who care for their child at home for 12 months (Chapter 3). This will help local governments (in particular, Copenhagen) that, because of supply constraints, are unable to guarantee a child-care place for all children as from their first birthday to reduce demand for formal childcare. This choice of solving the "problem" through extending leave and effec-tively giving parents, usually the mother, the right to care for their own children for a prolonged period of time or pay for childcare at home rather than expanding for-mal childcare does imply a preference for home-based care for young children that has not been present in public policy for some years.[8]

4.2.3.2. *Part-time leave and return to work in the Netherlands*

The high costs and childcare capacity constraints in the Netherlands mean that formal childcare is used on a part-time basis, if at all, and by their nature informal care arrangement are often used on a part-time basis (Chapter 3). In addition Dutch legislation of different sorts facilitates the use of part-time employment solutions. Equal rights to part-time workers and other workers on flexible contracts (Chapter 6), the Adjustment of Hours Act and the design of leave programmes on a part-time basis illustrate the role of part-time work in the Dutch policy model. These policy signals contribute to explaining the popu-larity of part-time employment in the Netherlands, especially among mothers with children (Chapter 2).

In the Netherlands part-time parental leave is usual. Unlike typical leave ben-efits in other countries, long-term leave programmes in the Netherlands are designed to facilitate parents actually to stay at work on a part-time basis (propos-als for the introduction of long-term carers' leave also involve leave on a part-time basis, see Box 4.1). Workers are further helped by legislated access to a variety of leave benefits to carrying out their caring commitments.

Significantly, the design of parental leave ties in with the Adjustment of Hours Work Act that allows an employee to adjust his/her overall working hours, for whatever reason (Chapter 6). All employees in enterprises with more than ten employees who have been at least one year in employment can choose the right to work longer or shorter hours. Employees have to adhere to due administrative process (ample notice), in asking for adjustment of their contractual working week, which can be refused by employers under certain conditions. But as the burden of proof lies with employers, request by employees are generally granted.

The current functioning of the relatively short period of full-time paid leave in Netherlands, followed by a period of subsidised adjustment to limited hours,[9]

Box 4.1. **The Work and Care Act in the Netherlands**

Recent reform in the Netherlands has led to an integration of different types of leave to care for children and other relatives, spouses and partners, in one encompassing framework: the Work and Care Act. The Act includes the right to paid maternity leave (16 weeks), paid paternity leave (two days), unpaid parental leave (for a maximum of 6 months on a part-time basis, see Background Annex for detail) and provisions in case of adoption and multiple births. In addition to these specifically child-related leave benefits, provisions to care for family or household members include:

- *Emergency leave*: paid leave of short-duration at full wages to cover for unforeseen emergency situations at home, *e.g.* death of family members.

- *Short-term carers' leave*: a maximum of ten days per year to care for sick children or the employees' spouse or partner. Leave is paid at minimum wage level or 70% of full wages whichever is the highest.

- *Career break leave* is paid for 6 months at € 444 per month (70% of the minimum wage), although duration can be longer, subject to employer agreement. However, the use of career-break leave is conditional on the employer replacing the worker with a benefit-recipient. This condition as well the low pay rate and the relatively limited awareness off this benefit have contributed to its limited take-up. When introduced in October 1998, it was expected that about 56 000 persons would use career-break leave during the next five years, whereas in 2000 alone only 211 workers used this scheme (LISV, 2001).

Although not in the Work and Care Act, in related developments the Dutch government gave employees the opportunity to use their holiday entitlements in a more flexible manner. Holiday entitlements can now be used without loss over a period of five years with the possibility to build up extended paid leave periods. "Leave saving" is also possible, employees can save earnings or leave worth up to 10% of gross annual earnings to use at a later stage for a period of at maximum one year. The saved amount can be paid out as salary during the period of leave.

Also under consideration, having been approved by Cabinet, is legislation concerning *Long-term carers' leave*: in the case of assisting a dying partner, child or parent, or to care for a child with a life threatening disease. Leave would be on a part-time basis and entitlement would be six times the number of contractual working hours, to be taken over a 12-week period. Leave is proposed to be paid at 70% of the minimum wage.

thus smoothes family income towards a situation where one of the adults in couple families works part-time. It has logic in the Dutch system where the nature of childcare provision and legislation fosters part-time work and is such an important way of helping families balance work and family life.

135|

4.2.3.3. Australia: income support to families in need

The Australian social protection system is not based on insurance principles. It provides income support to people in times of need, as identified through family-based means and income tests (Background Annex to the review). In line with these principles, the Australian social protection system contains some benefits that provide income support during the child-related leave period for some workers. First, there is income-tested Maternity allowance lump-sum payment. Second, Family Tax Benefit, Part A is a per child amount to assist with the costs of the child; Part B is for single income families and assists when the mother is not in the workforce. Third, for low-income families with partners earning up to about 50% of APW-earnings, the Partnered Parenting Payment is available (see Background Annex to the review for relevant programme rules). In all, including FTB(A), and assuming a 14-week period, the mother in a low-income family could receive payments during maternity leave equal to about 35% of average earnings, all of which are financed out of general taxation. Higher income households receive much less.

Several alternatives for introducing pay during child-related leave in Australia are under discussion [see, for example, HREOC (2002) for a discussion of issues, policy objectives and financing options]. One option raised in the debate is to introduce a mandatory insurance-based system for workers. Such a system does not fit neatly into the Australian social protection system, although it would not be without precedent.[10] Another option suggests moulding existing elements of the benefit system into a general tax-financed paid leave programme. For example, that part of the family benefit which is paid to the adults in a household with no or low earnings, regardless of spousal earnings [FTB(B)] could be "rolled up" into a maternity/parental leave payment of some duration. Recent New Zealand reforms in a social system that has some similarities to that of Australia reflect another alternative.[11]

The government has recently announced the introduction of a First Child Tax Refund (Howard, 2001) which will give a parent that drops out of the labour force the right to claim back one fifth of the tax he, or more usually, she paid in the year up to childbirth per year for up to five years.[12] Obviously, such a measure will help in income-smoothing over the life cycle of the family. Indeed, in many respects it mimics the effects of an insurance-type system, with a minimum benefit of around A$ 500 per year and a maximum of A$ 2 500. The potential payment is much lower than the public payments in Denmark and the Netherlands, but the duration of payment is significantly longer than envisaged in other countries.

However, despite the possible introduction of the First Child Tax Refund, it is apparent that the Australian government continues to believe that financial support while on leave should be provided in a complementary way through the industrial and social protection systems. As described above, employer-provided paid leave is only available to a limited group of workers. More recently, however, there have been signs that more employers are thinking of introducing paid maternity leave. For example, the retailer E*sprit* has introduced 12 weeks paid leave, a significant development, as this is the first employer of any significance in the female-employment-dominated retail sector, while the Australian Catholic University introduced paid maternity leave for 12 months in 2001. Hoping to exploit the interest in the topic, the ACTU has been campaigning for introducing a case for the Australian Industrial Relations Commission to consider for the introduction of 14 weeks paid maternity leave. Nevertheless, if this case is not successful, it remains likely that for some time yet employer-provided paid maternity/parental leave will not be widespread in Australia.

4.2.4. *Gender equity*

That men's use of prolonged child-related leave is so rare (see above) is a source of concern for two reasons. First, it both contributes to and is indicative of the gender segregation in childrearing. Getting fathers more involved in childcare early on in the child's life may change male attitudes and may even be good for child development, but either way requires men to take more leave.

Second, if males took more leave any possible bias in the labour market against women as being potentially more expensive employees (because they are more likely than men to take advantage of leave provisions) would be reduced. For example, when choosing between two otherwise identical workers, employers will have an incentive to hire that employee who is the least likely to use child-related leave and incur relevant costs. As women are more likely to use leave benefits, employers have incentives not to hire female workers of childbearing age. In practice, such incentives are tempered by a number of effects. Equal opportunities legislation can no doubt limit some of the worst cases of discrimination (Chapter 6). Furthermore, women may gravitate towards employers who are less likely to discriminate (*e.g.* the public sector), leading to occupational segregation, which may harm the efficiency with which labour is allocated in the economy. There remains considerable unexplained variation between male and female earnings. For example, the gender wage gap in Australia is about 10% (Chapter 2). Factors such as educational attainment and occupational sorting account for only 39% of the wage variation, unexplained differences account for 61% of the wage variation in Australia (Reiman, 2001).

However, getting men to take more leave is difficult, as men usually feel that taking prolonged leave damages their career prospects. Men returning to their career after leave are more likely to encounter a prejudice that they do not "take work seriously" than women in similar circumstances. Thus, even when leave benefits are fully paid to either parent, the long-run household opportunity costs will

137|

be higher if a man takes leave because the harm it may do to his career-prospects. Even in Denmark with its long history of public pursuit of gender equitable policies, taking prolonged parental leave still seems to endanger male career prospects. As long as male behaviour remains largely traditional, economic incentives predict that mothers will remain the predominant users of prolonged parental leave periods and thus that caring will remain primarily a female activity. As taking parental leave for an extended period may deteriorate labour market skills, and damage future career paths and earnings, taking prolonged leave hampers future female career prospects and is harmful gender equity (Box 4.2).

The financing of leave arrangements

From a gender equity perspective it matters how income support during leave is financed. If individual firms pay income support directly, or contributions are based on the "risk profile" of firms, then firms with high propensity to employ (young) women would still pay more than employers of predominantly male workforces. If, on the other hand, contributions are based on employment of men as well as women, or are paid by all employees (social insurance systems), or are covered by government out of general taxation, then the costs of pay during leave are not borne by an individual employer, reducing their incentive to discriminate.

Maternity pay in the Netherlands is financed through unemployment insurance contributions that are the same for all private sector employers and employees. Hence, the cost of public maternity pay is equally shared among all employers, regardless of the proportion of their female workforce. This not only spreads the costs, it also avoids risk-selection and potential discrimination among workers.

Redistribution across employers in the Danish system is more restricted. In Denmark, individual employers and unions operate separate funds along occupational lines. The government covers maternity, paternity and parental leave payments up to about 55% of average earnings while the remainder of the cost of leave is thus born by employers and employees within a certain sector, but not across sectors. Male-dominated unions are not necessarily progressive in attitude towards pay during maternity/parental leave. For example, the Danish metal workers union runs its own maternity scheme that is relatively cheap, as only 1 to 2% of its workers are female. Other unions with a larger proportion of female workers aspire to arrange for a comprehensive pooling of resources across all sectors, but thus far, to no avail.

4.3. Conclusions

For (future) parents who prefer simultaneously to be in employment/pursue their career and establish/have a family, it is of great value to be able to take time

---

Box 4.2. **Prolonged leave from work and the impact on female earnings**

Taking parental leave for an extended period may deteriorate labour market skills, and damage future career paths and earnings [see Edin and Gustavsson (2001) for an overview of studies on the negative relationship between work interruptions and skills]. These patterns are reflected in Australian mothers' lifetime income. Mothers from all educational backgrounds are likely to earn less than two-thirds of the earnings of their childless peers over a lifetime, and because pension entitlements usually depend on work histories, such differences persist into old age. However, because Australian mothers are more likely to return to the workforce and do so more quickly after childbirth than previously, the family gap in lifetime earnings between childless women and those with children more than halved between 1986 and the end of the 1997. Nevertheless it remains considerable at about A$ 160 000 (Chapman *et al.*, 2001).

In marked contrast, a recent Danish study finds that children do *not* on average seem to have any long-term effect on their mother's wages compared to non-mothers (Datta Gupta and Smith, 2002). The birth of a child does lead to a slower wage growth of the mother compared to non-mothers, reflecting the depreciation of human capital while the mother is on leave, but the effect is temporary and mothers' earnings catch up with non-mothers a few years after returning to the labour force. While the methodologies in the Australian and Danish studies are not entirely compatible, it is reasonable to suppose that the differences across countries reflect differences in the likelihood of women returning to full-time employment shortly after childbirth.

The effect of human capital depreciation has the strongest impact on life course earnings of high-skilled workers in Denmark, and also contributes to the existing wage differentials with men. The gender wage gap has remained fairly stable in Denmark at about 10% over the last 15 years. But while low-skilled women have reduced their wage gap to low-skilled men, female Danish high-skilled workers seem to have fallen behind to their male counterparts (Datta Gupta *et al.*, 2002). Obviously, the effect of leave on human capital accumulation and depreciation is strongest for high-skilled workers. Moreover, high-skilled female workers are often employed in the public sector and not in the private sector where wage growth has been more pronounced. Finally, at higher earnings ranges women in Denmark still work fewer paid hours than men, while doing more unpaid housework further hampering their career prospects.

---

off around childbirth without the risk of losing employment. Access to income support during this period maintains disposable household income close to earnings levels, and if followed by return to the work on leave fosters a relatively smooth income pattern while household costs are likely to increase. In Denmark, mothers generally return to the labour force as soon as a childcare place becomes available, receiving at least some income in the interim. In effect, the Danish system guarantees (one of the) working parents the right to care for their own child. The Dutch system provides for a smooth transition from full-time to part-time employment and is logical, as part-time work is such an important way of helping families balance work and family life.

Social support in Australia is provided to all households in need, but has not been tied to labour force attachment, although the First Child Tax Refund initiative will provide modest help in smoothing income over the lifecycle and compensating mothers for the time they take off (or reduce working hours) associated with childbirth. Recently, there has been public debate about pay while on maternity/parental leave. Any expansion of paid parental leave is likely to have to come from industrial bargaining. Whilst such agreements may become more common, they do not seem likely to extend to a great proportion of the Australian workforce.

Extending paid leave arrangements could attract female workers into the labour force by increasing their returns to work. However, as female labour supply of younger women is already high, such gains are likely to be small. The planned Danish reform is designed to be neutral in terms of labour supply, but projections do not account for potential pressure on employers to extend the top-up period of benefits. High labour costs also limit the room for extending leave generosity in the other two countries.

Leave arrangements upon childbirth have been or are a policy issue in both Australia and Denmark. But their relevance to the work and family reconciliation issue should be considered in the context of other social policy objectives (female independence, and family income effects), its cost and alternative policies that may be more effective in increasing labour supply among low-income families (Chapter 5).

In fact, badly designed paid leave arrangements can be harmful to gender equity. If paid leave is financed on a fair redistributive basis (though contributions or general taxation), then the costs of pay during leave are not borne by an individual employer, reducing their incentive to discriminate. In line with these principles the Dutch financing system is more gender equitable than the Danish one.

In all three countries current take-up patterns are deemed unsatisfactory from a gender equity perspective. Interestingly, the Danish reform abolishes the "father quota" of leave, used by about 20% of fathers. It is hoped that by extending benefit generosity fathers will make more use of the scheme. But that does not seem to be an altogether realistic assumption. As long as the careers of fathers are negatively affected by taking leave, the long-run household opportunity costs will be lowest when the mother uses parental leave. In all three countries, a culture shift in the workplace seems to be needed to bring about a more gender equitable use of parental leave arrangements.

Leave for a long period damages the future earnings prospects of mothers. If only for that reason, paid leave can only cover a short period of child rearing. With the important exception of Dutch part-time leave, it only postpones the point where parents have to confront the real difficulties of balancing work and family commitments. The policy interest it generates seems disproportionate to its utility.

141

Notes

1. Chapter 6 discusses employer-provided care days, holidays or otherwise used to care for sick children

2. Paternity leave only became a legal right in the Netherlands on 1 December 2001, with the introduction of the Work and Care Act. Until then most fathers received one or more days leave on basis of collective agreements. In 1999, 15% of the new fathers had no access to paternity leave.

3. Almost two-thirds of workers who use parental leave are public sector employees, no doubt because public workers often receive a top-up to 75% of earners during the leave-period, while parental leave in the private sector is generally unpaid (Arbeidsmarktinspectie, 2001). Fiscal measures were introduced in 2001 to stimulate take-up in the private sector.

4. The public payments equal about 55% of APE-earnings and lead to spending of 0.36% of GDP. On average the top-up to full wages will thus be equal to 45% of APE-earnings, and is paid to about 80% of the workers. Hence, the value of benefits to recipients paid by employers is about 0.23% of GDP.

5. Maternity leave upon childbirth also allows for breastfeeding of the infant more easily at home than is achievable in many workplaces.

6. Leave will be paid at 100% of the maximum UI payment benefit and at maximum for only 32 weeks. If leave is taken for 48 weeks (40 weeks is the maximum for unemployed mothers), payment rates per week will be adjusted accordingly (32/48*100 UI benefit). The extra cost in 2002 is projected be a spending increase by about 15% to almost DKK 5.8 billion, and is financed out of budgetary spending cuts on other items (*e.g.* a reduction in the size of the civil service). The reform is projected to have no, or limited, impact on effective labour supply (Finansministeriet, 2002).

7. All eligible parents with children being born before 1 January 2002 are still entitled to childminding leave and as this can be taken until the child is 9 years of age, childminding leave will only cease to exist in 2010.

8. The Danish National Council for Children advocates that it is beneficial to children if they receive full-time parental care until their first birthday.

9. Rather than adjusting working hours immediately, parents have a financial incentive to use the parental leave benefit first, as during this period contributions to private occupational pension schemes are covered in full, and do not reflect the adjustment in hours.

10. There are compulsory contributions to "superannuation schemes" for pensions.

11. The new New Zealand Paid Parental Leave Scheme, introduced from 1 July 2002 and provides for up to 12 weeks paid leave at a rate of approximately 70% of average

female weekly earnings or 100% of previous earnings, whichever is lower (New Zealand Government, 2002). The parent will be able to take unpaid leave for the remaining period up to 52 weeks after the birth (as in Australia). The payment will be financed out of general tax revenue and spending on both paid parental leave and the existing income-tested parental tax credit (for low-income families) will amount to about 0.12% of GDP.

12. The carer must stay at home to look after the child. The refund will be paid at the end of each tax year as part of the parent's tax assessment (ATP, 2001).

Chapter 5

Promoting Female Employment

This chapter considers how policy may influence the decisions of parents (and mothers in particular) to work or not. It considers the financial incentives embodied in the tax and benefit system, but also the *requirements* placed on parents to seek work, and the help given to jobless parents to find work.

5.1. Introduction

In Denmark, policy takes for granted that, apart from the initial period after childbirth, parents wish to work full-time. In Australia, the situation is somewhat more nuanced. It is probably fair to say that social attitudes favour mothers looking after their children full-time when they are pre-school aged (Chapter 2). However, both childcare policy and benefit policy (for lone parents, at least) have been altered to make work (including part-time work) more financially attractive. The Dutch situation is even more complex. As in Australia, there is still a social presumption that young children are best looked-after by their parents. However, work by both parents is increasingly common, with women often working part-time. A "one-and-a-half earner" model is common. Gender equity objectives underlie a desire for a more equal distribution of paid work across both parents, and a "two two-thirds earners model" does influence some aspects of policy.

This chapter examines government policy towards the work patterns of parents. Policy areas of relevance include the tax system, the benefit system and programmes to help those out of work find employment.

5.2. The financial incentives to enter work

People seek paid employment (or not) for many reasons, including self-esteem, social pressure, social contacts, etc. People may well take a job even if they are worse off working rather than receiving social benefits for these reasons and because they believe that even badly-paid work is the best way of getting established in the labour market, leading to higher incomes in the long run. It follows that looking only at the financial returns of working can never give a full picture of whether a particular individual or family will seek paid employment.

145

Equally, however, it is reasonable to assume that the financial incentives to work are an important reason why people work, and that, other things being equal, changes in the financial incentives will affect employment rates.

5.2.1. Incentives for second earners to work

One way of comparing the financial returns facing the second earner in a household across countries is to assume that the primary earner has a fixed level of earnings, and then to see how net incomes change with an additional earner. This approach implies that the labour supply of one earner is entirely independent of the labour supply of the second earner. This is unlikely to be completely true. Nevertheless, this approach does expose the workings of the tax/benefit system.

Table 5.1 compares how taxes, benefits, and net incomes change when a second adult starts earning ⅓ of average earnings (which might be interpreted as moving into part-time work) in a couple with two children where the other adult earns the average level of earnings in the economy. All numbers are expressed as a percentage of average earnings. The three countries differ enormously in whether they have allowances (as in Denmark and to a lesser extent the Netherlands); local taxes (more important than central government taxes in Denmark); social security contributions (more important than taxation in the Netherlands, but significant in Denmark), etc. It follows that focussing on *one* aspect of the system (*e.g.* family benefits) can be very misleading if other parts of the tax/benefit system have offsetting effects. Rather than look at the detailed structure of the tax system, therefore, it is more revealing to focus on differences in *net* income, and total payments net of benefits to the government.

Line 12 of Table 5.1 confirms that *net* transfers to the government (*i.e.* taking off taxes and social security contributions, but adding in cash benefits paid to one-earner couples) vary substantially across countries. Whilst a one-earner couple on average earnings with two children in Australia makes net transfers to government of little more than 11% of gross earnings, in the Netherlands the net transfers are over 21% and in Denmark over 30%.

If the partner of the primary earner in the household enters the labour force to earn ⅓ of average earnings, total taxes in Australia barely change (Line 10) – an additional 3.3% of average earnings is required in tax, or only 10% of the additional earnings. However, the loss of Family Tax Benefits (Line 11) is significant, over halving in total value. Hence gross earnings of ⅓ average earnings increases household net income by about 23%, with an average effective tax rate on the second earner of 31%.

In Denmark and the Netherlands, cash benefits are not affected by the second earner entering work, but the total taxes and social security contributions certainly are. In Denmark, the net return to the low earnings second earner are just

Table 5.1. **Financial returns for second earners with low earnings**

Item	Australia		Denmark		Netherlands	
	100-0	100-33	100-0	100-33	100-0	100-33
Wage level (first adult – second adult)						
1. Gross wage earnings	100.0	133.3	100.0	133.3	100.0	133.3
2. Standard tax allowances						
Deduction for social security contributions and income taxes			9.3	12.6	2.8	2.8
Work-related expenses			2.4	4.8		
Total	0.0	0.0	11.7	17.4	2.8	2.8
3. Tax credits or cash transfers included in taxable income	0.0	0.0	0.0	0.0	5.7	7.8
4. Central government taxable income (1-2+3)	100.0	133.3	88.3	116.0	102.9	138.3
5. Central government income tax liability (exclusive of tax credits)						
Income tax	21.6	24.6				
Medicare levy	1.5	1.8				
Total	**23.1**	**26.4**	**5.5**	**7.2**	**9.6**	**10.7**
6. Tax credits			1.4	1.4	1.3	1.5
7. Central government income tax finally paid (5 – 6)	**23.1**	**26.4**	**4.1**	**5.8**	**8.3**	**9.2**
8. State and local taxes			21.8	30.9		
9. Employees' compulsory social security contributions			11.7	17.4	19.2	28.4
10. Total payments to general government (7 + 8 + 9)	**23.1**	**26.4**	**37.5**	**54.1**	**27.6**	**37.6**
11. Cash transfers from general government	11.9	4.8	6.7	6.7	6.1	6.1
FTB(B)	6.4					
For two children	5.5	4.8	6.7	6.7	6.1	6.1
12. Take-home pay (1 – 10 + 11)	**88.8**	**111.7**	**69.1**	**85.9**	**78.6**	**101.8**
13. Employers' compulsory social security contributions			0.6	1.2	16.2	21.1

Source: Calculations based on OECD (2002f).

16.8% of average earnings – an effective overall tax rate on the second earner of 50%. In the Netherlands, the equivalent overall tax rate on the second earner is about 30%.

Table 5.2 performs the same calculation, but this time assumes that the second earner receives gross wages equivalent to two-thirds of average earnings. The effective tax rates on the second earner entering the labour market at this higher level of earnings are very similar to those on the lower earnings already described. In Australia, the additional earnings would increase net family income by 47% of average earnings, meaning that the effective tax rate on the second earner is 30%. In Denmark, the equivalent effective tax rate is 50% (as it was for the lower level of earnings by the second earner) and in the Netherlands the effective tax rate is 33%.

147

Table 5.2. **Financial returns for second earners with moderate earnings**

Item	Australia 100-0	Australia 100-67	Denmark 100-0	Denmark 100-67	Netherlands 100-0	Netherlands 100-67
Wage level (first adult – second adult)	100-0	100-67	100-0	100-67	100-0	100-67
1 Gross wage earnings	100.0	166.7	100.0	166.7	100.0	166.7
2 Standard tax allowances						
Deduction for social security contributions and income taxes			9.3	15.6	2.8	3.8
Work-related expenses			2.4	4.8	0.0	0.0
Total	**0.0**	**0.0**	**11.7**	**20.4**	**2.8**	**3.8**
3 Tax credits or cash transfers included in taxable income	0.0	0.0	0.0	0.0	5.7	9.9
4 Central government taxable income (1 – 2 + 3)	100.0	166.7	88.3	146.3	102.9	172.7
5 Central government income tax liability (exclusive of tax credits)	0.0	0.0	5.5	10.9	9.6	12.7
Income tax	21.6	33.3				
Medicare levy	1.5	2.5				
Total	**23.1**	**35.8**	**0.0**	**0.0**	**0.0**	**0.0**
6 Tax credits	0.0	0.0	1.4	1.4	1.3	1.6
7 Central government income tax finally paid (5 – 6)	**23.1**	**35.8**	**4.1**	**9.5**	**8.3**	**11.1**
8 State and local taxes	0.0	0.0	21.8	41.0	0.0	0.0
9 Employees' compulsory social security contributions	0.0	0.0	11.7	20.4	19.2	38.7
10 Total payments to general government (7 + 8 +9)	**23.1**	**35.8**	**37.5**	**70.9**	**27.6**	**49.7**
11 Cash transfers from general government	11.9	4.7	6.7	6.7	6.1	6.1
FTB(B)	6.4	0.0				
For two children	5.5	4.7	6.7	6.7	6.1	6.1
12 Take-home pay (1 – 10 + 11)	**88.8**	**135.7**	**69.1**	**102.5**	**78.6**	**123.1**
13 Employers' compulsory social security contributions	0.0	0.0	0.6	1.2	16.2	26.8

Source: Calculations based on OECD (2002f).

Interpreting what these charts mean is not straightforward. Clearly, the effective tax rates on the second earner of around 30%, 30% and 50% for Australia, the Netherlands and Denmark respectively are consistent with an assertion that having a second earner is more financially worthwhile in the first two countries than in Denmark. However, the marginal returns to work are not all that matter in determining the incentives to work. The richer is a household, the more "leisure" it is able to afford, and so a rich household may choose to only have one earner, with the second adult in the household not *needing* to work. It follows that the high average rates of tax in Denmark might have the opposite effect: despite the relatively lower net returns to being a two-earner household when compared with the other two countries, it is nevertheless *necessary* to have two earners in order to achieve a desirable standard of living.

Denmark is to many the archetype "individual rights" country in its treatment of two adult families. However, it has near-fully transferable allowances, a system more commonly associated with the male breadwinner model. To some extent, the existence of the near-fully-transferable tax allowance is possible *because* of the high rates of tax. The disincentive to second earners arises not simply because the allowances are transferable, but also because the marginal rate structure is pro-gressive. In Denmark, whilst the marginal rate structure is progressive, it is not sharply so, because high amounts of tax revenue must be raised even from those with relatively low incomes. Hence, at two-thirds of average earnings, a taxpayer will already face a marginal rate of 45%; this rises to 50% at average earnings and 63% at 166% of average earnings (OECD, 2002f). Around average earnings, there-fore, where most earners are concentrated, there is very little progression in mar-ginal rates. At higher levels of income of a primary earner, when it might be expected that there would indeed be a big difference in marginal rates and a dis-incentive for the second earner to work, the ability to transfer the allowance is restricted.

The incentive to work for second earners in both Denmark and the Netherlands is fairly insensitive to the earnings of the partner. For example, if the partner earned two-thirds of average earnings, then the tax rates facing a second earner with one-third of average earnings would still be around 50% in Denmark, and would be 32% in the Netherlands. However, the Australian system is income tested. At two-thirds of average earnings, a single earner couple with two children would be entitled to a significant amount of income-tested family benefits. The partner entering work would reduce these. Hence, whereas the average tax rate on a second earner with one-third of average earnings when married to a spouse earning average earnings was around 30%, it would rise sharply to 58% were the same person to be married to someone with two-thirds average wages (and to 64% if the partner was on the minimum award wage). In other words, the incentive for a second earner to work in Australia declines sharply the less the primary earner receives. This effect is common to all systems, which involve means-tested bene-fits being paid to those in work. It has the unfortunate effect of meaning that the incentive for second adults to work is lowest in those families where a second earner would be particularly useful in raising incomes and providing income secu-rity. It is perhaps important to note that the lack of work incentives for low-wage second earners is in large part a reflection of the lack of work incentives for all low-wage workers.

Childcare costs also affect the incentive to work and are of particular impor-tance when considering those facing second earners. Table 3.5 in Chapter 3 illus-trated a case where there was a single adult working, earning average wages, with a second adult looking after two children. They then considered the conse-quences of the second adult starting work, earning two-thirds of average earnings,

149

and using childcare to look after the two children. These childcare costs amounted to 40% of the net increase in earnings in Australia, 57% of the increase in Denmark and 61% of the increase in the Netherlands. Putting both the tax/benefit changes and childcare costs together, the family income of the Australian couple would go up by 40% of the earnings of the second earner; in the Netherlands the couple would keep just 26% of the increase in earnings, and in Denmark just 22%. If there were just one child needing formal care, the returns to work for the second earner would be higher, as she would keep 49, 36 and 31% of her earnings after deducting childcare costs in Australia, the Netherlands, and Denmark respectively.

The two-earner household considered in the previous paragraph has a relatively high income. In Denmark, subsidies to childcare costs are inversely proportional to incomes, as are net taxes, so considering lower earnings levels affects the absolute returns to work, but not really the percentage of extra earnings which a family will keep. In the Netherlands, this is also, broadly, the case (though there is a small element of progressivity in both the effective tax rate and the childcare subsidy). In Australia, the childcare subsidy is in effect inversely proportional to income. However, because the tax/benefit system is strongly progressive, returns to work for a second earner after childcare costs fall sharply the lower are the earnings of the spouse. If the first earner in a family with two children requiring formal care earns ⅔ of average earnings, then in all three countries the net returns to work of the second earner are similar – 30% in Australia, 25% in the Netherlands and 24% in Denmark.

There are typical case calculations, and as such are always open to criticism.

- Not that many families have two children under school age. But some do, and anyway Chapter 3 showed that net childcare costs for two children are usually a lot less than double the costs of one child;

- The assumption that the second earner receives just two-thirds of the earnings of the first earner could be challenged. But Chapter 2 noted that women working in Denmark earned on average just 70% of the earnings of their spouse, a figure which was just 26% in the Netherlands and 44% in Australia;

- Not all (or even many, in the case of Australia and the Netherlands) families use formal childcare full-time. They use informal carers, such as family and friends, or use part-time childcare. Given that taxes, benefits and formal childcare take such a large proportion of their earnings, this is hardly surprising.

The discussion of work incentives so far has been based around the idea of holding the earnings of the primary earner constant, and then seeing what the returns to a second earner starting to work might be. It is possible, however, to imagine other decision-making processes within a family. For example, there might be a decision that the family needs a given net income, but has a choice about whether it achieves this through a male-breadwinner approach, through a combination of full-time and part-time work, or by both partners earning equal amounts. To the extent that the tax/transfer system is not neutral between these choices, public policy might influence how work is distributed within a household.

Table 5.3 illustrates the effects of the distribution of earnings across a couple on net incomes. Exactly how earnings are distributed between two adults has an enormous impact on the total taxes paid in both Australia and the Netherlands, but in each case there are offsetting effects in either social security contributions or family benefits. In the Netherlands, the differences in taxes paid according to the distribution of earnings within a household are remarkably high, but these are all but entirely offset by equally large differences in social security contributions. As described above, the tax system is based on the individual. Tax rates in the bottom income tax bracket are very low. Only when taxable income takes an individual into the second tax bracket (as is the case at 133% of average earnings) does taxation become significant. However, although some social security contributions are levied on gross earnings, as in most countries, some are levied on income in the first tax bracket. When there is only one earner, that means that only one set of earnings faces such contributions; when there are two, these social security contributions are correspondingly higher.

The recent Australian tax reform benefited most one-earner families, who gained more on average from the reform than any other household type. A key reason for this was the introduction of Family Tax Benefit, Part B [FTB(B)].[2] This is mainly paid to one-earner households and is gradually withdrawn from families the more the *second* earner receives in wages. Hence benefits are less for a household

Table 5.3. **Average tax rates at 133% of average earnings**

Primary earner (% of average earnings)	Secondary earner (% of average earnings)	Average tax rate	Average social security payments	Total taxes, minus transfers
Australia				
1.33	0.00	26.8%	0.0%	19.9%
1.00	0.33	19.8%	0.0%	16.2%
0.67	0.67	19.0%	0.0%	15.4%
Denmark				
1.33	0.00	31.2%	11.0%	37.2%
1.00	0.33	27.6%	13.0%	35.6%
0.67	0.67	27.6%	13.0%	35.6%
Netherlands				
1.33	0.00	14.3%	13.8%	23.5%
1.00	0.33	6.9%	21.3%	23.6%
0.67	0.67	3.4%	22.6%	21.4%

Source: Calculations based on OECD (2002f).

with an even distribution of earnings across the couple than it is when there is a split between a main and a secondary earner, and the single earner household receives the highest level of benefit. But this effect is *less* important in determining net household payments to government than the fact that the tax system is fully individualised and relatively progressive. Because a single earner will be in a higher tax bracket, with higher average tax payments, the more evenly are earnings distributed in a household, the lower will be the average tax rate. Hence, there is a mild overall "bias" in favour of two earner households in Australia despite the existence of FTB(B).

It follows from this that simplistic analysis of the effects of the tax/transfer system can be very misleading. Denmark has a tax structure which formally appears to favour one-earner households, but in practice the high average tax rates on all families and the limitation on the transferability of the allowance for high-income earners means that it does not. Australia has a benefit system which seems to favour one-earner households, but in reality the combination of an individual tax system and a progressive rate structure means that two-earner couples are "helped" as much or even more. And the Dutch system, too, is carefully balanced so that households with similar levels of income make very similar net contributions to the government.

The final word in this section however, has to be that where women with partners who are already working use formal childcare, they can only expect to receive a fraction of their gross earnings. Only women with high incomes will have a significant portion left after meeting childcare costs. They may still work – because they want to, because when the children go to school the net returns to work will increase, because some increase in family incomes is better than none – but few women in these circumstances will be under any illusion that they are getting "a good deal".

5.2.2. *Incentives for one earner households to work*

For the majority of families with children, the key labour supply question is whether there should be two earners in a household or just the one earner. For a minority of families, however, there may be no adult in employment.

Benefit incomes for jobless households can depend on a variety of factors, including the family structure, the age of the children, the duration of time spent in receipt of benefit and the earnings before losing employment. The net incomes of a two adult-two children family during the first month of benefit receipt when no adult is working, expressed as a ratio of the income that the family would have were one adult to work full-time earning average wages (the net replacement rate), varies between about 60% in Australia, to over 70% in Denmark and over 80% in the Netherlands (OECD, 2002g and 2003 forthcoming). This assumes that one

152

adult in the family qualifies for unemployment insurance in Denmark and the Netherlands: if they do not, and the family qualifies for social assistance, then the net replacement rates can be a little higher in Denmark and a little lower in the Netherlands. Lone parents have roughly the same net replacement rates as two-adult families in Denmark, slightly lower replacement rates in the Netherlands, and significantly lower replacement rates in Australia.

These net replacement rates were calculated in comparison with average earnings in each country. Were the only available jobs to be paid less, then the difference between out-or-work and in-work incomes would be somewhat smaller. Furthermore, local governments in the Netherlands are permitted to pay supplements to certain groups in order to reduce poverty levels. One group particularly likely to benefit is families with children, and lone-parent families in particular, and replacement rates are consequently that bit higher.

In both of the European countries, therefore, there are limited immediate financial returns to work for families with children, and this is particularly so for low-skilled workers. This does not mean that they will not seek to find work: work provides social contact, may be important for self worth, and working even in low-paid jobs may be the best way eventually to find better-paid jobs. Nevertheless, the low returns to work means that the formal requirements to look for work and to participate in labour market programmes can be important in determining the behaviour of benefit recipients, and this topic is returned to below.

5.3. Effects of the tax benefit system on those already in work

If the marginal rate of tax is high, the incentive to work an extra hour, or to invest in upgrading your education or skills in order to increase your marginal wage rate, is reduced. Equally, if benefits are related to income, then increasing earnings might just lead to reduced benefit receipts. The combination of both the tax and the benefit effects gives the marginal effective tax rate (METR), which is the amount by which any increase in earnings is reclaimed by the government in increased taxes or reduced benefits.

METRs are important in designing family policies, because not only are some benefits, tax allowances and subsidies targeted on families with children, they are also often targeted on *low-income* families with children. Because the benefit or tax concession is withdrawn from families at some point, they potentially face higher METRs than families without children. Whereas high METRs for men probably have little influence on behaviour – men work full-time, because that is what social norms say that men should do – high METRs may have an important influence on whether women seek part-time or full-time work.

In Denmark, between DKK 41 600 and DKK 101 200, the marginal tax rate is 47%; it rises to around 52% up to DKK 260 000, and then rises to 65%. But on top of

153|

this, the housing benefit is withdrawn (at between 11 and 19% of any increase in income) and the subsidy for childcare is withdrawn at about 19%.[3] Potentially, METRs can exceed 80%. The maximum possible METR used to be higher than this, but a reform in the late 1990s reduced the maximum rate – at the cost of extending the marginally lower but still high METR to more people.

Chart 5.1 illustrates the effects. Whereas single people without children predominantly face METRs of under 55%, most lone parents face METRs of over 60%, and 10% have METRs of over 70%. There is less difference in the distribution of METRs for couples with and without children, but still, METRs for those with children are generally higher. The implication of these results is that some parents,

Chart 5.1. **METRs in Denmark, 1996**

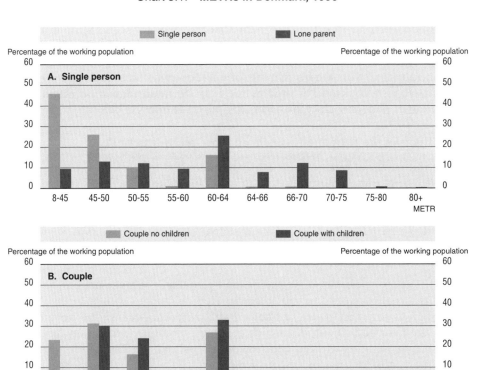

METR: Marginal effective tax rate.
Source: Calculations based on "Danish Law Model".

particularly lone parents, will see relatively little difference in incomes when working part-time, as opposed to working full-time.

In Australia, "A New Tax System" (ANTS) was implemented from 1 July 2000, reducing personal income tax and/or raised the tax threshold for low to medium income families and reduced the withdrawal rate for FTB(A) from 50% to 30% and for Parenting Payment – Single from 50% to 40%. This was partly in response to similar concerns about high METRs. Chart 5.2 shows the distribution of METRs before the tax reform. As with Denmark, the METRs for single parents were significantly skewed to the right when compared with single people more generally, and that METRs for couples with children were slightly higher than for couples without children. As a result, of those with METRs of over 60%, 54% were couples with children and 22% were lone parents.

The reforms reduced the 50% taper for family tax benefit to 30%, so many of the highest METRs will now be lower. However, this will have extended the FTB much further up the income distribution. This effect will have been reinforced by the higher level of FTB (so there is more benefit to withdraw) and by a higher "free area" before any benefit is withdrawn. In other words, whilst the highest levels of METRs will have been reduced, the slightly lower (but still high) level of METRs will have been extended. Hence whilst those receiving FTB under the old system have METRs 20% lower than under the new system, Beer and Harding (1999) estimated that 85 000 single earner families (16% of the total number of single earner families) will have become newly entitled to FTB, and their METRs will have increased by 17-26 percentage points. They are better off than previously – even considerably better off – but face higher marginal effective tax rates.

Low income two-earner couples have not seen much change in METRs from the reform, but, for example, two earner couples with two children and incomes between (very approximately) A\$ 500 and A\$ 650 saw their METRs fall, but those with incomes from A\$ 650 to A\$ 800 became eligible for FTB(A) at an increased rate and their METRs rose. Under the old system, it was possible for a family where the primary earner had a very low income (around half of average earnings) and the spouse was working part-time to face METRs of well over 100%. This is now less likely. However, the cost of removing this absurdity has been that METRs have been increased further up the earnings distribution, and may well affect the decision of spouses of partners who themselves have low earnings to move from part-time to full-time work [Beer and Harding (1999) estimate that those in this range of the earnings distribution will have seen METRs rise by maybe 30%]. Sole parents in receipt of benefit under the old system have gained from the reduction in taper rates, but the very reduction in rates has made more people eligible for benefit, so facing higher METRs than previously.

155|

Chart 5.2. **METRs in Australia, 2001**

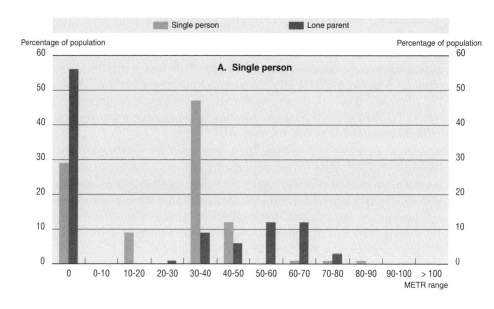

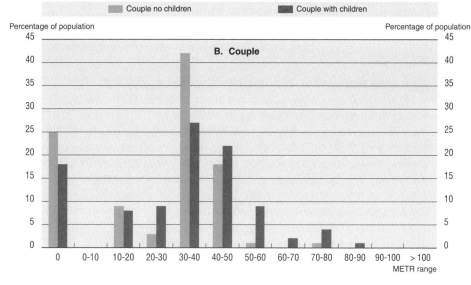

Note: METRs of zero reflect non-working households or those working a trivial number of hours. The population
includes all working age males aged 15 to 64 and females 15 to 61. Couples are counted separately. The self-
employed are excluded.

Source: Tabulations provided by DFACS.

METR calculations are sometimes rather inadequate to describe the incentives facing families in work. Suppose an extra hour of work requires an extra hour of child-care. As described in Chapter 3, in Denmark and to a lesser extent the Netherlands and Australia (in both childcare can be purchased by the half day), childcare is "lumpy" and a family may find in difficult to purchase one extra hour. More likely, they have to purchase more hours of care than they need, so in practice there are no additional costs to extra work, but rather greater usage of a service they were already paying for. If, however, they did find it necessary and possible to buy additional childcare, the subsidy from the state would go up proportionally.

METRs are a classic example of the "bulging balloon" dilemma – solve a problem in one area of the earnings distribution, and another one appears somewhere else in the distribution. That said, some choices about *where* high METRs should be applied are better than others. In general, the Australian reforms can be said to have improved the structure of the system. Lone parents in particular may not find full-time work feasible or desirable, and the reforms have made part-time work look more attractive than previously. METRs of over 100% are morally undesirable and send a message about the irrelevancy of personal effort in improving family well-being which governments do well to avoid.

5.4. Evidence of incentive effects

Australia

In 1980, 46% of women in Australia married to working men were working. By 1997, this had increased to 66% (ABS, 2000e). However, employment varies enormously according to the number of children in the household. Those with four or more children generally are less likely to work than the average, as would be expected given the greater caring responsibilities and the higher rates of benefit paid to those with large families. The increase has also been lower – from 40% to 46% over the same period.

Redmond (1999) traces the replacement rates facing both one-earner households and, to the extent possible, second earners since 1980, and suggests that some of the differences in employment rates over time can be explained by such factors. To summarise crudely an extraordinarily convoluted history of changes, the general approach has been to have at least one payment which is withdrawn fairly rapidly as incomes rise, and another form of support which reaches much of the earnings distribution. The general tendency through the 1980s and the 1990s was to increase the net incomes of families through steadily greater use of means-tested benefits. This is important because, as in many other countries, earnings did *not* rise for much of this period, particularly at the bottom end of the earnings distribution.

157|

As a result, the ratio of out-of-work incomes to incomes of the same family were it to have earnings rose sharply between the mid and late 1980s, particularly for low earnings levels and for larger families. However, in the early 1990s, incomes out of work fell in comparison with incomes in work, though since then the trend has been upwards once again.

Redmond argues that the "premium gained by women taking up low paid work where their husbands are already in low-paid full-time employment is small, and has fallen steadily since the early 1980s" (Redmond, 1999). In particular, he finds the ratio of income of the household where the woman does not work to that where it does rising from around 85% in 1980 to well over 95% by the end of the 1990s for a two child household. These estimates do not take into account childcare costs. As reported by the then Department of Health and Family Services Annual Reports, in 1993 net childcare fees for a low income household and one person in part-time work were A$ 22 per week, rising to A$ 30 per week by 1996, and for higher income households, a constant A$ 40-45 per week. Were these costs added into the equation, then for a low-income household there was no net gain to a second earner entering the workforce for low-income households.

More generally, studies of the *aggregate* trends in labour market behaviour of women indicate that women are *less* likely to work full-time the higher are (after tax) wage rates in the economy, and are more likely to work the less affordable are mortgages (Connolly and Spence, 1996; Connolly, 1996). This is because, other things being equal, a small but significant proportion of women work full-time when the household needs money, but otherwise appear to prefer non-participation or part-time work. Connolly and Badhni (1998) estimated no significant impact from childcare costs on female part-time participation rates (a result common to other Australian findings – *e.g.* Debelle and Vickery, 1998).

Denmark

A recent Finance Ministry report (Finansministeriet, 2001) looks at the development of the "income gap" – the difference in incomes of those in work with what they would receive were they to be on benefit. It suggests that there has been a steady decline in the number with a small income gap (and hence little financial incentive to work), from over 11% in 1993 to a projected 7% in 2002. Perhaps a bit more than 2 percentage points of this decline is related to policy changes in the mid-1990s. Single parents are one of the identified group which sometimes have small incomes, and their number has declined in line with the changes in the population more generally. However, these numbers assume that parents use childcare both when working but also when not working. On the alternative assumption that day care is purchased *only* when all parents present in the household work, the low income rate in 1993 would have been 3 percentage points higher, and 1.6 percentage points higher in 1997. In other words, childcare costs do reduce the financial incentive to work noticeably, but that they became *less* of an issue during the period covered. This is consistent with the changes in childcare pricing structures described in Chapter 3.

However, such studies are dependent on assumptions. For example, income is defined to include the value of pension contributions as future income. This is a contestable approach that differs from most other studies. Pedersen and Smith (2001) suggest an *increase* in the number of people who are *worse* off working rather than being on benefit between 1993 and 1996, from 7.4% of the total labour force to 9.6%. One of the striking findings of this study (and of the Finansministeriet study) is the gender difference in labour market incentives. Whereas 5-6% of men face a replacement rate of over 100%, for women the ratio went from 9% to 13% between 1993 and 1996. Indeed, "in 1996, 18.5% of the male workforce and no less than 40% of the female workforce had compensation rates exceeding 90%" (Pedersen and Smith, 2001). There is some evidence, reported in this study, that exits from employment are related to the size of the incentive to work, at least for women. This is consistent with international evidence (*e.g.* OECD, 1994) that women are more sensitive to economic incentives than are men.

A cross-national study by Callan *et al.* (1999) suggests that in Denmark, having young children does *not* affect participation rates by women in Denmark (unlike in most other countries they consider). This result is also found in many national studies (see *e.g.* the survey in Graversen and Smith, 1998). This is posited to be an effect of the universality of childcare provision (though the presence of young children is found to affect whether married women work part-time or full-time). The study also provides evidence about the effects of the tax system on second earners. This study models the effects of imposing the British tax system (lower average tax rates, individual taxation) and the Irish tax system (relatively high average tax rates, joint taxation) on Danish couples. They estimate that the move to joint taxation would cause many second earners to drop out of the labour force, with participation rates of married women potentially falling as low as 50%. The British system would also cause a drop in labour force participation by married women. However, in this case the reason is quite different: it is because the lower average tax rates would have an income effect, which would mean that fewer Danish women would *need* to work. Hence the study confirms that the Danish tax system supports dual earners, despite not being a fully individualised system, because of the level of taxation.

159

The Netherlands

Much of the Dutch social assistance benefit system is linked to the level of minimum wages. In order to increase the employment prospects of low-skilled workers, the general approach has been to let minimum wages gently decline as a percentage of average wages. However, whether this actually results in lower wage costs is complicated by the fact that the actual wage scales agreed by the social partners usually start significantly above the minimum wage level. Hence the government has sometimes resorted to exhorting the social partners to extend pay scales downwards. Because social assistance is linked with to the minimum wage level, the level of out-of-work income has been declining when compared with average earnings (but not, of course, the minimum wage). This has caused some tensions about whether the result has been an increase in poverty. Local governments have therefore been given some flexibility to increase benefit payments for some groups, if necessary (OECD, 1998a). The tax system has also been repeatedly reformed, in order to increase the incentive to work. The most recent changes are described in Box 5.1.

The consensus of most commentators has been that these changes have contributed to the improved Dutch employment performance over the past twenty years, but that they have had subsidiary impact when compared with other reforms, to the wage bargaining structure in particular. Nickell and van Ours (2000) provide a typical summary when they report estimates that the tax/benefit changes from the early 1980s to the mid-1990s accounted for a fall in (structural, *i.e.* discounting the effects of the economic cycle) unemployment of 0.65 percentage point (compared with a total decline of 4.5 percentage points).

5.5. Labour market programmes

This section looks at how governments help those parents who are not in employment to seek work. Obviously, many labour market programmes are open to a broad range of people who are not in work, regardless of their family situation. These are not considered in any detail. Rather, two particular issues are treated: the requirements placed on parents to participate in labour market programmes; and the implementation of programmes specifically for helping parents to find work.

5.5.1. Parents and conditionality

There has, generally, been a tightening of conditions placed on benefit recipients to seek work across many OECD countries. This has also been the case in the three countries under consideration. However, attitudes to requiring *both* parents in a two-parent household to seek work, or lone parents to work, vary both across countries and over time.

Box 5.1. **The tax reform in the Netherlands**

Since 2001, the Dutch tax system is an almost completely individualised system with tax credits rather than allowances, though some elements depend on family circumstances. If one partner is *not* working then unused credits *cannot* be transferred to the spouse. But the non-working spouse can get the general individual tax credit paid out in cash, as long as spousal earnings are sufficiently high (if not, then the cash payment to the spouse is proportionally reduced). How this works in practice varies enormously according to a whole range of factors, but as an example, most non-working women whose spouses earn more than half average earnings will receive nearly NLG 3 500 (US$1 600) per year. However, if both spouses are working, then some of the family related credits (Child Tax credit and the Supplementary Child Tax credit) are awarded to the partner with the highest earnings. Hence, not only is the barrier of high marginal tax rates reduced compared to the old tax system, but there is an implicit subsidy to second workers taking work (above the threshold set by the cash payment in lieu of the general tax credit).

The net effect of these changes over the previous system has been evaluated by the Centraal Planbureau (CPB, 1999) and are summarised in Table Box 5.1. Because there was a substantial cut in average tax rates, all household types gained from the reform. However, working households gained more than non-working households, so one of the aims of the tax reform – to increase the returns to work – appears likely to have been achieved. The pattern of which household types did best from the reform is more complex. As low levels of incomes, one-earner households gained substantially. At higher level of incomes, two-earner families start to gain by more than one-earner families.

Table Box 5.1. **Effects of the Dutch 2001 tax reform: percentage increases in household income**

Income level	Type of household		
	One-earner couple households	Two-earner couple households	Single person households
Earnings < 150% of minimum wage	5.5	4.25	5.75
Earnings 150-250% of minimum wage	4.0	4.25	4.25
Earnings > 250% of minimum wage	3.75	4.75	5.5
Benefits < 120% of minimum wage	2.75	2.25	2.25
Benefits > 120% of minimum wage	2.0	2.25	2.0

Source: CPB (1999).

Australia

In Australia, the traditional attitude has been that if a household wishes to have a parent at home full-time, this is not something which the benefit system will seek to change. If both parents were without work in a two-parent household, job-search requirements will only have been applied to one of the parents, the other parent having a right to a benefit in his (or usually her) own right as a full-time carer. Lone parents have not been required to look for work until their children are 16. The level of benefit has not been high, and the standard of living of parents who relied on benefit alone for their income would hardly be comfortable. Nevertheless, the option has been there.

The problems in getting back to paid work faced by parents who have been out of the workforce for a long period of time while they are caring for their children have been increasingly recognised. Whilst government policy remains open to the possibility of parents being full-time carers whilst receiving benefit, the emphasis is increasingly on informing such people of their labour market options, with renewed emphasis on encouraging and assisting people to make the most of opportunities for combining family responsibilities with workforce participation.

The most prominent discussion of these issues has been an independent commission, usually referred to by the name of its chairman as the McClure report (McClure, 2000). This commission, made up of representatives of government, employers, unions and the NGO community, argued that giving parents the possibility of *not* working sometimes results in choices which are not in the best interests of the individuals concerned. For example, 65% of jobless families in Australia are headed by lone parents (see Chapter 2). This in turn is related to the fact that under half of lone parents are working at any point in time,[4] and that 50% of all children in poverty are in lone-parent families.

The "Australians Working Together" package takes steps to deal with this issue (Vanstone and Abbott, 2001). It provides additional support and assistance to help parents re-entering the workforce and provides some mild new activity requirements for those receiving parenting payment. From when the youngest child is school age onwards, parents who are full-time carers in receipt of benefit will be obliged to attend an interview once per year, at which their labour market options will be discussed. As from July 2003, when the youngest child is 12 or more, parents will be required to participate in about 6 hours activity per week (on average) in one or more of a significant range of options *e.g.* training, structured job search, employment assistance, education, voluntary work, part-time employment.

The compulsory interview only starts from when the youngest child is 6. The rationale is that society believes that there is a substantive difference between pre-school children (who are reckoned to be best looked-after by their mothers) and school-age children (where the maternal presence is deemed somewhat less necessary). However, this argument is largely irrelevant. Even beyond the age of 6, mothers are not being *required* to participate in work; they are just being given information, asked to consider their possibilities when they do go back to work, and warned that the longer they remain without work, the harder will it be to find work when they need it. Parents who wish may also draw up a return to work plan and undertake some labour market related activities. However, all this is as valid for the parents of pre-school children as they are for those of children in school. Indeed, the case for intervening earlier on in a period of parenthood is that the mother is more likely to have usable labour market skills and contacts. Helping to develop a strategy for re-entry into the labour market is likely to be much easier for younger mothers even where this is balanced with parental choice about providing care and development opportunities for their young child(ren) in the home. All new applicants will be given additional information and will be able to access participation planning interviews, even when the children are younger, but nevertheless the new policy could have a greater early-intervention focus, keeping the mother in touch with the labour market from an earlier stage.

The new approach is advertised as providing tailored help for each individual, yet to do this properly requires trained assessors of individuals. While an emphasis has been placed on staff selection and training within Centrelink, the government has in fact been moving out of the business of advising individuals about their labour market opportunities, this being a service now more usually provided by Job Network[5] providers. The ratio of clients to staff will be crucial. It is a common theme of much of the evaluation of labour market programmes that poorly designed programmes can be counter-productive, both because they waste the time of programme participants which could have been spent more productively, and because they can dent the self-esteem and confidence of individuals in their ability to find a job. If mothers are to be required to participate in activities, then it is necessary for these to be of good quality. It is a reasonable presumption that the new clientele will be harder to deal with (and therefore more expensive) than those participating in the JET programme. Increased funding has enabled additional places in education, training and employment services to be provided, however, a comprehensive programme will have to deal with those who have deep-rooted problems; not just those who need a little push to get them job ready.

Finally, there is a risk that because everybody "must" do something, individual tailoring of interventions becomes nominal rather than real. The challenge will be to ensure that the activity to be carried out is appropriate to the objective of encouraging participation, rather than coming to be seen merely as a further compliance requirement. Already some NGOs are expressing some disquiet that mothers will be volunteering to work with them to satisfy their activity requirements, whereas the NGOs themselves consider that many of those who have been without work for very extended periods of time, and often on low incomes, would normally be their target *clientele*, not a pool from which they would expect to recruit help.

The Netherlands

In the Netherlands, couples with children are treated the same as people without children when applying for social benefits. If neither parent is working, then in principle they *both* have to look for work with the objective of becoming financially independent of the benefit. Lone parents with the youngest child under 5 have no obligation to re-enter employment. Those with a youngest child aged between 5 and 12 years have an obligation to be in or be looking for part-time work (defined as 12 hours per week). Beyond 12, parents face the same job-search requirements as everyone else – for full-time work. The underlying principle of welfare reform in the Netherlands has not just been in order to free them from poverty and social isolation; it has had a clear objective of liberating lone parents from their status as housewives for emancipation reasons (Knijn and van Wel, 2002).

In practice, however, the situation is more complicated. For jobless couples, there is still a tendency to consider the husband as being the primary candidate for finding a job, rather than there being equal pressure on both members of a couple to seek work. Some local governments do seek to persuade lone parents with very young children to attend courses in order to prepare themselves for future labour market participation. Compulsion is not applied, so to that extent there is little difference from the JET programme in Australia, but because lone-parent benefits are covered in part by local governments, sometimes significantly more effort is put into the promotion of activities by lone parents than under the JET programme (see below). On the other hand, those who are not interested in voluntarily pursuing reintegration are generally seen only maybe once every 18 months.

Most importantly, however, the apparent requirement to be seeking part-time work when children reach the age of five is very misleading. The relevant law requiring labour market activity of social assistance claimants says "the new rules are in principle applicable to all welfare claimants", but it also states that "municipalities will have to consider the presence of young children". This means that the local authorities have the option of exempting individual lone parents from the obligation if there are some reasons why it would be inappropriate.

According to a survey undertaken by Knijn and van Wel (2002), 60% of lone mothers on social assistance who do not have children under 5 are exempted from "normal" job-search requirements. The reasons lie both in the attitudes of lone parents, the skills mix of lone parents and the incentives facing local government officers.

Health problems, inability to find childcare, and relationship difficulties are all common reasons for *not* applying the obligation. In addition, lone parents on social assistance in the Netherlands generally have low educational attainment and poor labour market prospects. Van Wel and Knijn (2000) suggest that a woman with lower education would have to work a minimum of 32 hours to earn more than welfare. In other words, part-time work is not going to make a material difference to living standards,[6] but full-time work conflicts with a belief by some mothers, supported by a significant portion of public opinion, that they are best placed to look after their children. Furthermore, employers may be reluctant to take on lone parents in full-time jobs because they will be expected to pay a significant amount of childcare costs, as described in Chapter 3 (Knijn and van Wel, 1999).

Faced with a strong reluctance on the part of many lone parents to look for full-time work, benefit officers generally appear to accept unconditional benefit receipt. In behaving in this way, benefit officers are not wilfully subverting public policy, but are instead responding to the various conflicting pressures which they face. First, benefit officers are under local government control, and some local governments are controlled by politicians who do not believe that mothers who wish to care for their children should be prevented from doing so. Although under administrative control of local government, 75% of the finance of social assistance benefits comes from Central government, so local governments face no particular financial incentive to push claimants off benefit. Second, benefit officers do see their function as helping their clients, not telling them that their views about childcare and work are unacceptable to the rest of Dutch society. As a result, benefit officers are much happier "stimulating" lone parents to engage in labour market activity, rather than *requiring* them.

Third, even when the policy of requiring labour force participation is in place, it is a dead letter unless it is credibly backed by sanctions for non-co-operation. Sanctions are a very difficult policy to enforce for lone parents. By definition, those lone parents in receipt of social assistance have little or no other income, and virtually no assets. Reducing benefit rates is tantamount to condemning a family to a standard of living which society – and more particularly benefit officers – find unacceptable. Hence the usual practice of local authorities is to go a long way in avoiding being put in a position to impose sanctions. Even those local governments which claim to take sanctions policy very seriously indeed will have a system of written warnings first.

Fourth, the policy itself is sufficiently vague to leave itself open to a number of interpretations. The requirement is to search for 12 hours work a week, but the jobs that do fall into that category are reported as being low-skilled with few

165|

career prospects. On average, part-time work is for 20 or so hours (and indeed, it is commonly reported that those lone parents who do seek part-time work are looking for around this amount of hours). Is a lone parent who claims to be looking for 12 hours work, so rejects job opportunities which involve 20 hours work to be sanctioned? As a result, sanctioning lone mothers for insufficient job search happens only occasionally, if at all.

Fifth, if a lone parent does accept part-time work, she is unlikely to get off benefit completely. The benefit officer is left with a great deal of administrative work – calculating residual benefit receipt, finding part-time childcare etc. As found by a survey of benefit officers (Knijn and van Wel, 1999), benefit officers often simply do not consider the effort involved is worth it, especially given that so many lone parents do not *want* the work.

Given that anyway local governments cannot seek to cover their entire stock of lone-parent benefit recipients – the cost would be too great, there is a strategic choice which most local governments make – to target such programmes at those who are most likely to benefit from them – usually those who are co-operative and who voluntarily wish to seek employment.

In a decentralised system such as that of the Dutch, it would be a mistake to assume that it is possible to make general statements about the behaviour of benefit officers in applying the work obligation across the entire country. There certainly are cases where the rules are applied in a general way. In The Hague, 10-20% of the social assistance caseload are estimated to suffer a sanction at some point in their benefit period. If a client does not co-operate with the benefit authorities, they first receive a warning, and then suffer a reduction in benefit of 10% for between 1 and 3 months. This can be done repeatedly until the benefit is reduced to zero.

More commonly, however, it is reasonable to assume that the pressure imposed on lone parents whose youngest child is between 5 and 12 is very light indeed. There is no evidence at all that there has been any increase in the rate of exit from social assistance into employment [indeed, Knijn and van Wel (2002) suggest that with only 12% of the stock of lone parents leaving the rolls in the past year, the rate of exit has arguably declined, and that with a buoyant economy!].

This is not to say that the policy is necessarily a total failure. After all, one reason why the policy may be implemented in form rather than substance is the lack of acceptance that work for this group of people should be the norm. Changing this belief cannot be done overnight, and the official statement that they *should* work may contribute to that process, and encourage local governments to put in place the policies, both labour market, financial and childcare, that will facilitate it. In other words, this is a policy for the long haul, and will require some hardening of policy concerning the hours requirement and the resources available for labour market programmes before any substantial effect on lone-parent employment over and above that caused by labour market changes more generally will likely be observed.

Finally, the advantages of the efforts which have been made in the Netherlands towards achieving a clearer allocation of functions to different administrative units may help the reintegration of lone parents into work. In particular, local governments now have clear responsibility for labour market programmes for lone parents, some ability to alter benefit systems to help marginal groups (see Chapter 3) and for childcare. They can start taking a more holistic approach to the barriers facing lone parents – ensuring that special income support measures do not act as a barrier to work, arranging childcare, including after-hours care and structuring programmes for parents of young children. The lack of administrative clarity in helping lone parents has in the past undoubtedly contributed to the relatively poor labour market participation rates of lone parents. Whilst there is, so far, little tangible evidence that more coherent systems are improving exit rates, at least the incentives for local governments to create such structures have gradually started falling into place.[7]

Denmark

Denmark does *not* have any special rules concerning lone parents or even parents more generally. Those on benefit are required to search for work (unless covered by maternity or child-minding leave). Caring for a child is not an activity which exempts someone from such requirements, except during the first year the child's life (though the proposed new benefit for childcare at home may extend this). The high employment rate means that few people end up on local social assistance. Furthermore, the strong tax base of local governments means that they have had the resources to monitor activity requirements through compulsory attendance in labour market programmes. Childcare is not a barrier to working, in that the social norm and benefit policy of requiring benefit recipients to put their children into local authority childcare whilst looking for work are both compatible with one another.

This picture of indifference to family situation has not got that long a pedigree. Even relatively recently, it was possible to use the moderately generous child-minding benefit (originally set at 80% of the unemployment insurance rate, which itself replaces a high proportion of previous incomes of low-income households, though has much lower replacement rates for higher earners) for a succession of children. Counties were sufficiently aware that some mothers could be out of the labour force for extended periods to have introduced programmes specifically targeted at such groups. As described in Chapter 5, government responded by reducing the replacement rate to 60% of UI entitlement, and this is reported to

167

have reduced the number of people prepared to "play the system" in order to claim benefits for an extended period.

One local employment service office examined how common it was for recidivism in UI receipt or cycling from UI benefit to leave. It was found that 300 (out of 4 000) female unemployed persons had moved from UI onto a period of child-related leave. This hardly suggests a huge abuse of the system: whilst such mothers may have been ill advised to choose this particular time to have their children, it falls well within the bounds of normal fertility patterns.[8]

Even so, the benefit recipiency rates of lone parents with children under the age of 6 are higher than those whose children are older (30% of lone parents with children aged under 6 are non-employed), which suggests that a few, at least, manage the system in such a way as to keep their benefit entitlements without seeking work. Some of those close to the system believe that benefit officers are not as strict with lone parents as with some other groups; equally, some local PES officers are adamant that they make no distinction between lone parents, mothers and others when determining whether sanctions should be applied.[9]

5.5.2. Labour market programmes

In Denmark, all jobseekers (regardless of whether they are eligible to UI, public assistance or in employment seeking other jobs) can register with the PES during an initial contact lasting about 10 minutes. In the weeks following registration, clients are invited to attend a more intensive interview during which information on client characteristics is gathered. Subsequently, clients are invited to an information session lasting about 2 hours and attended by 20-30 clients at one time, during which individual rights and obligations are outlined.

UI benefits can last up to four years in theory. After 12 months all UI clients are *obliged* to attend job-training and education programmes (there are pilot programmes underway in some regions on basis of activation after 6 months of benefit receipt). However, the regional labour market councils can decide that some client-groups can access education and job-training prior to having been unemployed for one year and two regional employment services in Denmark act as a pilot case in that they start to activate unemployed from the first day onwards.

The employment service is involved in job matching, counselling and buying-in training for its clients: it does not hold interviews to check on job-search activity. UI funds, however, hold regular interviews to check on job-search activity of their members. Employment training and job support measures during the activation process (after the first year) are not available to public assistance clients. Local governments are responsible for the labour market integration of their clients. The services they provide are similar: both the PES and local governments tend to buy in services from outside contractors. Activation of anyone who has been on benefit for more than a year is general.

The one substantive difference between the services of the PES and those of local governments of relevance to this study is that the PES has no right to deal with social problems – they can only deal with the labour market problems. If someone "needs" social work, then in principle they are not ready for the labour market, so are not entitled to UI. Hence the PES does not employ social workers, or psychologists, etc.[10] Local governments, by contrast are responsible for social services, so are particularly well-placed to offer an integrated package of social services and employment aids.

In the Netherlands, UI lasts for just one year, so parents attempting to care for their children without working are much more likely to be in receipt of social assistance, currently operated by local governments. Up to 60% of the social assistance caseload are lone parents. At present, there are parallel structures for unemployment insurance clients and social assistance clients. This will change: as of 2002, new "Centres for Work and Income" (CWI) will become the first point of call for all applicants for both social assistance and social insurance. CWI will carry out a client assessment, which will allocate the client into one of four streams or phases:

- able to find work;
- pathway within one year (*i.e.* expected to be able to find work within one year);
- longer pathway required; and
- unable to work – requiring social activation or welfare aid.

The CWI will be responsible for helping the Phase 1 clients. Depending on local agreements with other organisations, it may also have responsibility for those who fall into Categories 2 and 3. The payment offices will assess the type of programme intervention required, and will generally contract for that with private sector suppliers – though a market has yet to really emerge for this. Clients are generally expected to sign "contracts" which set out actions which the client will follow in order to find work. Typical expenditures on labour market reintegration per client are somewhere between € 1 500 and € 10 000 per year, depending on the pathway followed. In each year perhaps only a quarter of the caseload receive help.[11]

The trend since 1994 has been for the number of social assistance cases to fall, but that more and more of those that remain have social problems. This has permitted local governments to allow caseloads per caseworker to fall: in the Hague they are now about 60-100 per staff member. A high proportion of the social assistance clientele has family responsibilities. For example, of the 23 000 social assistance clients in the Hague,[12] 11 000 are "women returners" to

169

the labour market, and 6 500 are lone parents. Because of the numbers of lone parents in the social assistance caseload, special programmes are often created specifically for them.

Several Australian programmes are designed to help mothers overcome barriers to work.

The Return to Work Scheme

The *Return to Work* (RtW) programme has a target group of non-income support recipients, but is open to all carers seeking to participate in the labour market. Participation is voluntary. The average cost of the programme is A$ 600 per client (US$315). Of this, A$ 250 is used to pay the provider for skills assessment, assistance with access to training and the development of a return to work plan. Providers manage training funds, and can spend up to A$ 1 500 on any one participant's training. Even so, with this limited amount of resources, it is clear that RtW does not involve case management. At December 2000, 34% of participants had gained employment within 3 months of leaving the programme (5% full-time and 29% part-time[13]).

Until recently, the RtW programme was not available to income support recipients who had access to Jobs, Education and Training programme (JET). This means that the RtW did not service the Parenting Payment customers who will be the subject of the new Australians Working Together initiative "Helping Parents Return to Work". The RtW programme has rather serviced women who have been out of the workforce for some time, but whose partner's income has precluded them from income support payments.

Despite this difference in customer groups, some of the problems experienced by the RtW programme may be of relevance in the application of the new initiative. One problem with RtW has been that some women have faced very negative attitudes from their husbands, who fear loss of (financial) control over their wives were they to find paid work. The compulsion inherent in activity testing may prove beneficial in overcoming such attitudes.

In some of the RtW sites, there have been problems because there is no system of brokering childcare places of matching vacancies with parents. This is not an issue for parenting payment customers, because the JET programme has arrangements in place to broker childcare places for its customers. Childcare for teenagers is a problematic issue. However, under the Helping Parents Return to Work measure, parents with teenage children can do their required activity during school hours and school terms unless they choose to do otherwise, so will not necessarily need childcare.

The RtW is being transformed into a new Transition to Work (TtW) programme. This will cover more clients than those currently in the RtW, but otherwise will remain essentially similar, bringing together the RtW programme and some pre-vocational training funds of the JET programme (see below). However, it is not clear that participation in TtW will be sufficient to satisfy the "mutual obligation" requirements which those on benefit must fulfil to keep their entitlements. Presumably it will. The TtW may be an appropriate option for some parents on income support who have activity requirements. The TtW programme will need to build up expertise in dealing with these customers, who may have lower motivation levels than current RtW customers who nominate for the programme on a voluntary basis.

Job Network/Intensive Assistance

Parents without work in Australia and in receipt of benefit will qualify for labour market assistance. In two-adult households where one partner receives Newstart Allowance (an activity tested payment), one (at least) of the parents will be required to look for work, and that in practice means that they are required to co-operate with labour market service providers who will help them with job-search or, if necessary, will put them into Intensive Assistance (IA) which can provide help with training, social and personal skills, address social problems – pretty much anything which the service providers believe will improve their employment prospects. This process is described in much detail in OECD (2001j), and is therefore not considered in any detail here. However, it is of relevance to note that the choice of successful service providers (collectively known as the Job Network) is dependent, in part, in the providers showing sensitivity to the needs of their potential clientele, so ability to deal with migrant or indigenous peoples and maybe a relationship with childcare providers would do no harm to their prospects.

The decision about whether benefit recipients are required to participate in IA is made through the Job Seeker Classification Instrument (JSCI) which assesses the barriers which someone faces in seeking employment. This operates on a points basis: amount of time outside the labour force, education level, health problems, etc. all give points, which, if high enough, give access to IA. Having a child does *not* give points. The rationale for this is that the JSCI points are given only when whether employment prospects are affected by some factor. Being a parent does not hamper prospects in the labour market, according to the research upon which the JSCI is based, so no points are given. In other words, the JSCI is *not* supposed to reflect the social costs or consequences of people out of work being found work, an approach which, if followed, would presumably result in greater importance being attached to helping parents achieve a decent income rather than their childless peers.

Lone and partnered parents are *not* required to participate in IA, because no conditions have been put on receipt of benefit until the recent Australians Work-   171|

ing Together initiative. But they are entitled to it if they wish and if the JSCI indicates that they are in need of it. It is suggested by benefit staff that most lone parents who seek IA generally do qualify. However, take up is low. Job Network providers generally report that lone parents do not fit well into the IA programmes. Because participation is voluntary, they do not have the same goals as a JN provider. The latter are very focussed on "getting an outcome" – work, or sometimes education – as this gets them money. For example, if a regular IA customer wants PT work, the JN provider would remind them of their legal requirements to be seeking full-time work (which is also what the provider gets paid for). But for lone parents, this sort of pressure is irrelevant.

Jobs, Education and Training (JET)

The JET programme is designed to improve the financial circumstances of parents and certain other customer groups by assisting with entry or re-entry into the workforce. Services are accessed on a voluntary basis, and are provided through individual interviews with JET advisers. The approach is not intensive, given that each worker has around 550 clients on their books (a typical IA worker might have under 200). The JET counsellor can access other benefits, such as Employment Entry and Education Entry payments on behalf of their clients. They can also help customers identify opportunities for and barriers to employment and to develop a return to work plan, as well as provide information services and assistance available to prepare for employment, and broker employment, education, training, childcare and support services. A JSCI assessment will be performed if appropriate, in order to register customers for Job Network services-Job Matching, Job Search Training, Intensive Assistance. The JET advisor can work with JET childcare resource workers who may be able to assist with a childcare place and/or costs. All lone parents will receive an invitation to talk to their JET adviser when their youngest child reaches school age, and again when they enter secondary education. Contact can be more regular. Perhaps 40% of those lone parents on benefit access JET at some point in time.

Personal Support Programme (PSP)

Australia does not have a tradition of having an extensive social worker network, organised at local government level. The Community Support Programme, which is being transformed into the Personal Support Programme (PSP), is designed to help overcome problems such as addiction, minor psychological complaints, etc. There is heavy (and, since budget changes in the early period of the current government, increasing) reliance on the Community sector to provide services. This programme will be extended in order to cope with the increased demands arising as a result of the increase in activity testing for mothers of children aged over 12. It will be more intense, and there will be an increased budget [up from A\$ 2 000 to A\$ 3 000 (US\$1 600)] per person. The total number of people assisted is estimated to increase from 15 000 people in 2000/2001 to 45 000 in 2004/2005. However, because the new clients may not all be voluntary attendees, they may prove more time-consuming to deal with. Furthermore, there will be some difficult issues as to how to deal with those formally in breach of their conditions. These issues have not been resolved.

5.6. Conclusions

The objective in all countries is to provide quality child development experiences – in the home or through childcare – as these are positively linked to outcomes for children later in life. It is hardly surprising that governments are nervous about the consequences of joblessness, not only for the parents, but also for their children. In Denmark the policy is clear, and has been for some time: having children does not exempt you from strict requirements to work. The result is that jobless households with children are rare: the employment rate of lone parents is even higher than for couples with children.

The other two countries have more complicated attitudes towards requiring mothers (in particular) to work. In theory, the Netherlands has moved a long way towards a general work requirement from when the youngest child is 5, but in practice these requirements are hardly applied. In Australia, conditions on benefit receipt for parents caring at home full-time are being introduced, but only really for those families where the youngest child is aged more than 12. Quite aside from discussions about the resources necessary to make this approach a success, it is unfortunate that such a long period of absence from the labour force is allowed before interventions (which would almost certainly be more effective were they to take place earlier) are introduced.

But this focus on lone parents and hard-to-employ groups should not entirely distract from the bigger picture (bigger in the sense that more people are involved) concerning two adult households. The tax and benefit systems of the three countries are not particularly biased for or against single earner or two-earner households, despite all having some individual provisions that appear to act in one way or another. In effect, the various "biases" in the system cancel each other out.

That is not to say that the tax/benefit system is irrelevant. First, the level of taxation varies dramatically across the countries. The returns to second earners in Denmark is low because the tax rate is high, but they nevertheless work because (among other reasons) this is the best way of achieving a desired standard of living. Second, the structure of the tax/benefit system affects incentives to work different hours. The effective tax rate on moving from part-time to full-time work for

173

second earners in Denmark is relatively low, for example, reinforcing the full-time work norm. In Australia (and, to a lesser extent, the Netherlands), part-time work is enabled by the tax/benefit system. Third, because the Australian system is strongly income tested, the incentives to work for the spouses of high income earners are significantly higher than they are for the spouses of low income workers. Those families most in need of two earners are those where the disincentives to having two earners are the highest.

There is another angle to the figures reported in this chapter about the returns to work for second earners after taking account of childcare costs, tax payments and reductions in benefit. This is that, under not obviously unreasonable assumptions, second earners "keep" less than half their earnings in Australia (and much less than this if spousal earnings are low), and between 20 and 30% of their earnings in Denmark and the Netherlands. Quite apart from any impact on labour supply (which of course will be mitigated by longer-run considerations, social norms, etc.), these figures suggest that many mothers do not get much immediate financial return for their participation in the labour market.

Notes

1. There is a danger that discussions of incentives become rather mechanistic, giving the impression that just because there is a potential financial incentive to behave in a particular way, families will understand this and respond accordingly. In practice, tax/benefit systems are very complicated, and few people fully understand the consequences of their actions. This is perhaps particularly relevant given the recent tax reforms in Australia and the Netherlands.

2. This replaces a dependant spouse rebate, and consolidates various other family benefits.

3. The amount of childcare which a family purchases is presumed to be invariant to their work decisions. But because the childcare subsidy is related to income, a marginal change in earnings will affect the amount of subsidy.

4. As shown in Chapter 2, 44% of lone parents worked in 1990. By 2000, this ratio had risen to 47%.

5. Job Network is a network of community, private and public providers which deliver employment services. See OECD (2001j).

6. For higher educated lone parents, not only are expected wage rate rates higher, but also receipts of alimony are much higher (van Wel and Knijn, 2000).

7. However, local governments still only contribute 25% of the marginal cost of the benefit of a lone parent on social assistance. Increasing this percentage would certainly help to concentrate efforts (see OECD, 1998a).

8. Supposing that all births take place when the mother is aged between 20 and 40 (teenage pregnancy being unusual in Denmark), then a fertility rate of 2 would be consistent with a 10% probability of childbirth per year. Assuming that all 4 000 female unemployed persons were of this age range and assuming that each leave period lasts a year, and it would be expected that 400 women would have been sampled as having moved from UI to leave. If either a shorter average period of leave, and/or some of the unemployed were assumed to be aged over 40, then the expected number of women moving to leave were pregnancy entirely random in its timing would be lower. Hence the 300 observed cases cannot be assumed to be evidence of women timing their pregnancy to maximise their leave arrangements, at least on any large scale.

9. The fact that no distinction is made between family types in determining sanction behaviour is consistent with both strict and lax sanctioning policy in general. A complaint of the employment services is that the latter is quite common for UI recipients. As UI funds are managed by competing agencies (unions), they are reportedly reluctant to sanction, as they would in effect be expelling a person likely to be a future contributor to the fund.

10. However, they do sometimes use the career counsellors as surrogate social workers, pushing people towards the communes with their social workers and relationship counsellors.

11. This ratio seems common to both the Hague and Zoetermeer local governments, for example.

12. For purposes of comparison, the population of the Hague is 421 000.

13. Information provided by the Department (DEWRSB).

Chapter 6

Family-friendly Work Practices

This chapter looks at how workplace practices respond to and build on the framework of public policies in place to help families reconcile work and family life.

6.1. Introduction

This chapter first briefly describes the labour market institutions in each country. It looks at the motives of employers and employees when coming to agreement on workplace practices. The penetration of family friendly work practices in the three countries is assessed. Finally, the chapter considers the role of public policy in influencing workplace practices.

6.2. The institutional framework for industrial relations

6.2.1. *Australia*

Australia has a system of industrial bargaining which results in workers being covered by three types of legal structures or contractual arrangements: under various State and Federal jurisdictions, awards,[1] collective enterprise agreements, and individual agreements. In practice there is considerable overlap, with legislation and awards providing a basic set of provisions extended by collective or individual agreements. Only a brief outline is provided here: OECD (2001j) provides an extensive discussion.

Awards set down legally enforceable conditions for workers. They may be made at the State or Federal level. Until 1974, award decisions were made taking into account "family welfare". In effect, this meant that awards assumed that workers had to support a family, so the "male breadwinner" model was entrenched in industrial relations. Wages were to be high enough to achieve this, and part-time work and other flexible employment practices were *de facto* discouraged. There were even different (and lower) minimum wages for women.

Awards nowadays are not designed to uphold some vision of family life which no longer bears much relation to actual practice, and explicit discrimination between the genders has long gone. Indeed, awards were used to enforce "equal pay for work of equal value", leading to a rapid rise in female earnings relative to males

Some standards in relation to leave have been established through test cases in the Australian Industrial Relations Commission, which have then been incorporated in awards. This has happened, for example, in the giving of a formal right to maternity leave for women in 1979 and adoption leave in 1985. Some more recent examples are given in Table 6.1.

Awards have been a declining influence on industrial relations in Australia. In 1990, two-thirds of those employed had their pay setting arrangements determined by awards; by 2000, this had fallen to less than a quarter of the workforce. Registered collective agreements have become much more important, now covering 35% of employees. Collective agreements must offer individuals a deal which is as least as good as the award (the "no disadvantage" condition).[2]

Individual agreements between employers and individual workers became much easier after the 1996 Workplace Relations Act. This allowed for "Australian Workplace Agreements", which now cover 2% of all Australian workers, a number which appears to be increasing. As with collective agreements, the "no disadvantage" test applies.

Awards and agreements often provide for both permanent and casual employment. Casual employment has increased its share of the number of total

Table 6.1. **Some key awards in the Australian industrial relations system**

Key awards	Rights given to employees
Parental leave (various over 20 years)	52 weeks of (unpaid) leave with the right to return to the same post (or similar). Either parent may take leave, but not both at the same time (except for 1 week). These rights are now embodied in legislation via the 1996 Workplace Relations Act (WRA).
Maternity leave for casual employees (May 2001)	Casual employees who have been regularly employed by the same employer for 12 months or more get the same rights to unpaid leave as permanent employees.
Carers' leave (1994, 1995)	Employees may use up to five days of their own sick leave entitlement to provide family care. Some measures were also introduced to sometimes facilitate annual leave to be taken in single days for caring purposes. Some State test cases extend this more widely.

Source: DEWRSB.

employees from 16 to 27% between August 1984 and August 2000 (ABS, 2001c). Indeed, over 60% of all the jobs growth that has taken place in Australia since the 1980s has been in casual employment. The term can be misleading – "casual work" may be regular, full-time work with a single employer and their terms and conditions are laid down in awards. In Australian statistics, however, casual workers are counted to be those who are not entitled to (paid) holidays and sick days. Instead, they receive a "loading" which compensates them for the absence of these rights. Loadings vary from industry to industry, but typically a casual worker might have an hourly wage rate of around 115-120% of non-casual workers.

Over half of all those who are "casual" workers have been with the same employer for more than one year, and one in eight remained with the same employer for five years or more (ABS, 2000a). There is a heavy overlap between casual workers and part-time workers, and between part-time workers and female workers. 67% of those casual workers who work part-time are women (ABS, 2001c).

6.2.2. Denmark

Employers negotiate a *framework agreement* with the unions. At one level down from these, there are 600 collective agreements (industry and enterprise agreements). Some ten of these agreements cover about 80% of the workforce, and the remaining negotiations tend to follow their lead. 54% of companies are attached to the employer's organisation covering about one/third of the workforce. Labour unions cover 85% of the workforce. The relationship between the centre and the collective agreement is best described by the distinction between guidelines and practice.

Some sectors "lead" developments in other sectors. For example, following an agreement in principle, the sectoral collective agreement made in 1989 introduced full pay for public employees on leave. The financial sector has paid full pay for all on maternity and paternity leave for some years. It was only in 2000, that the collective agreement for the industrial sector extended full wages to those on maternity leave for up to 14 weeks.

6.2.3. The Netherlands

There are three (or even four levels) to industrial agreements in the Netherlands. First, employers and unions come to an agreement under the auspices of the STAR (a private bipartite labour organisation). These discussions are similar in form to the framework agreements which take place in Denmark: they result in recommendations as to the topics considered by unions and employers at the level of individual sectors. For "fair competition" reasons the government often extends these sectoral agreements to cover all employees in a sector of industry, regardless of whether they or their employers were involved in the negotiations. Such "administrative extension" has the force of law. Partly as a result, collective agreements made at the sectoral level cover 90% of employees, even though unionisation rates – at only 20% of employees – are low.

Agreements made at the sectoral level often leave certain issues to be negotiated at the company level. Indeed, the importance of discussions at the company level seems likely to increase, as the agreements made at the sectoral level themselves increasingly take the form of *frameworks* rather than containing detailed provisions which have to be followed.

Negotiations take place in the context of the so-called "Poldermodel". This approach to policy-making is built around a desire to preserve social consensus. As described by den Dulk (1999):

> "The government [...] can be characterised as stimulating, leaving social partners and organisations relatively free in their decision to implement work-family arrangements. In the view of the government, they are the right actors for developing facilities that meet the needs of both employers and employees. The role of the government is to remove existing barriers and to stimulate the development of work-family arrangements in collective agreements."

However, the government reserves the right to impose its views. For example, the government considered that a proportion of childcare costs should be borne by employers. It remained up to the unions and employers to come to an agreement. Progress was insufficient, in the view of the government, who then eventually intervened, expanding state-financed provision, while increasing the pressure on employers to fall into line by exempting employer contributions for childcare costs from social security contributions. This has the effect of significantly tilting the balance of negotiations: to provide the cash equivalent of € 100 of childcare subsidies to an employee at average wages would cost the employer € 135, given the level of employer and employee taxes and social contributions.

6.3. Motives

6.3.1. Unions

Union leaderships are often male and traditional (with of course some notable exceptions); union members are predominantly male; part-time workers are less likely to be unionised (and even less likely to be active in a union). For all these reasons, unions are often not particularly active in demanding family-friendly provisions. Such demands may be "on the table" at the start of the negotiations, but are not strenuously pursued. Even when unions do take seriously the problems of part-time workers, it is difficult to define a policy: defending an 8 hour day is not what their members want, but defining what they *do* want is relatively difficult (Probert, Ewer and Whiting, 2000).

180

Conflicts can arise within the union movement, reflecting differences in the membership of different unions. In Denmark, many employers provide maternity pay, which in effect makes employing women relatively more expensive. Some unions would like to arrange for employers to make collective provision for maternity pay, so that males as well as females contribute to the costs. However, the metalworkers union opposes such collective provision, instead running a scheme for provision of maternity pay just for their members. Given that only 1-2% of the members of this union are women, the necessary levy is very low. Compared with the current situation, collective provision across industries would involve net transfers from male-dominated sectors to female-dominated sectors, so it is in the narrow interests of the members of the metalworkers union to provide relatively generous benefits to their female members at relatively low costs to their male members.

Even within a particular union, it is a mistake to imagine that a clear view on the desirability of family-friendly policies is likely to emerge, particularly if the impression is gained that the union is pursuing a narrow sectional interest. In Denmark, some unions have felt that they should push for women returning to work to be entitled to reduce their hours worked for a time, in a similar way to that which is common in the Netherlands.[3] However, other members of the union have argued that all should have similar rights to reduce their working hours, reducing the chance of success.

6.3.2. Employers

Employers have an interest in offering family-friendly provisions to their workforce for a number of reasons:

- Family-friendly provisions might reduce staff turnover.
- Employers sometimes want flexibility in hours worked, as well as employees.
- Being known as the employer with good family-friendly employment practices may give employers the choice of the best workers among those who value such provisions highly.
- Some policies may improve the motivation and productivity of the workforce.

6.4. The extent of practices in the workplace

Cross-country comparisons of family-friendly work practices are hampered by conceptual and empirical problems. Empirically, few surveys cover *employees* in a comprehensive manner. Rather, the unit of analysis is either the firm, or collective agreements (each one of which may cover many firms in the Netherlands) or, in

181

the Australian context, a sample or census of awards or workplace agreements. A further complication is that in the Netherlands, the social partners have the option of "opting out" of the publicly-provided scheme and providing equivalent (or better) benefits through collective agreements. This means that a clause in a collective agreement covering, for example, maternity leave can mean *either* that the employer is providing exactly what would otherwise be covered by public provision, *or* that the employer is providing leave in addition to the statutory requirement. For example, 39% of the collective agreements in the Netherlands include stipulations to maternity leave. Only in 15% of these agreements does it concern leave provisions that are more generous than the legal requirement (Arbeidsinspectie, 2001). Furthermore, a comparatively low or high penetration of a particular family-friendly provision has to be interpreted in the light of public provisions which may (or may not) render policies at the workplace redundant.

The tables in the annex to this chapter give evidence from the various national studies of the penetration of family-friendly work practices, other than part-time work. In the light of the problems identified, they have to interpreted with due caution. Nevertheless, some patterns emerge.

6.4.1. *Family-friendly work practices*

Flexible working hours

Employees may seek flexible working hours so as better cope with work and family responsibilities. Some control over working hours can be especially important for working parents. However, flexibility in hours is not always in the interests of parents if it means them sometimes being required to work hours which do not fit with family responsibilities. Regular hours facilitate childcare arrangements; irregular hours worked at the behest of employers may put particular strains on parents. Flexible hours certainly *can* be a family-friendly provision, but are not inherently so.

In Denmark, the general culture of the workplace is that the vast majority of employees start and finish at fixed times. However, some collective agreements provide scope for making agreements on "flexitime" schemes in individual workplaces. Table 6A.1 suggests that under 30% of enterprises have such provisions in their formal agreements with employees. A somewhat paradoxical finding which comes out of Danish research on flexible working hours is that those who have access to such arrangements use them to work *more hours than* those who do not (Sondergaard, 1999).

In Australia and the Netherlands, part-time work is much more common than in Denmark. Table 6A.2 suggests that in at least a third of Australian federally certified agreements, there are family-friendly provisions relating to working time flexibility.[4] Such provisions cover 14% of individual contracts. However, caution is needed in interpreting these figures: informal arrangements may be common.

Teleworking/home working

Teleworking/home working involves work that can typically be carried out at a distance from the usual workplace. In Australia, only a small number of Federal and State collective agreements (2 and 5% respectively; see Tables 6A.3 and 6A.5 in the annex to this chapter) had provisions for working from home. However, these covered a higher proportion of the population (14% in the case of Federal provisions). A survey from 1995 carried out by the National Institute of Occupational Health showed that between 5 000 and 10 000 Danes work at home. In 1997, framework agreements were made in several sec-tors (including central government) about the collective agreement coverage of teleworking/home working.

Leave arrangements

Allowing for extended leave in some circumstances or for providing income payments from the employer whilst on leave are the most common form of family-friendly provision. Leave arrangements around childbirth (pregnancy, maternal, paternal and parental) are discussed in more detail in Chapter 4, but briefly it can be noted that:

- In Australia, paid maternity leave remains uncommon, being found in 4% of individual agreements and 30% of federal collective agreements.

- In Denmark, the State guarantees a proportion of previous salary whilst someone is on maternity or parental leave up to a certain maximum. This is topped-up by employers in over 60% of cases, rising to nearly 90% in the case of large enterprises.

- Maternity pay in the Netherlands is also a proportion of last earnings, but the government maximum payment is much higher than in Denmark. Hence, in the Netherlands, only 5% of employers top-up public benefits to those on maternity leave. Paternity leave is common, though only in 14% of cases does it extend for more than two days. Provisions for parental leave are found in half of all agreements, though it is paid leave in only 5% and only one agreement in ten gives parental leave of more than 8 months duration (Arbeidsinspectie, 2001).

Caring for sick children

In Denmark, it is a statutory right for a parent to take off work the first day of illness of a child; thereafter it is assumed that parents will be able to make other arrangements. Almost 40% of workplaces give additional time to parents to look after their sick children (over and above the first day of illness) and a third permit workers to bring children to work if there is some disruption to their normal care arrangements (Pedersen, 1998).

Family or carers leave is the most common family-friendly provision provided in Australian collective agreements, covering about half the relevant employees. These agreements sometimes permit parents to use up some of their annual quota of sick days; sometimes give them days off to look after sick children in addition to the parent's own allocation of sick days.

The Netherlands has just introduced legislation covering care for sick children (Chapter 4) which previously were covered in many, but by no means all collective agreements. For example, "unforeseen circumstances" leave and care leave can be found in about 25% of agreements, it being paid in ½ to ¾ cases (Arbeidsinspectie, 2001). In addition, there are some initiatives which allow individuals to "save" leave from one year to the next which they can then use subsequently to enable them to study. In a minority of cases, these savings can also be used for caring activities. There are similar arrangements in Australia.

Childcare

In a very small number of cases in Australia (perhaps 1% of collective agreements) employers provide help with childcare for their employees. In Denmark, childcare very rarely is mentioned in collective agreements. In each case, this reflects the dominant role played by the public sector in providing subsidised childcare (in Denmark) or providing income-related benefits to parents (in Australia). In the Netherlands, employers play a much more prominent role, with 65% of all agreements in 1998 providing some help with the childcare costs of employees. Looking just at larger firms (den Dulk, 1999), the increase in childcare provisions actually took place largely in the early 1990s – in 1990/91, just 15% of employers offered help with childcare, compared with 54% in 1996.

6.4.2. Regular hours of work

Part-time work

Part-time work is simultaneously a response to the absence of particular institutions which might support a reconciliation of work and family life (such as childcare); a balanced way of pursuing familial and career goals; and a possible way of undermining "good" full-time well-paid jobs. The institutional details concerning part-time work matter. In particular, in Australia and Denmark, hours worked are a matter which employers and employees must agree on. This is not the case in the Netherlands, since July 2000 many employees have a *right* to change their working

184

hours (down to part-time or up to full-time), with employers only being given a veto if they can show that it is impractical or solvency-threatening.

Given the controversy about part-time work in other countries, this law seems surprisingly widely accepted by employers. Indeed, the general attitude of employers is that part-time work is already so common, with 70% of women working part-time and even 13% of men (the highest proportion in the OECD after Australia), that most employers are well-used to finding ways to structure their work practices around their employees working practices. Furthermore, as similar arrangements have been in place in some collective agreements for several years (den Dulk, 1999) the legislation is to some extent "levelling the playing field", rather than introducing some unfamiliar new right. Table 6A.6 in the annex shows that 67% of Dutch agreements currently contain formal provisions permitting workers to reduce their hours of work in some circumstances (such as returning to work after childbirth). 17% of agreements permit an increase in hours as well (Arbeidsinspectie, 2001).

Up to 25% of women working part-time are doing so *involuntarily* and form a group which potentially could demand to increase their hours. Not all these women are mothers with young children, and among that group of workers the desire to work more seems limited: only 3% of the fathers and mothers with young children have used provisions to increase hours work. 87% of working mothers reduce hours to care for children, in over half of the cases through reducing hours with current employers, and a quarter of the mothers also use part-time parental leave. About 10% of the mothers change jobs to be able to reduce hours work (Commissie Dagarrangementen, 2002). 27% of fathers of young children also reduce hours. This is more often for a short period of time, whereas mothers tend to remain in part-time work.

Both employers and employees representatives are firmly of the view that lack of childcare places, uncertainty of school hours and short-notice cancellations of school classes do sharply curtail the hours women are able to work. Tackling these problems could increase labour supply in terms of the number of mothers and average hours worked.[5]

In most parts of the Danish labour market, part-time work has not been common and indeed has sometimes been actively discouraged. Since the passing of an Act on Implementation of the Part-time Directive (agreed at the EU level), part-time rights are generally secured by collective agreements though in some sectors – for example construction and transport – provisions in collective agreements explicitly prevent part-time employment. Possibilities for part-time work are also sometimes limited by provisions stating that the number of full-time employees must not drop because a part-time position is established. In total, 35% of the collective agreements allow for part-time work; another 59% allow part-time work for new entrants. 6% of the collective agreements do not facilitate part-time work.

185|

Most part-time friendly provisions are not general: in the financial sector, there is a right for employees to work part-time after childbirth, but only for a few months.

The definition of part-time work in Denmark is based on the respondent's own classification. On this basis, 35% of women work part-time. However, using the usual international cut-off of 30 hours, only a little over 20% of working women are doing so part-time. In other words, while women often work fewer hours than men – even in Denmark –, they often work just a few hours less. In fact, most persons who work less than 15 hours per week are under 30 years of age, often students who combine short hours of work (10-15 per week) with their studies.

It is unarguable that workplace culture is not especially congenial to those seeking part-time work. One company's guidelines state baldly: employees are required to work full-time. In fact, 10% of their staff work part-time, but the underlying assumption is that full-time work is what is normal, part-time work is somewhat exceptional, usually agreed for a fixed period (one year, say), with the presumption that people will then revert to full-time. Working part-time is likely to delay career progression, and managers simply do not work part-time. In another firm, those seeking to work part-time are invited to discuss it with a human resource adviser, who will endeavour to determine whether there is some underlying problem with which the company can help. Only when the Human Resource adviser agrees will the possibility be discussed with the line manager. The reason for this process is to avoid any suggestion that part-time work is a right for staff members. Furthermore, some managers note that part-time workers tend to work the hours that they contract to work, whereas full-time workers can be expected to work unpaid overtime. Again, the result is that only women support staff work part-time, no men and no managers. Overall, based on the national definition of part-time work (less than 37 hours work per week) only 9% of women who are top managers work part-time, compared with 20% of female high earners, 40% of medium earners and over 50% of female "earners at the basic level".[6]

Part-time work is now an essential part of the Australian labour market, but it is mixed-up with other features of the labour market. Around 44% of all female employment is part-time compared with 35% in the early 1980s (Chapter 2). For mothers of dependent children, 57% of working women with a partner work part-time, as do 53% of employed lone mothers. Average part-time hours were just over 18 hours per week in 2000. When the international definition of part-time work (30 hours or less) is used, the growth in part-time work has been less rapid for women – from 34% of the total female employment in 1980, to just over 40% in 2000. There has therefore been a significant growth in the number of women working 30 to 35 hours per week (Chapter 2).

There has been growth in the part-time work of men as well, which has been even more rapid (6% a year), but from a much lower base. This has taken the proportion of males employed in part-time work from 5% to 13% of total male employment from 1980 to 2000 (and to 15% on the slightly different international basis – the highest proportion in the OECD). Because of these increases in part-time employment rates, but also because female employment has grown more rapidly than male employment, the ratio of part-time workers in the economy has exploded – from 16% of the total in 1980, to 27% in 2000. Around ⅔ of part-time jobs are *casual* (ABS, 2001c). Hence whereas most males work in "regular" full-time permanent employment, a significant minority of females work in part-time casual employment.

There has been a bias within many Australian awards against part-time work, reflecting the historical role of the awards in ensuring that jobholders would earn enough to support themselves and their family. It followed that part-time work might affect the ability of workers to command a high-enough salary to do this.

The public policy response has been in two parts. First, regular part-time work is encouraged by requiring awards where appropriate to include such provisions and to end the practice in some awards of having a maximum ratio of part-time to full-time workers. About three-quarters of them provided for regular part-time work towards the end of 2000. However, in one sixth of cases only those returning after parental leave are entitled to such arrangements. Permanent part-time work with regular hours appear in only 22% of Federal and 7% of State collective agreements (though these cover perhaps 30% of those covered by collective agreements). The second approach is to extend provisions which help casual workers to reconcile work and family life, for example the federal award standard for parental leave now provides that casual workers who have worked with the same employer for 12 months are entitled to one year of unpaid maternity leave under the Workplace Relations Act.[7]

Table 6.2. **Proportion of part-time employees receiving standard employment benefits in main job**

August 2000

Standard benefit	Proportion of part-time employees entitled to benefit (%)		
	Males	Females	Persons
Annual holiday leave	18.7	39.3	33.6
Sick leave	18.6	39.8	34.0
Long service leave	14.3	33.9	28.5
None	35.6	20.1	24.4

Source: ABS (2001c).

187

Long hours

15% of Danish men work 49 hours a week or more, and 2% of women.[8] In Australia, 25.5% of full-time workers worked more than 49 hours a week in 2000, up from 20.4% a decade earlier.[9] In the Netherlands, the ratio is lower: just 1.7% of employees worked more than 46 hours in 1996, the lowest proportion in the European Union (Eurostat, 1997). It is self-evident that an individual working such hours has correspondingly less to devote to caring activities.

The Australian Living Standards Survey, conducted in 1991-92, suggested that 55% of women working full-time felt that "working hours interfered with time for children" (Glezer and Wolcott, 1998). Under one-third of part-time women workers felt similarly, and 27% of fathers believed work affected their ability to be a good parent. The Australian Family Life Course Study (AFLCS) found that nearly 80% of women working part-time were happy with their hours of work, but satisfaction decreased with increasing working hours. Most women with children under 12 expressed a preference for working fewer hours (Glezer and Wolcott, 1997). Only 10% of both men and women in the AFLCS said that family demands interfered with work, but 44% of men and 28% of women said that work interfered negatively with family.

Dissatisfaction in work/family balance is highest among those working long hours, employed in high-status jobs (Glezer and Wolcott, 1999). Gollan (2001) found that 57% of all managers report such a recent deterioration in the work/life balance, compared with 47% of technical staff, 32% of intermediate clerical staff, and 20% of labourers and cleaners. In effect, senior staff are working more hours than they want to.

The Australian Council of Trades Unions believes that there are 1 million hours of overtime worked each year, of which two-thirds is unpaid, though ACCIRC argues that 60% of those who work more than 49 hours a week are *not* managerial. There is a case before the Australian Industrial Relations Commission, initiated by the ACTU, dealing with reasonable hours, including limits on overtime, paid and unpaid, of 60 hours a week for 4 weeks, or 54 hours over 8 weeks, or 48 hours over 12 weeks.

In the Netherlands, many two-earner households are in a "one-and-a-half" earner model – the male works full-time, and the female works half time and takes responsibility for much of the caring and household tasks. This lack of gender neutrality worries some. The Dutch Equal Opportunities Council developed an alternative model of society in which male full-time hours are reduced to allow them more time for unpaid activities outside the labour market, in turn allowing their partners to increase hours worked (Emancipatieraad, 1996). This approach is official government policy (SZW, 1997 and 1999). To a great extent, this policy remains aspirational rather than being something that is being implemented (Plantenga *et al.*, 1999), but it nevertheless has influenced discussions of working time, with 36 hour weeks being common in the public sector and spreading elsewhere in the economy.

6.4.3. *The penetration of family-friendly policies in the labour market*

Over 40% of collective agreements in Australia contain at least one family-friendly initiative, and if flexible working hours are included, this figure exceeds 70%. In Denmark, over 60% of agreements have some family-friendly policy. In the Netherlands, paternity leave alone is in 91% of agreements. The provisos given at the beginning of this section apply: the absence of a formal agreement does not necessarily mean the absence of family-friendly practices. For a number of reasons, ranging from paternalistic employers, to a wish to preserve the flexibility which comes from keeping arrangements informal, the actual extent of family-friendly practices is likely to be far higher than that indicated by formal provisions. However, it is equally apparent that many initiatives are introduced in a minority of agreements, and that the existence of an agreement is not equivalent to saying that all employees are in a position to use the provisions contained therein.

There has been a move towards decentralisation of industrial bargaining in all three countries under review. Opinion is very divided on whether this has promoted the penetration of family-friendly work practices, or hindered it. Box 6.1 outlines some key features of the Australian debate.

6.5. The scope for expanding family friendly work-practices

6.5.1. *The bottom-line case for family-friendly work practices*

There is a cost to losing members of staff, not just in advertising for, recruiting and processing new employees, but also the skills which have been developed whilst working for the firm are lost. A family-run dental practice in Brisbane estimates the cost of losing a dental assistant as being A$ 30 000 (US$15 800). Given an industry average duration in employment of just 22 months, the gains from reducing turnover are potentially large. In the Australian retailing sector, anecdotally, attrition rates are in the region of 30-40% in the first 6 months after being taken on. Recruitment of a new member of staff costs A$ 1 200-2000. At the other end of the jobs market, a leading law firm estimates that it costs A$ 100-150 000 (US$53-80 000) to replace a lawyer in terms of lost contacts and knowledge. In the Netherlands, the "Daily Arrangements" Committee estimates the average cost of labour turnover across the economy was NLG 50 000 (US$20 000) on average. The Dutch subsidiary of a management consultancy believes that talk of the costs of recruiting and training new staff vastly underestimates the opportunity cost of losing one of their senior consultants. Instead, the lost income which would have

189|

Box 6.1. **Have industrial relations reforms in Australia affected the introduction of family-friendly work practices?**

Individual agreements, known as the Australian Workplace Agreements (AWA) are highly regulated. No worker can be forced to move onto an AWA (though new employees may not be given the option of any contract other than an AWA). The Office of the Employment Advocate (OEA) is charged specifically to monitor whether AWAs are legal and to check that the "no disadvantage" condition is satisfied. Hence in principle employers should not be able to use AWA to undermine workers' rights to work-life reconciliation policies or indeed any other employment conditions.

Indeed, the OEA argues the opposite, on the basis of a survey it has undertaken (Gollan, 2001) on whether employees (both with and without an AWA) think that the work/family balance has got better or worse. Of those employees *without* an AWA, 20% say that conditions have worsened because of changes at work, with 10% claiming that on the contrary things have got better. 20% of those employees *with* an AWA also report a degradation of the balance due to work, but 15% report an improvement because of changes at work. This difference between the two samples is interpreted by the OEA as showing that AWA employees generally have more control over their working hours and start/finish times than other employees.

Whitehouse (2001) uses the ADAM database developed by ACCIRT to look at the inclusion of work-life reconciliation policies in AWAs. She finds that between 1997 and 1999, on average 12% of AWAs had at least one provision which might be counted as such, excluding working time flexibility. There was a decline in the prevalence of such provisions between 1998 and 1999, though little can be inferred on the basis of such a short time-span.

The big increase in enterprise agreements means that many workers are no longer directly covered by awards. The evidence cited above and in the annex to this chapter refers to the proportion of firms with or employees benefiting family-friendly work provisions. However, when looking at *trends* in the penetration of family-friendly provisions, Whitehouse (2001) reports that there was a surge in the percentage of agreements referring to work/family measures in collective agreements in 1997/98, but that since then the proportion has fallen off sharply, and this pattern is found even within sectors and States. The data on which this conclusion is based are, however, contradicted by the official Workplace Agreements Database, based on a census of federally certified agreements (see table below). This not only shows very different levels of penetration of work-life reconciliation policies in the workplace (family leave is found in just 3% of agreements according to the ADAM database used by Whitehouse, *op cit.*), but also shows little trend over the five-year period since 1997, except in part-time work, where there is a strong upward trend.

Box 6.1.   **Have industrial relations reforms in Australia affected the introduction of family-friendly work practices?** (*cont.*)

Table Box 6.1.   **Work/family-friendly provisions in Federal certified agreements, 1997-2001**

Provision	1997	1998	1999	2000	2001	Total
Family/carers leave	30	27	29	24	30	28
Paid maternity leave	4	10	9	6	7	7
Paid paternity leave	2	3	2	3	5	3
Paid adoption leave	2	1	1	2	3	2
Extended unpaid parental leave	2	*a*	1	1	3	1
48/52 career break	1	2	2	2	3	2
Part-time work*b*	16	20	24	23	27	22
Jobsharing	2	2	2	2	3	2
Working from home	1	2	1	1	1	1
Child care	2	1	*a*	1	1	1
Family responsibilities	2	3	4	4	3	3
Total of agreements	5 122	7 007	6 161	6 876	6 672	31 838

a) Represents less than 1%.
b) Excludes casual part-time work. Between 4-8% of certified agreements specifically provide for regular part-time hours
Source: Workplace Agreements Database.

Finally, the expansion in casual work contracts referred to above has obvious consequences for the penetration of family-friendly policies in the workforce. More than a quarter of all Australian workers are on casual contracts, and may not benefit from family-friendly provisions available to the core workforce. It is sometimes suggested that enforcement of award provisions is anyway not that tight (*e.g.* Burgess and Campbell, 1998). Evidence suggests that whilst some can use casual work as a stepping-stone onto permanent contracts, this is by no means a general experience.

been generated had the person remained should be counted, and this could be as much as NLG 5 million (US$2 million).

A large Australian corporation, AMP, believes that it has achieved a 400% return on investment in making their workplace more family friendly, mainly through increasing staff return after maternity leave. The Commonwealth Department of Finance and Administration saw turnover fall from 23% to 15% per year after reforming its work practices, with sick leave down and productivity up in addition. A property management company, Lend Lease had a return-to-work rate of women employees after childbirth of just 27%: this has now been increased into the 80s.

There are other, less easily quantifiable, reasons why businesses might introduce family-friendly work practices. Good staff can be attracted through offering what is in effect a better, less-stressful lifestyle, rather than higher pay. More generally, firms in all three countries have to cope with demographic shifts which are affecting the structure of the labour force. A firm which restricted itself to recruiting from a declining demographic group (prime aged males) will put itself as a disadvantage compared with those who can offer work practices which are compatible with the aims of a greater proportion of the potential labour force. Finally, many family-friendly work practices are congruent with (and therefore introduced at the same time as) "modern" techniques for workforce organisation. For example, giving employees more control over how they do their work, including how they organise their time so as to get the work completed, may increase worker productivity.

6.5.2. Why are family-friendly work practices not more common?

The occasionally strikingly high rates of return which some employers claim to have realised from introducing family-friendly work practices raises the question as to why such practices are not *more* prevalent than they appear to be. There are several possible explanations: that the business case given above is overstated; that workers preferences for family-friendly provisions are not represented in negotiations; and that there are structural reasons preventing the introduction of such provisions even when they are desirable. Furthermore, it may be that they are unaware of the potential benefits which such policies may bring.

The business case for family-friendly policies is overstated

The small amount of evidence presented above suggested some remarkable rates of return being achieved by businesses which introduced family-friendly work practices. Yet whether such returns can be generalised across the population may be challenged from several directions (Glass and Estes, 1997; and Dickens, 1999).

The particularly high rates of return referred to above are driven by the costs of high rates of labour turnover. If these costs are high, this must be because either skills are very firm-specific, or there is a general lack of appropriately skilled labour. For low-skilled work, the costs of high labour turnover are likely to be less, suggesting that the incentives for firms to introduce family-friendly work practices are likely to be concentrated in high-skilled professions. Evidence does indeed suggest that there are more likely to family-friendly work practices in companies with high ratios of professional staff, and high earners (Whitehouse and Zetlin, 1999; Glass and Fujimoto, 1995; Osterman, 1995). And because the costs of *not* having family-friendly work practices are higher the greater is turnover, and this in turn is likely to be related to the gender balance of the organisation, it is to be expected that the more female workers there are, the greater the likelihood of workplace practices being family-friendly. There is evidence that this is indeed the case.[10]

There are some striking counter-examples where employers of low-skilled workers have been in the vanguard of introducing family-friendly policies. Again in Australia, retailers such as Coles and Woolworths have introduced family-friendly work practices as part of a package to reduce the distinction between a core work-force and a highly unstable mass of temporary workers. ALCOA, a large Australian mining enterprise in a traditionally male-dominated industry, is interested in improving the work/life balance for a mixture of related reasons: attracting staff (fostering diversity extends the pool of labour from which can be hired), and moti-vating existing staff to improve productivity.

A further reason for being cautious about the generality of high rates of return in introducing family-friendly work practices is that many such policies depend on being able to pool and share risks. Offering workers flexibility is simpler to man-age when workers can cover for one another and staff can be rearranged to cover absences. This is less easy for small businesses than for larger ones, suggesting that without intervention, family-friendly work practices are more likely to make headway in large firms than small ones. This is a hypothesis which is partly con-firmed by the evidence from Denmark in Table 6A.2 of the annex. Den Dulk (1999) reports that Dutch data shows the same pattern. In Australia, leaving aside flexible working hours, 35% of agreements in large firms have at least one family friendly measure, compared with just 8% of small firms.[11]

Workers preferences for family-friendly policies may be overstated

In all three countries, whereas family-friendly work practices are often on the table at the start of negotiations, unions often withdraw their demands when it comes down to a choice between them and more money (Sloep, 1996, Probert, Ewer and Whiting, 2000). Whether this reflects underlying demand for such prac-tices may be doubted. Simplifying somewhat, but not outrageously so, unions are predominantly male and represent full-time workers. Unions in the past were rela-tively uninterested in reconciling work and family life, because their core mem-bership was not interested in such issues. The question not so much whether this has changed (it clearly has in many cases, though some unions represent workers in male-dominated industries), but rather finding an appropriate approach.

Structural reasons prevent employers from realising the advantages of family-friendly policies

The idea that a firm has a single viewpoint in deciding whether to introduce a family-friendly package of policies is a gross simplification. In practice, firms are

193|

compartmentalised into cost centres, as this is the only realistic way to run large complex organisations. This can have the unintended effect of diffusing the potential benefits of introducing family-friendly work practices across a number of departments, preventing any single overview of the advantages of having such practices from emerging.

For example, industrial relations in Australia in particular takes place in a complex area of jurisprudence, with Commonwealth and State law, and the award system giving a large number of potential frameworks within which agreements can be made. As a result, industrial relations departments often exist independently of Human Resource departments. This dichotomy has been pointed to as a possible reason why Human Resource departments often appear to be persuaded of the bottom-line merits of introducing family-friendly policies, yet agreements realising these benefits are not as common as might be expected.

Leadership

"Leadership" has two effects on the implementation of family-friendly work practices. First, high-level commitment is necessary to overcome internal institutional barriers to introducing such measures. Second, without such leadership from senior management, the workforce will not take advantage of any measures which are put in place.

In practice, firms do *not* usually appear to introduce family friendly practices because they have engaged in some hard-nosed assessment of the costs and benefits. Instead, they are introduced because someone very high up in the organisation takes a leadership decision about how the company should behave as an employer. This is partially confirmed by two pieces of evidence: first, when asking firms which do have a strong commitment as to why they introduced their programmes:

- "There clearly is a bottom line advantage, but we had not modelled the effects before we introduced our various policies – it was a strategic decision."

- "Introducing family-friendly policies was all part of "doing the right thing."

- "We did not explicitly set ourselves up to be family friendly – it resulted from treating people with respect."

Second, although the "business case" for introducing family-friendly work practices makes clear predictions about which firms should introduce such policies (female workforce, highly trained, large organisation, etc.) which are partly confirmed by the evidence, nevertheless the overall predictive power of the model seems very small.[12] That leaves much of the variation in introducing such measures to be explained by intangible factors, of which leadership seems likely to be the most important.

Even in the public sector, the role of leadership is critical. The decision that the Australian Department of Finance and Administration should aim to become an employer of choice was made by a new Secretary to the department: it was not a response to detailed evidence of potential savings.[13]

Part of the reason why the extension of family-friendly work practices so dependent on the personal vision of a senior individual in an organisation is no doubt because only a leader can overcome the compartmentalisation and narrowness of vision that is inevitable in large complex organisations. Another reason, however, is because only very senior officials can take responsibility for some of the consequences of family friendly work practices. For example, clients of lawyers and management consultants may be expected to accept that exceedingly long hours will *not* always be worked, that their contacts will sometimes be on parental leave, that sometimes their accounts will be managed by two part-time workers, and not a single person. Because some family-friendly practices are sufficiently unusual, someone high up in command has to take responsibility for the workforce to feel that they *can* take advantage of the provisions without compromising the business objectives of the organisation and their own careers.

Because of the apparent importance of leadership in promoting family-friendly work practices, the issue of the glass ceiling is relevant. According to the Australian Council of Trades Unions, only 1.3% of senior executives are female. In Denmark, too, there is evidence that the glass ceiling remains (Datta Gupta *et al.*, 2002) and it is referred to as an issue in the Netherlands .

It is all well and good for an informed and concerned human resource department to introduce state-of-the-art work practices, but if the workforce does not take advantage of them, there is little point. In practice, men do *not* take advantage of family-friendly provisions, be they parental leave (though paternity leave, which of course is much shorter, may be taken), caring for sick children, or part-time work. It is the culture of many businesses that, for men at least, work should come first. For women, the pressure is reported to be less intense, and it is more acceptable to use provisions (Probert, Whiting and Ewer, 2000). However, this may therefore have the effect of confirming gender roles and the "unsuitability" of women for management positions: it is the structure supporting the glass ceiling.

It is noticeable that firms which do claim to have significantly altered the work culture of their organisation have focused attention as much on the management as on "the shop floor". For example, various companies have referred to the following events as being "breakthroughs" which brought home to the workforce more generally that the management was serious about family-friendly policies: the promotion of a woman even whilst she was pregnant; the promotion of a

195

woman to a more senior management post even though she was working part-time; a male partner of a law firm choosing to work part-time. In addition to such evidence about the role that managers play in setting an example that it is "all right" to take advantage of family-friendly provisions, there is also evidence that such practices need systematising and recording to promote their usage (Russell, 1999; Whitehouse and Zetlin, 1999).[14]

6.6. The role of government

6.6.1. Publicising the benefits of family-friendly work practices

There is little point in persuading or requiring employers to introduce family friendly work practices if individuals do not take advantages of the provisions. Fathers may want to take-up paternity leave, for example, but they feel that this would damage their career prospects. In this case it may be a legitimate role of government to overcome resistance by managers. In addition, if the failure of men in general to take up provisions designed to help them play a greater role as parents (continues to) leads to greater stress on women bearing the burden of dual roles, there is a gender equity case for public intervention towards greater use by men of family-friendly provisions.

The Australian Federal Department of Employment and Workplace Relations Work and Family Unit, has as its objective the promotion of FFP provisions in workplaces, including increasing the awareness of opportunities available in the agreement-making process. The Unit provides information on best practice, publicises model clauses and distributes resources. It is conducting a project in the retail sector, a significant employment sector with no FFP tradition, looking at issues such as optimal rostering, part-time management positions, etc. This model is replicated in some States, and other agencies may be involved in similar tasks at the State level. The objective is to make resources available for employers to enable them to develop responses.

At the Commonwealth and State levels, prizes for family-friendly employers are used as a way of publicising the potential benefits to employers of introducing such practices. By giving awards in a variety of categories, including those industries which are predominantly male, the message is given that family-friendly policies can be appropriate for all sorts of business.

The various governments may also be active in promoting employee awareness of family-friendly provisions. The Office of Workplace Services is a federal service, with a state network providing information to employees regarding their entitlements. Working Women's Centres have an advocacy role, representing women in industrial tribunals, reflecting the low penetration of union membership in many predominantly female occupations.

The Equal Opportunities for Women in the Workplace Agency is a statutory authority that sits within the Employment, Workplace Relations and Small Business portfolio. Its role is to assist organisations to achieve equal opportunity for women, principally through compliance with reporting requirements. The organisation generally finds that there are few overt problems of discrimination in areas such as recruitment and selection, or harassment, reflecting the large size of the companies which are their client group. However, they do find indirect problems, such as promotion; training and development ("women are trained for their current jobs, but men are trained for their next job") and work organisation (women opting out of jobs which have family-unfriendly hours, thereby often opting-out of promotion prospects).

In the Netherlands, the Daily Arrangement Committee is one organisation that plays a role in promoting family-friendly work practices. "E-Quality" is another such organisation: approaching the issue from both a gender and ethnicity perspective.[15] The Daily Arrangements Committee argues that the reconciliation of work and family life in the Netherlands can be substantially improved by through better spatial planning (where are crèches in relation to schools and workplaces?) and co-ordination of opening times of schools, crèche and after-school clubs. There are some positive models. One company with whom they work reported a halving of absenteeism, an increase in productivity and an increase in job satisfaction from such a system. Another firm reports a fall from 14% to under 1% in their absenteeism rates.

6.6.2. Altering the cost/benefits of introducing family-friendly work practices

The Netherlands uses employer-based subsidies in order to influence the content of collective agreements. The origin of this approach lies in the distribution of responsibilities between the government and social partners. The "polder model" of government stresses the importance of consensus between social partners as to the best way to balance the competing demands of different social groups. However, whilst the government believes that some issues *should* be resolved through negotiation and compromise, this does not mean that they inevitably *are*. Faced with the absence of an agreement on parental leave, the response of the government has been to "oil the machine" through reducing the cost to employers of making concessions. Hence, employer expenditures on paid parental leave or childcare payments are not subject to social security contributions, effectively making them some 10-15% less costly than a wage payment of similar net value to employees. There is a cost to the public budget of such provisions: the childcare subsidy to employers costs NLG 113 million (US$46 million) and the parental leave subsidy just NLG 18 million (US$7.3 million), reflecting the fact that the penetration of such provisions into collective agreements and practice remains low.

6.6.3. Over-riding the outcomes of industrial bargaining

Sometimes public policy takes the line that particular policies are sufficiently important that they cannot be left to the social partners. Hence in the Netherlands, whereas parental leave has been something which is the responsibility of employers and employees to agree upon, this has not been the case for maternity leave. In Australia, the giving of unpaid leave is mandatory, but whether it is paid or not is left for negotiation.

However, sometimes the motivation for overriding any potential outcome of collective bargaining is because of some core societal values. Legislation reflecting fundamental rights of individuals influences workplace practices in all three countries. Relevant human rights legislation includes: equal pay for equal work; harassment; non-discrimination on grounds of gender; non-discrimination on grounds of pregnancy; and non-discrimination on the grounds of family responsibility. The three countries have different ways of ensuring that these rights are upheld and in ensuring that necessary amendments to legislation are introduced.

In Australia, the Human Rights and Equal Opportunities Commission (HREOC) can intervene in a tightly restricted number of areas where there is discrimination – on grounds of sex, pregnancy or potential pregnancy, marital status, family responsibilities (but for dismissals only[16]) and harassment. On these issues, they can investigate cases, and engage in conciliation between employers and employees (at which point most cases are settled). If judicial hearings are required, HREOC can be a "friend of the court". For example, they recently intervened in the unpaid parental leave hearings (for casual workers) of the industrial relations commission.

HREOC is not just concerned with the judicial application of human rights legislation; they also have a leadership role in identifying whether current practices reflect basic rights. Recent work has focussed on pregnancy and work. They have found that there is sometimes great misapprehension about the medical consequences of pregnancy which can result in bizarre employer attitudes. Despite legislative prohibition of some 15 years standing, discrimination and harassment still exists.[17] Renewed emphasis on employer responsibilities and the issuing of "pregnancy guidelines" were among the steps flowing out of this report (HREOC, 1999).

Many of the most difficult issues they address, however, relate to indirect discrimination. For example, if some employee is forced to start work at 8 am every morning, without any flexibility, this arguably might be indirect discrimination against those with family responsibilities. Precedent has developed such that it now seems clear that employers are under an obligation to *consider* the possibility of flexibility in working hours in such cases, though they are not under an obligation to prove that such provisions are not feasible.

In the Netherlands, the Equal Treatment of Working Hours Act (1996) provides for equality treatment of employees, irrespective of full-time or part-time status. Employees, employers and unions can seek a review by the Equal Treatment Commission (which was established much earlier). It has the ability to make non-binding recommendations, but those recommendations do hold weight if the matter is pursued in the Courts.

Denmark has a rather different historical approach to ensuring gender equity. The strategy of many women's groups has not been to seek legislation which "protects" women, but rather to get women into positions of power. Introduction of equal rights for part-time workers therefore has been introduced mainly in response to the EU directive on this topic, rather than any strong domestic pressure for such a change.

6.7. Conclusions

In Denmark, legislation determines leave periods. Childcare is provided without employer involvement. Where there might be a role for bargaining – in hours of work, and particularly the use of part-time work – there is relatively little interest from either employers or employees, or at least their representatives. The key issue in workplace relations is the funding of the leave period. The topping-up of wages by employers – likely to become more important, following the introduction of new leave arrangements as described in Chapter 4 – puts a burden on employers of women. Assuming that there is no large change in the leave-taking practices of men, there is a need to find a way of spreading the costs of paid leave more equitably across the population.

Workplace practices are much more central to the reconciliation of work and family life in the other two countries. In the Netherlands, government in effect directs the social partners to come up with an agreement on topics it considers important. If the response is insufficient, it will then legislate. This is a powerful incentive to make an agreement, and as a result, agreements on the right to part-time work, childcare, leave etc. have all taken place (though have nevertheless been supplanted by legislation in some cases).

In Australia, government keeps most workplace practices at arms length, confining its role to setting up the frameworks in which bargaining takes place. For the past few years, this has involved relegating awards to a platform, upon which more decentralised bargaining – either collective or individual – can build. Federal legislation nevertheless is used sometimes – to cover the protection of fundamental rights, for example, or to provide minimum entitlements such as 12-months unpaid parental leave. Government activity is restricted to influencing the content of the safety-net awards, and to promoting the adoption of "best practice" by employers.

199

Leaving aside those areas where legislation is present (or threatened, in the case of the Netherlands), it is difficult to avoid the conclusion that the spread of family-friendly work practices is at best "patchy". Unions are still in the process of a transition from supporting a full-time breadwinner model, and have not worked out the best way of reflecting the needs of part-time and/or female workers. Businesses are sometimes not structured in such a way that the gains from introducing family-friendly work practices can be realised. Employers will keep up with the pack – where there has been a concerted attempt to get employers to top-up maternity pay, for example, failure to do so would mark employers out as being "bad", and this is avoided. Some practices – flexible hours, for example, can clearly be in the interests of both employers and employees, and are introduced. But although best practice is very good, many family-friendly policies are a minority interest. Prizes and publicity for good employers are no doubt valuable in educating employers about what is possible, but do not, as a matter of fact, appear to have led to great inroads in spreading such practices to "difficult groups", such as small employers, or employers of low-skilled workers. Hence the penetration of family friendly policies is highly uneven. Relying on "the business case" as the main way of promoting family-friendly work practices risks the outcome that such provisions are restricted to the public sector and to highly-skilled high-paid professionals.

Annex to Chapter 6

Table 6A.1. **Denmark: Family-friendly initiatives by enterprises, 1997**

Initiative	Number of employees in enterprise			Total
	1-50	61-200	Over 200	
Care day in excess of child 1st day lost through sickness	37	38	41	37
Special hours for parents	27	32	37	28
Bring the children on the job	32	35	33	32
Work at home if children have needs	13	19	34	14
Full or partly wage top-up on maternity (parental) leave	60	84	87	62
At least one of the initiatives above	60	70	70	61

Source: Sondergaard (1999).

Table 6A.2. **Multiple family-friendly provisions, federal collective agreements in Australia, 2000 and 2001**

Number of family-friendly provisions	Certified agreements with family-friendly provisions[a]		Certified agreements with family-friendly provisions and flexible working hours[b]	
	Number	% of agreements	Number	% of agreements
1	2 244	16	5 079	37
2	1 348	10	2 270	17
3	892	7	1 155	8
4	592	4	722	5
5	336	2	454	3
6	159	1	413	3
7	106	1	288	2
8	67	*	200	1
9	24	*	162	1
10	11	*	69	1
11	12	*	38	*
12	1	*	27	*
13	#	#	13	*
14	#	#	8	*
15	#	#	3	*
16	#	#	2	*
Total	**5 792**	**42**	**10 903**	**80**

a) Family friendly provisions used in this analysis are: flexible use of annual leave, access to single days annual leave, 48/52 week career break, unlimited sick leave, all purpose paid leave, paid family leave, access to other paid leave for caring purposes, unpaid family leave, extended unpaid parental leave, paid maternity leave, paid paternity leave. Paid adoption leave, part-time work, job sharing, home based work, family responsibilities and childcare.
b) Flexible hours provisions used in this analysis are: make up time, time off in lieu at either ordinary rates or penalty rates, hours averaged over an extended period, compressed hours, flexible start/finish time, flexitime system, negotiable hours of work, hours decided by majority of employees, and banking/accrual of rostered days off.
Agreements recorded a maximum of 12 family-friendly provisions.
* Less than 0.5%.
All percentage figures have been rounded.
Source: DEWR, data drawn from Workplace Agreements Database.

Table 6A.3. **Work/family provisions in federal collective agreements in Australia, 2000-2001 average**

Provision	% of agreements	% of employees covered
Family-related leave		
Family/carer's leave	27	59
Access to other leave for caring purposes	19	40
Paid family leave	3	15
Unpaid family leave	9	23
Paid maternity/primary carer's leave	7	32
Paid paternity/secondary carer's leave	4	16
Paid adoption leave	2	14
Extended unpaid parental leave	2	6
Access to single days annual leave	13	23
Flexible annual leave	6	10
48/52, career break	3	17
All purpose paid leave	3	9
Unlimited sick leave	1	2
Assistance with children		
Childcare provisions	1	7
Other family-friendly provisions		
Part-time work[a]	25	67
Regular part-time work[a]	7	28
Job sharing	3	16
Family responsibilities clause	3	17
Home-based work	1	10

a) "Part-time work" refers to all part-time employment provisions. "Regular part-time work" refers to a commitment to and/or provisions that encourage regularity and stability in part-time working hours.
Source: DEWR Workplace Agreements Database which contains all federal agreements.

Table 6A.4. **Work/family provisions in Australia workplace agreements, 1998-99 average**[a]

Provision	% of employers	% of employees
Family-related leave		
– Sick/personal/carer's leave[b]	..	26
– Paid maternity leave	4	17
– Paid paternity leave	4	15
– Extended unpaid parental leave	..	4
Working-time flexibility		
– Rostered days off	..	3
– Employee choice over distribution of hours	..	14
– Start and finish times not set by agreement	..	14
Number covered		81 932

a) For caveats relating to estimates of provisions in AWAs and the number of employees affected, see DEWRSB and OEA (2000).
b) Increased compared to award provisions.
.. Data not available
Source: DEWRSB and OEA (2000) drawing from Australian Workplace Agreements Management System and Australian Workplace Agreements Research Information System.

Table 6A.5. **Work/family provisions in registered State collective agreements in Australia, 2000**

Provision	% of agreements
Family/carer's leave[a]	34
Paid maternity leave	5
Paid paternity leave	2
48/52	5
Career break	0.5
Permanent part-time work	7
Job sharing	3
Working from home	5
Child care[b]	0.5
School fees paid	*
Elder care referral services	*
Employee Assistance Programs	11
Number covered	598

a) Family/carer's leave is defined here as any reference to one or more of: family/carer's leave taken as part of or additional to sick leave; family/carer's leave taken as part of other leave (*e.g.* annual, bereavement, rostered days off, time-off-in-lieu); more than five days family/carer's leave; employee may also be granted leave without pay, leave on half-pay, leave on reduced pay. It should be noted that this is a broader definition than that used for the Workplace Agreements Database and reported for federal agreements.
b) Includes childcare facilities at the workplace or subsidised places.
* Less than 0.5%.
Source: ADAM database, ACIRRT, unpublished data, June 2001; a sample of 598 State agreements commencing in 2000.

Table 6A.6. **Percentage of collective agreements with family-friendly work provisions in 1998 and coverage of employees in the Netherlands**

Measure	% collective agreements	% employees
Opportunity to change work hours	67	62
Either up or down	17	8
Down	42	
Up	8	
Any request is in principle acceptable	12	
Pregnancy/maternity leave	39	40
With wages top-up	5	
Paternity leave	91	79
Leave of more than 2 days	14	
Adoption leave	40	42
Leave of more than 2 days	14	
Parental leave	50	41
Paid leave	5	
Leave of more than 8 months	11	
Unforseen circumstances leave	24	29
Paid leave	18	
Leave of more than 3 days	12	
Care leave	19	21
Paid leave	10	
Leave of more than 1 month	5	
Special activities leave	18	25
Paid leave	2	
Leave savings scheme	6	
Leave savings scheme	28	42
Only for study	19	
Only for care	6	
Child Care	55	57
Just for the 0-4 age group	19	25
Just for the 0-12 age group	18	18
Help with child care is subject to conditions[a]	8	5
Direct financing of the cost by employers	17	
Financing of the cost via a collective fund	22	
Total	132 collective agreements	4.7 million workers

a) For example, in February 2000, 5% of collective agreements stipulated that child care benefits were paid for female workers only.
Source: Arbeidsinspectie (2001).

Notes

1. An award is a legally binding industrial instrument registered in an industrial tribunal at federal or state level. Awards usually cover multiple employers and establish minimum standards across substantial sections of an occupation or industry. The award system not only regulates terms and conditions of employment by directly covering employees, it also forms the basis for establishing 'no disadvantage' for employees entering into agreements at the enterprise level. Through state legislation, some awards will apply to all employees. The exception is the State of Victoria which abolished its own legislation, and where employees not covered by a federal award or an agreement have minimum wages specified in the federal legislation.

2. The no disadvantage test is global: individual terms and conditions can be less generous than under the award or legislative benchmark, but the overall package of employees' terms and conditions has to be at least as generous as the benchmark.

3. Meanwhile, while collective agreements in Denmark increasingly include options to part-time employment its incidence has in fact fallen – see Chapter 2.

4. The figures here refer to collective agreements, which may provide family-friendly working arrangements *additional* to those available through either legislation or the award system. The data in the annex refers to registered collective agreements which cover 35% of employees (Tables 6A.2, 6A.3, 6A.5 in Chapter 6), while a further 2% are covered by registered individual agreements (Table 6A.4).

5. An increase of maternal labour force participation by 3.5% in numbers, while mothers increasing their number of hours worked by 2 hours per week, is estimated to generate gains of €1.3 billion per annum in the Netherlands (Commissie Dagarrangementen, 2002). However, the required increase of spending on improving the infrastructure to facilitate this improvement of the reconciliation of work and family life (school hours, out of school care, childcare capacity, etc.) is unclear. Nevertheless, *potentially* gains appear substantial.

6. Ministry calculations based on statistics from Statistics Denmark, StatBank Denmark, Labour Force Survey.

7. Agreements are often no comprehensive so conditions of employment in a workplace may be provided by both an agreement and an award.

8. *Source*: Statistics Denmark, StatBank Denmark, Labour Force Survey.

9. DERWSB research into long working hours in Australia shows that while there was a general increase in hours worked over the last 30 years, this trend has eased since the mid-1990s. Average weekly hours for full-time employees rose by 1.4 hours between 1982 and 1988, 0.9 hour between 1998 and 1994 and 0.4 hour between 1994 and 2000 (DEWRSB communications).

10. Whitehouse and Zetlin (1999) report that over 20% of agreements with employers where more than 65% of the workforce is female have non-hours-related family-friendly work provisions. This ratio falls to 10% if the workforce is equivalently male-dominated. Interestingly, even after controlling for male dominance, some industries (construction, metal working) are particularly unlikely to have family-friendly work practices, suggesting that cultural stereotypes continue to play a strong role.

11. Multivariate analysis has also suggested that workplace size has a large effect on whether there are family-friendly practices in Australia [Glass and Fujimoto (1995); Osterman (1995); Seyler *et al.* (1995); Whitehouse and Zetlin (1999)].

12. Whitehouse and Zetlin (1999) explain 27% of the variation in the introduction of family-friendly work practices which, as they note, is signfiicantly higher than in most other similar studies.

13. Whitehouse and Zetlin (1999) report that in Australia, 26% of public sector collective agreements and 37% of public sector AWAs have family-friendly work practices compared with 10% of private collective agreements and 7% of AWAs.

14. Attitudes to taking different types of provisions vary. For example, a survey of insurance and banking employees in Australia (Probert, Whiting and Ewer, 2000) found that colleagues were particularly likely to be unsupportive of measures such as leaving on time/declining overtime/etc. A quarter thought co-workers were unsupportive of these rights and 30-37% of managers. Gollan (2001) suggests that more generally 10% of workers are not confident that they would be able to use leave entitlements without negative attitudes from managers.

15. Their mission is to achieve more legal equality for women and men of different ethnicities, by work at three levels – individual, structural and symbolic. E-Quality wants to promote economic independence for women, but they also want this balanced with the caring role as well. They work with particular employers in some circumstances, including, for example, the police.

16. On family responsibilities, HREOC's role is limited to dismissals only. This reflects the lack of agreements about the role of Commonwealth and states at the time the measure was introduced.

17. A survey undertaken for the report of employees at a construction site in the State of Queensland gives some idea of the attitudes held by some workers. 45% said that if they were an employer, they would be less likely to employ a woman of childbearing age and 22% thought it a waste of time for a woman to do an apprenticeship if she had future plans to have children.

References

ABORIGINAL and TORRES STRAIT ISLANDER COMMISSION (1999),
"Submission to the Human Rights and Equal Opportunity Commission Inquiry into Rural and Remote Education in Australia", Canberra.

ABS (1998),
Forms of Employment August 1998, Cat. No. 6359.0, Australian Bureau of Statistics, Canberra.

ABS (1999),
Australian National Accounts: National Income, Expenditure and Product, Cat. No. 5206, Australian Bureau of Statistics, Canberra

ABS (1999a),
Population – Special Article, Aboriginal and Torres Strait Islander Australians: A Statistical Profile from the 1996 *Census*, Australian Bureau of Statistics, Canberra.

ABS (2000),
Year Book Australia 2000, Australian Bureau of Statistics, Canberra.

ABS (2000a),
Forms of Employment, Cat. No. 6359.0, Australian Bureau of Statistics, Canberra.

ABS (2000b),
Child Care, Cat No. 4402.0, Australian Bureau of Statistics, Canberra.

ABS (2000c),
Labour Market Statistics in Brief: Australia, Cat. No. 6104.0, Australian Bureau of Statistics, Canberra.

ABS (2000d),
Occasional Paper: Labour Force Characteristics of Aboriginal and Torres Strait Islander Australians, Experimental Estimates from the Labour Force Survey, Cat. No.6287.0, Australian Bureau of Statistics, Canberra.

ABS (2000e),
Labour Force Status and other Characteristics of Families, Australia, Cat. No. 6224.0, Australian Bureau of Statistics, Canberra.

ABS (2001),
Births, Cat. No. 3301.0, Australian Bureau of Statistics, Canberra.

ABS (2001a),
"Family-Family functioning: Looking after the children", *Australian Social Trends* 1999, Cat. No. 4102.0, Australian Bureau of Statistics, Canberra.

ABS (2001b),
Employee Earnings and Hours, Australia, Cat. No. 6306.0, Australian Bureau of Statistics, Canberra.

ABS (2001c),
Employee Earnings Benefits and Trade Union Membership, Catalogue 6310.0, Australian Bureau of Statistics, Canberra.

ABS (2001d),
Working Arrangements Australia, Cat. No. 6342.0, Australian Bureau of Statistics, Canberra.

ABS (2001e),
Managing Caring Responsibilities and Paid Employment in New South Wales, Cat. No. 4903.1, Australian Bureau of Statistics, Canberra.

ACIRRT (1999),
Agreements Database and Monitor, Australian Centre for Industrial Relations Research and Teaching, No. 22, University of Sydney.

ACOSS (2001),
Unpublished tables: Persons not in the Labour Force for Childcare Reasons (based on unpublished ABS tables), Australian Council for Social Services.

ADEMA, W. (2001),
"Net Total Social Expenditure – 2nd Edition", Labour Market and Social Policy Occasional Paper Series, No. 52, OECD, Paris.

AIHW (2001),
Australia's Welfare 2001, Australian Institute of Health and Welfare, Canberra.

AIHW (2001a),
Trends in the Affordability of Child Care Services, Welfare Division Working Paper No. 20, Australian Institute of Health and Welfare, Canberra.

ANTECOL, H. (2000),
"An examination of cross-country differences in the gender gap in labour force participation rates", Labour Economics, Vol. 7, pp. 409-426.

ARBEIDSINSPECTIE (2000),
De Positie van Mannen en Vrouwen in het Bedrijfsleven en bij de Ocerheid, 1998, Ministerie van Sociale Zaken en Werkgelegenheid, The Hague.

ARBEIDSINSPECTIE (2001),
Arbeid en Zorg in CAOs 1999, Ministerie van Sociale Zaken en Werkgelegenheid, The Hague.

ATP (2001),
First Child Tax Refund, Australian Tax Practice Weekly Tax Bulletin, Issue 2001/48, 15 November 2001.

BARNES, A. (2001),
"Low Fertility: A discussion paper", DFaCS Occasional Paper No. 2, Department of Family and Community Services, Canberra.

BEER, G. and HARDING, A. (1999),
"Effective Marginal Tax Rates: Options and Impacts", Paper presented to the Centre for Public Policy Conference on "Taxation Reform: Directions and Opportunities", 18 February 1999.

BERTELSMANN FOUNDATION (ed.) (2000),
International Reform Monitor, Issue 3.

BERTHOUD, R. and ROBSON, K. (2001),
"The Outcomes of Teenage Motherhood in Europe", Innocenti Working Papers, No. 86, United Nations Children's Fund, Innocenti Research Centre, Florence.

BOND, K. and WHITEFORD, P. (2001),
"Trends in the Rates of Receipt of Income Support and Employment Outcomes Among People of Working Age: Australia 1965-1999" (draft).

BOOCOCK, S.S. (1995),
"Early Childhood Programs in Other Countries: Goals and Outcomes", *The Future Children*, Vol. 5, No. 3, pp. 25-50, Los Altos.

BORCHORST, A. (1993),
"Working Life and Family life in Western Europe", in Carlsen and Elm Larsen (eds.), *The Equality Dilemma: Reconciling Working Life and Family Life, Viewed in a European Perspective – the Danish Example*, The Danish Equal Status Council, Copenhagen.

BOVENBERG, A.L. and GRAAFLAND, J.J. (2001),
"Externe Effecten van Betaalde en Onbetaalde Arbeid", *Christen-Democratische Verkenningen*, Nr. 10, October 2001, pp. 11-18.

BOVENBERG, A.L. and GRADUS, R.H.J.M. (2001),
"De Economie van Moeder Theresa", *Economische Statistiche Berichten*, 15 Juni, 2001, pp. 516-519.

BROOM, B. (1998),
"Parental Sensitivity to Infants and Toddlers in Dual Earner and Single Earner Families", *Nursing Research*, Vol. 47(3), pp. 162-170.

BUCHANAN, J. and THORNTHWAITE, L. (2001),
"Paid Work and Parenting: Charting a New Course for Australian Families", Australian Centre for Industrial Research and Training, University of Sydney, July.

BURGESS, J. and CAMPBELL, I. (1998),
"Casual Employment in Australia: Growth Characteristics, A Bridge or a Trap", *The Economic and Labour Relations Review*, Vol. 9(I), pp. 31-53.

BUTLER, B. (2000),
"Responses to Participation Support for a More Equitable Society: the Interim Report of the Reference Group on Welfare Reform", Aboriginal and Torres Strait Islander Commissioner for Social Justice.

CALLAN, T., DEX, S. SMITH, N. and VLASBLOM, J.D. (1999),
"Taxation of Spouses: A cross-country study of the effects on married women's labour supply", Centre For Labour Market and Social Research Working Paper 99-02, University of Aarhus, Denmark.

CBS (2000),
"Bevolkingsgroei voor twee derde allochtoon", September 2001. *www.cbs.nl*

CBS (2001),
"Sociaal-Economische Maandstatistiek", Vol. 18, Centraal Bureau voor de Statistiek, December, pp. 46-50, Vorrburg/Heerlen.

CBS (2001a),
"Statline Electronic Databank Statistics Netherlands", Table "Ouderschapsverlof van

werknemers, 1992/1994-1997/1999", Centraal Bureau voor de Statistiek, Vorrburg/ Heerlen. *www.cbs.nl*

CBS (2001b),
"Statline Electronic Databank Statistics Netherlands", Table "Ziekteverzuim Overheid", Centraal Bureau voor de Statistiek, Voorburg/Heerlen. *www.cbs.nl*

CBS (2002),
"Werkende Moeders", February, 2002. *www.cbs.nl*

CCCH (2000),
A *Review of Early Childhood Literature*, Centre for Community Child Health, prepared for the Department of Family and Community Services as a background paper for the National Families Strategy, Canberra.

CPB (1999),
Economische gevolgen van de Belastingherziening 2001, Werkdocument No. 115, Centraal Plan- bureau.

CENTRELINK (2001),
A *Guide to Commonwealth Government Payments*, 1 July 2001-19 September 2001.

CHAPMAN, B., DUNLOP, Y., GRAY, M., LIU, A. and MITCHELL, D. (2001),
"The Impact of Children on the Lifetime Earnings of Australian Women: Evidence from the 1990", *Australian Economic Review*, Vol. 34, No. 4, pp. 373-389.

CHILD SUPPORT AGENCY (2000),
Child Support Scheme: Facts and Figures 1999-2000, ACT.

CHILD SUPPORT AGENCY (2001),
Child Support Schemes: Australia and Comparisons.

CHRISTENSEN, E. (2000),
Det 3-arige barn (The Three Year Old), Danish National Institute of Social Research, Vol. 00:10, Copenhagen.

CHRISTOFFERSEN, M.N. (2000),
"Who Choose Teenage Childbearing? A longitudinal study of 1966 to 1973 birth cohorts in Denmark", Working paper based on results of the National Child Development Survey, Danish National Institute of Social Research, Copenhagen.

CHRISTOFFERSEN, M.N. (2000a),
"Growing up with Unemployment: A study of parental unemployment and children's risk of abuse and neglect based on national longitudinal 1973 birth cohorts in Denmark", *Childhood*, Vol. 7:4.

CHRISTOFFERSEN, M.N. (2000b),
Trends in Fatherhood Patterns – the Danish Model, Seminar at the Centre for Populations Studies, London, 16 November 2000.

CHRISTOFFERSEN, M.N. (2000c),
Will Parental Work or Unemployment Influence Pre-School Children's Stress Reactions?, A paper for the 10th Nordic Social Policy Research Seminar, 17-19 August 2000.

COMMISSIE DAGARRANGEMENTEN (2002),
Advies van de Commissie Dagarrangementen, The Hague, January.

CONNOLLY, G. (1996),
"Causality between Consumer Loan Affordability and the Female Full-time Participation Rate in the Australian Labour Force", *Australian Bulletin of Labour*, Vol. 22, No. 3.

CONNOLLY, G. and BADHNI, S. (1998),
"Part-time Participation and Unemployment in Australia", paper to the 27th Conference of Economists, University of Sydney, 28 Sept./1 Oct., 1998.

CONNOLLY, G. and SPENCE, K. (1996),
"The Role of Consumer Loan Affordability and Other Factors Influencing Family Decisions in Determining the Female Full-Time Participation Rate in the Australian Labour Force", Paper to the 25th Conference of Economists, Australian National University, 22-26 September 1996.

COSTELLO, P. (1998),
Tax Reform – not a new tax, a new tax system, Canberra.

COUNCIL OF EUROPE (2001),
Recent Demographic Developments in Europe, Strasbourg.

DANISH CENTRE FOR DEMOGRAPHIC RESEARCH (1999),
Research Report No. 11, Copenhagen.

DATTA GUPTA, N. and SMITH, N. (2002),
Children and Career Interruptions: the Family Gap in Denmark, Economica, *forthcoming*.

DATTA GUPTA, N., CHRISTOFFERSEN, M.N. and SMITH, N. (2001),
"Maternity Leave, Facts and Myths", *Politiken*, July.

DATTA GUPTA, N., OAXACA, R. and SMITH, N. (2002),
"Swimming Upstream, Floating Downstream – Trends in the US and Danish Gender wage gaps", Economica, *forthcoming*.

DEBELLE, G. and VICKERY, J. (1998),
The Macroeconomics of Australian Unemployment, Reserve Bank of Australia, Sydney.

DEWRSB (1998),
Federal Industrial Relations and Legislation Framework, Work and Family Unit, Department of Workplace Relations and Small Business, Canberra.

DEWRSB and OEA (2000),
Agreement Making in Australia under the Workplace Relations Act 1998 and 1999, Department of Workplace Relations and Small Business and the Office of the Employment Advocate, Canberra.

DFACS (1999),
Annual Report 1998-99, Department of Family and Community Services, Canberra.

DFACS (2000),
Stronger Families and Communities Strategy (information kit), Department of Family and Community Services, Canberra.

DFACS (2000a),
Interim Report of the Reference Group on Welfare Reform: Technical and Other Appendices, Department of Family and Community Services, Canberra.

DFACS (2000b),
1999 Census of Childcare Services – Summary booklet, Department of Family and Community Services, Canberra.

DFACS (2001),
Annual Report 2000-2001, Department of Family and Community Services, Canberra.

DFACS/DEWR (2002),
"Australia's Country Note for the OECD Project – Family Friendly Policies: The Reconciliation of Work and Family Life", Commonwealth Departments of Family and Community Services, Employment, and Workplace Relations, Canberra, *forthcoming*.

DICKENS, L. (1999),
"Beyond the Business Case: a three-pronged approach to equality action", *Human Resource Management Journal*, Vol. 9, No. 1.

DINGELDEY, I. (2001),
"European Tax Systems and their Impact on Family Employment Patterns", *Journal of Social Policy*, Vol. 30, No. 4.

DOBBELSTEEN, S.H.A.M., GUSTAFSSON, S.S. and WETZELS, C.M.M.P. (2000),
Childcare in the Netherlands between Government, Firms and Parents. Is the dead-weight loss smaller than in the public daycare system of Sweden?

DULK, L. den (1999),
"Work-family Arrangements in the Netherlands: the role of employers", in L. den Dulk, A. van Doorne-Huiskes en J. Schippers (eds.), *Work-Family Arrangements in Europe*, Thela Thesis, Amsterdam.

EDIN, P-A and GUSTAVSSON, M. (2001),
"Time Out of Work and Skill Depreciation", mimeo, Uppsala University.

EERSTE KAMER DER STATEN-GENERAAL (2001),
"Vaststelling van regels voor het tot stand brengen van een nieuw evenwicht tussen arbeid en zorg in de ruimste zin (Wet arbeid en zorg)", Sdu Uitgevers, 's-Gravenhage, The Hague.

EMANCIPATIERAAD (1996),
Concerns for a New Security: Recommendations for an Equal Opportunities Income and Social Security Policy, adv. No. IV/45/96, The Hague.

EUROSTAT (1997),
Labour Force Survey, Office for Official Publications of the European Commission, Luxembourg.

EVANS, M.D.R (2000),
"Women's Participation in the Labour Force: Ideals and Behaviour", *Australian Social Monitor*, Vol. 3. No. 2, October, pp. 49-57.

FINANSMINISTERIET (2000),
Hearings and Citizens Survey 2000 – Summary, Ministry of Finance, Copenhagen. *www.fm/uk/pubUK/summary24102000/indeex.htm*

FINANSMINISTERIET (2001),
The Danish Economy, 2001: Medium Term Economic Survey, Copenhagen.

FINANSMINISTERIET (2002),
Kommunernes Landsforening (budget), Copenhagen.

FÖRSTER, M. (2000),
"Trends and Driving Factors in Income Distribution and Poverty in the OECD Area", Labour Market and Social Policy Occasional Paper Series, No. 42, OECD, Paris.

GLASS, J.L and ESTES, S. (1997),
"The Family Responsive Workplace", *Annual Review of Sociology*, No. 23.

GLASS, J.L and FUJIMOTO, T. (1995),
"Employer Characteristics and the Provision of Family-responsive Policies", *Work and Occupations*, Vol. 22, No. 4.

GLEZER, H. and WOLCOTT, I. (1997),
"Work and Family Values: Preferences and Practice", *Family Matters*, No. 48, AIFS, Spring/ Summer, Melbourne.

GLEZER, H. and WOLCOTT, I. (1998),
"Parents' Preferences for Balancing Work and Family Responsibilities", *Work and Family*, Vo. 16, No. 4.

GLEZER, H. and WOLCOTT, I. (1999),
"Conflicting Commitments: Working Mothers and Fathers in Australia", in L. Haas, P. Hwang and G. Russell (eds.), *Organisational Change and Gender Equity: International Perspectives on Parents in the Workplace*, RussellSage, California.

GOLLAN, P. (2001),
AWA *Employee Attitude Survey*, Office of the Employment Advocate.

GRAVERSEN, E.K. and SMITH, N. (1998),
"Labour Supply, Overtime Work and Taxation in Denmark", Centre For Labour Market and Social Research Working Paper 98-08, University of Aarhus, Denmark.

GUSTAFSSON, S.S, WETZELS, C.M.M.P. and KENJOH, E. (2002),
"Postponement of Maternity and the Duration of Time spent at Home after first Birth", Labour Market and Social Policy Occasional Papers, OECD, Paris, *forthcoming*.

HARDING, A. and BEER, G. (2000),
"Effective Marginal Tax Rates and the Australian Reform Debate", in Petersen, H.-G. and Gallagher, P. (eds.), *Tax and Transfer Reform in Australia and Germany: Australia Centre Series*, Vol. 3, University of Potsdam, Potsdam.

HARDING A. and SZUKALSKA, A. (2000),
"Making a Difference: The impact of Government Policy on Child Poverty in Australia, 1982-1997-98". *www.natsem.Canberra.edu.au*

HARRISON, L. J. and UNGERER, J. A. (2000),
Children and Child Care: A Longitudinal study of the relationships between developmental outcomes and use of non parental care from birth to six, paper prepared for the Department of Family and Community Services, Panel Data Conference, Canberra.

HOWARD, J. (2001),
"Address at the Federal Liberal Party Campaign Launch", Sydney.

HREOC (1999),
Pregnant and Productive, Human Rights and Equal Opportunities Commission, Sydney.

HREOC (2002),
Valuing Parenthood: options for Paid Maternity Leave: Interim Paper 2002, Human Rights and Equal Opportunities Commission, Sydney.

INGLES, D. (1997),
Low Income Traps for Working Families, Discussion Paper No. 363, Centre for Economic Policy Research, Australian National University, Canberra.

INGLES, D. (2000),
Rationalising the Interaction Of Tax And Social Security: Part 1: Specific Problem Areas Discussion, Paper No 423, Centre for Economic Policy Research, Australian National University.

215|

KALISCH, D.W., AMAN, T. and BUCHELE, L.A. (1998),
"Social and Health Policies in OECD Countries: A Survey of Current Programmes and Recent Developments", in OECD Labour Market and Social Policy Occasional Papers, No. 33.

KAMERMAN, S. (2001),
"An Overview of ECEC Developments in the OECD Countries", in S. Kamerman (ed.), Early Childhood Education and Care: International Perspectives, The Institute for Child and Family Policy, Columbia University, New York.

KEUZENKAMP, S., HOOGHIEMSTRA, E., BREEDVELD, K. and MERENS, A. (2000),
De Kunst van het Combineren: Taakverdeling onder Partners, Sociaal Cultureel Planbureau, The Hague, October.

KNIJN, T. and van WEL, F. (1999),
Zorgen voor de Kost, Uitgeverij SWP, Utrecht.

KNIJN, T. and van WEL, F. (2002),
"Careful or Lenient: Welfare reform for lone mothers in the Netherlands", Journal of European Social Policy, Vol. 11, No. 2.

KNUDSEN, L.B. (1999),
"Recent Fertility Trends in Denmark – A Discussion of the Impact of Family Policy in a period with Increasing Fertility", Research Report 11, Danish Center for Demographic Research.

LANGEN, A. van and HULSEN, M. (2001),
"Schooltijden in het Basisonderwijs: Feiten en Fictie", ITS, Nijmegen.

LISV (2001),
Loopbaanonderbreking 2000 (Finlo), Landelijk Instituut Sociale Verzekeringen, Amsterdam.

McCLURE, P. (2000),
"Participation Support for a More Equitable Society, Final Report of the Reference Group on Welfare Reform", July 2000.

McDONALD, P. (1999),
"Social and Demographic Trends Relating to the Future Demand for Child Care", paper prepared for the Commonwealth Child Care Advisory Council, Commonwealth Child Care Advisory Council, Canberra.

McDONALD, P. (2000),
"The 'Toolbox' of Public Policies to Impact on Fertility – a global view", paper for the Annual Seminar 2000 of the European Observatory on Family Matters, Low Fertility, Families and Public Policies, Sevilla, Spain.

MINISTERIE VAN FINANCIEN (2001),
Taxation in the Netherlands, Ministry of Finance, The Hague.

MOREHEAD, A., STEELE, M., ALEXANDER, M., STEPHEN, K. and DUFFIN, L. (1997),
Changes at Work, The 1995 Australian Workplace Industrial Relations Survey, Longman, South Melbourne.

MOSS, P. and DEVEN, F. (1999),
Parental Leave: Progress or Pitfall, Research and Policy Issues in Europe, NIDI/CBGS Publications, Brussels.

NCAC (2001),
Family Day care Quality Assurance Handbook, National Childcare Accreditation Council, Canberra.

NCAC (2001a),
  Quality Improvement and Accreditation System Handbook, National Childcare Accreditation Council, Canberra.

NEDERLANDSE GEZINSRAAD (2001),
  Gezin: Beeld en Werkelijkheid, The Hague.

NEW ZEALAND GOVERNMENT (2002),
  Paid Parental Leave, www.executive.govt.nz/minister/harre/ppl/scheme.htm

NICKELL, S.J. and van OURS, J. (2000),
  "The Netherlands and the United Kingdom: A European Unemployment Miracle?, *Economic Policy*, No. 30.

NYFER (1999),
  Meer werken, minder zorgen, arbeid en zorg in wetgeving en CAO's, Breukelen.

OECD (1993),
  The Labour Market in the Netherlands, Paris.

OECD (1994),
  The OECD Jobs Study, Paris.

OECD (1996),
  Caring for Frail Elderly People – Policies in Evolution, Paris.

OECD (1998),
  Maintaining Prosperity in an Ageing Society, Paris.

OECD (1998a),
  The Battle against Exclusion, Vol. 2, Social Assistance in Belgium, the Czech Republic, the Netherlands and Norway, Paris.

OECD (1998b),
  The Battle against Exclusion, Vol. 1, Social Assistance in Australia, Finland, Sweden and the United Kingdom, Paris.

OECD (1999),
  A Caring World: The New Social Policy Agenda, Paris.

OECD (1999a),
  Country Note – Early Childhood Education and Care in the Netherlands, Paris.

OECD (1999b),
  Education Policy Analysis, Paris.

OECD (2000),
  Reforms for an Ageing Society, Paris.

OECD (2000a),
  OECD Employment Outlook, Paris.

OECD (2000b),
  Education at a Glance, Paris.

OECD (2000c),
  Trends in International Migrations, Paris.

OECD (2001),
  Towards a Sustainable Future, Press release on the OECD Council meeting at Ministerial level, 17 May, Paris.

OECD (2001a),
  Ageing and Income: Financial Resources and Retirement in 9 OECD Countries, Paris.

OECD (2001b),
  OECD Economic Outlook, No. 70, Paris.

OECD (2001c),
  Revenue Statistics, 1965-2000, Paris.

OECD (2001d),
  OECD Social Expenditure Database, 1980-1998, 3rd Edition, Paris.

OECD (2001e),
  Society at a Glance: OECD Social Indicators, Paris.

OECD (2001f),
  OECD Employment Outlook, Paris.

OECD (2001g),
  OECD Labour Force Statistics 1980-2000, Paris.

OECD (2001h),
  Education at a Glance, Paris.

OECD (2001i),
  Starting Strong – Early Childhood Education and Care, Paris.

OECD (2001j),
  Innovations in Labour Market Policies – The Australian Way, Paris.

OECD (2001k),
  Taxing Wages, 1999-2000, Paris.

OECD (2002),
  National Accounts of OECD Countries, Main Aggregates – Vol. 1, 1989-2000, Paris.

OECD (2002a),
  Main Economic Indicators, Paris.

OECD (2002b),
  OECD Economic Surveys – the Netherlands, Paris

OECD (2002c),
  Labour Market Statistics, CD-ROM, Paris.

OECD (2002d),
  OECD Employment Outlook, Paris.

OECD (2002e),
  Economic Surveys – Denmark, Paris.

OECD (2002f),
  Tax Equations, Paris.

OECD (2002g),
  Benefits and Wages: OECD Indicators 2002 Edition, Paris.

OECD (2002h),
  Taxing Wages, 2000-2001, Paris.

OECD (2003 forthcoming),
  Benefits and Wages: OECD Indicators 2003 Edition, Paris.

OECD/HEALTH CANADA (2002),
   Measuring Up: Improving Health System Performance in OECD Countries, Paris/Ottawa.

OECD/STATISTICS CANADA (2000),
   Literacy in the Information Age: Final Report of the International Adult Literacy Survey, Paris/Ottawa.

OR, Z. (2002),
   "Improving the Performance of Health Care Systems: From Measures to Action: A Review of Experience in Four OECD Countries", OECD Labour Market and Social Policy Occasional Papers, No. 57, Paris.

OSTERMAN, P. (1995),
   "Work/family Programs and the Employment Relationship", *Administrative Science Quarterly*, Vol. 40, No. 4.

OXLEY, H., DANG, T.-T., FÖRSTER, M. and PILLIZZARI, M. (1999),
   Income Inequalities and Poverty Among Children and Households with Children in Selected OECD Countries: Trends and Determinants.

PEDERSEN, L. (1998),
   Orlov, ledighed og beskæftigelse, Danish National Institute for Social Research (Socialforskningsinstituttet), Vol. 96, No. 10, Copenhagen.

PEDERSEN, P.J. and SMITH, N. (2001),
   "Unemployment Traps: Do Financial Dis-incentives matter?", Centre for Labour Market and Social Research Working Paper 01-01.

PLANTENGA, J. (2001),
   The Gender Perspectives of the Dutch National Action Plan of Employment, External report commissioned by and presented to the European Commission, Utrecht.

PLANTENGA, J., SCHIPPERS, J. and SIEGERS, J. (1999),
   "Towards an Equal Division of Paid and Unpaid Work: The Case of the Netherlands", *Journal of European Social Policy*, Vol. 9(2), pp. 99-110.

POWELL, L.M. (2002),
   "Joint Labour Supply and Childcare Choice Decisions of Married Mothers", *The Journal of Human Resources*, Vol. 37, No. 1.

PRESS, F. and HAYES, A. (2000),
   OECD *Thematic Review of Early Childhood Education and Care Policy – Australian Background Report*, Canberra.

PROBERT, B. (2001),
   "Grateful Slaves" or "Self-made Women": a matter of choice or policy?, Clare Burton Memorial Lecture, RMIT University.

PROBERT, B. and MURPHY, J. (2001),
   "Majority Opinion or Divided Selves? Researching Work and Family Experience", *People and Place*, Vol. 9, No. 4.

PROBERT, B., EWER, P. and WHITING, K. (2000),
   "Work versus Life: Union Strategies Reconsidered", *Labour and Industry*, Vol. 11, No. 1.

PROBERT, B., WHITING, K. and EWER, P. (2000),
   Pressure from All Sides: Life and Work in the Finance Sector, RMIT, Melbourne.

PURCELL, G. (2001),
   Promoting Substantial Public Investment in ECEC Services and Infrastructure: An Australian

Perspective, material presented to the OECD Thematic Review of ECEC Conference, Stockholm 14-15 June 2001.

REDMOND, G. (1999),
Tax-Benefit Policies and Parents' Incentives to Work: The Case of Australia 1980-1997, SPRC Discussion Paper No. 104, Social Policy Research Centre, Sydney.

REIMAN, C. (2001),
The Gender Wage Gap in Australia, NATSEM Discussion paper 54, National Centre for Social and Economic Modelling, Canberra, March.

REGERINGEN (1999),
"Danmark 2005 – en god start på det nye århundreded", Copenhagen.

ROSTGAARD, T., (2001),
Developing Comparable Indicators in Early Childhood Education and Care, Comparative Welfare State Research Working Paper 03:2001, The Danish National Institute of Social Research.

ROSTGAARD, T. and FRIDBERG, R. (1998),
Caring for Children and Older People – A Comparison of European Policies and Practices, Danish National Institute of Social Research, Copenhagen.

RUSSELL, G. (1999),
"International Trends in Approaches to Work and Family", paper to Work and Family Experts Seminar, Collected Proceedings, October 1999.

RUSSELL, G., BARCLAY, L., EDGECOMBE, G., DONOVAN, J., HABIB, G., CALLAGHAN, H. and PAWSON, Q. (1999),
Fitting Fathers into Families: Men and the Fatherhood Role in Contemporary Australia, Department of Family and Community Affairs, Canberra.

RUSSELL, G. and BOWMAN, L. (2000),
"Work and Family – Current Thinking, Research and Practice", prepared for the Department of Family and Community Services as a background paper for the National Families Strategy, Canberra.

SCP/CBS (2001),
Armoedemonitor 2001, Sociaal Cultureel Planbureau/Centraal Bureau voor de Statistiek, The Hague.

SEYLER, D.L., MONROE, P.A. and GARAN, J.C. (1995),
"Balancing Work and Family: the role of employer-supported child care benefits", *Journal of Family Issues*, Vol. 16.

SLOEP, M. (1996),
Het primaat van een mannenbolwerk: Emancipatie in cao-onderhandelingen, Emancipatieraad, The Hague.

SOCIALMINISTERIET (2000),
Early Childhood Education and Care Policy in Denmark, Background Report, Ministry of Social Affairs, Copenhagen.

SOCIALMINISTERIET (2000a),
Consolidation Act on an Active Social Policy (English version), Ministry of Social Affairs, Copenhagen. *www.sm.dk*

SOCIALMINISTERIET (2000b),
Social Assistance Consolidation Act (English version), Ministry of Social Affairs, Copenhagen. *www.sm.dk*

SOCIALMINISTERIET (2001),
The Danish National Report on Follow-up to The World Summit for Children, Copenhagen.

SOCIALMINISTERIET (2001a),
Consolidation Act on Benefits in the event of Illness or Childbirth (English version), Ministry of Social Affairs, Copenhagen. www.sm.dk

SOCIALMINISTERIET (N.D.),
Social Policy in Denmark, Ministry of Social Affairs. www.sm.dk/eng/dansk_socialpolitik/index.html

SONDERGAARD, J. (1999),
"The Welfare State and Economic Incentives", in T. M. Andersen, S.E. Hougaard Jensen and O. Risager (eds), Macroeconomic Perspectives on the Danish Economy, Macmillan.

STATISTICS DENMARK (2000),
"Daily Cash Benefits in Connection with Pregnancy, Birth and Adoption 1999", Social Conditions, Health and Justice, Copenhagen.

STEWART, W. and BARLING, J. (1996),
"Fathers' Work Experiences Effect Children's Behaviours via Job-related and Parenting Behaviours", Journal of Organisational Behaviour, Vol. 17, pp. 221-232.

SZW (1997),
Kansen op Combineren, Arbeid, Zorg en Economische Zelfstandigheid ("Opportunities for Combining"), Ministerie van Sociale Zaken en Werkgelegenheid, The Hague.

SZW (1999),
Op Weg naar een Nieuw Evenwicht tussen Arbeid en Zorg ("Towards a New Balance between Work and Care"), Ministerie van Sociale Zaken en Werkgelegenheid, The Hague.

SZW (2001),
A Short Surevy of Social Security in the Netherlands, as at 1 July 2001, Ministry of Social Affairs and Employment, The Hague.

TROUW (2001),
Opvoeddebat/Gedogen bij de kinderopvang, 7 November 2001. www.trouw.nl//artikelprint/1005028200246.html

UNITED NATIONS (2001),
World Population Prospects 1950-2050, 2000 Revision, United Nations, New York.

VANSTONE, A and ABBOTT, T. (2001),
Australians Working Together – Helping people to move forward, A Statement, Canberra.

VNO/NCW (2001),
"Nieuwe wet basisvoorziening kinderopvang", Arbeidsvoorwaarden, Sociale Zaken, No. 42, Vereniging van Nederlandse Ondernemingen, Nederlandse Christelijke Werkgevers, 14 December.

VWS and OC&W (2000),
Early Childhood Education and Care Policy in the Netherlands, Background Report, The Ministry of health Welfare and Sport and the Ministry of Education, Culture and Science, The Hague.

VWS (2001),
Cabinet Approves Childcare Bill, news release, Ministry of Health, Welfare and Sport, The Hague.

WEL, F. van and KNIJN, T. (2000),
Alleenstaande ouders over Zorgen en Werken, "s Gravenhage, Ministerie van Sociale Zaken en Werkgelegenheid/ Elseviers Bedrijfsinformatie.

WFU (1999),
Work and Family: State of Play 1998, Work and Family Unit Department of Workplace Relations and Small Business, Canberra.

WHITEFORD, P. (2001),
Benefits for Children: Australia, in Battle, K. and M. Mendelson (eds), Benefits for Children A Four Country Study, The Caledon Institute of Social Policy.

WHITEFORD, P., MORROW, I. and BOND, K. (2002),
"The Growth of Social Security Spending in Australia: Explanations and Comparisons" Department of Family and Community Services, Canberra, *forthcoming*.

WHITEHOUSE, G. (2001),
"Industrial Agreements and Work/family Provisions: trends and prospects under "enterprise bargaining"", *Labour and Industry*, August 2001.

WHITEHOUSE, G. and ZETLIN, D. (1999),
"Family-friendly Policies: distribution and implementation in Australian Workplaces" *The Economic and Labour Relations Review*, Vol. 10, No. 2.

YOUNG, C. (1990),
Balancing Families and Work: A Demographic Study of Women's Labour Force Participation, AGPS Canberra.

Background Annex to the Review

Main Family Assistance, Benefit Programmes
and Family Leave Programmes in the Three Countries

This annex briefly outlines the main family assistance and benefits programmes in the three countries as they apply to people of working age with children. It also outlines leave provisions for those in work needing to take care of very young children. Childcare benefits and child-related leave benefits are discussed in Chapters 3 and 4 respectively.

Family assistance

Family benefits subsidise some of the direct costs of children, and for low-income households play an important role in poverty alleviation. In all three countries child payments generally vary with age and are usually paid to the mother, except for the Dutch child tax credits. The Netherlands and Denmark both have universal family cash benefits. These mainly address horizontal equity objectives. The Netherlands also has a series of tax credits for families with children, including employment-contingent family assistance, through the Supplementary Single Parent Tax Credit and the Combination Tax Credit. Australia has income-targeted child benefits and payments to low-income earners. The main family payment [FTB (A)] is income tested, the targeting is gentle so that a portion is payable well up the income distribution. It therefore contributes more towards vertical equity objectives than the Danish and Dutch provisions (see Table A1).

Australia has a payment to single income families (both in one-parent and two-parent households). Denmark has payments for lone parents, but these are not income tested. The Netherlands has two tax credits available to single parents, but no separate cash benefits.

As shown in Table A2, the maximum family payment in Australia is set at a significantly higher level than those in Denmark, relative to average earnings, but this maximum level is only available to those families living on incomes less than around 69% of the average earnings. The Dutch rates are lower again than the Danish for young children, but within a similar range for older children.

In July 2000, Australia's complex set of programmes directing assistance to families was replaced with the Family Tax Benefit in reforms that aimed to simplify payment structures, improve work incentives, and support the choices families make in balancing their work and parenting responsibilities. The changes were part of the "New Tax System" (ANTS). The Family Tax Benefit is, in reality, two income-tested programmes that are delivered together. Family Tax Benefit, Part A [FTB(A)] is a per child payment to low and middle income families with dependent children.[1] The reform increased the income

Table A1. **Main family benefit programmes**[a]

Programme	Recipient group	Features
Australia[b]		
Family Tax Benefit A FTB(A)	All families with dependent children except high-income families.	Per child, age related payment. Income tested on family income, non-taxable. Can be received as a regular cash payment, reduction in income-tax or as an end-of-year lump sum.
Family Tax Benefit B FTB(B)	Single income families with dependent children, and those with low second incomes.	Per family, income test applies to second income only, non-taxable. Can be received as a regular cash payment, reduction in income tax or as an end-of-year lump sum.
Maternity Allowance	All families as under FTB(A) – at childbirth (or adoption).	Per child, lump sum payment to those eligible for FTB(A). Paid through the FTB system.
Maternity Immunisation Allowance	All families as under FTB(A) – at childbirth (or adoption).	Per child, lump sum payment to those eligible for FTB(A). Payable at 18 months for children who meet immunisation requirements; paid through the FTB system.
Denmark		
Family Allowance	All families with dependent children.	Per child, age related benefit. Not income tested non-taxable.
Ordinary Child Allowance	Single parents and parents who both receive a pension under the Social Pension Act – with dependent children.	Per child flat rate benefit. Not income tested, non taxable.
Extra Child Allowance	To single parents with dependent children.	One benefit per single parent (irrespective of number of children) Supplement to the ordinary child allowance. Not income tested, non taxable. Usually paid to the mother.
Netherlands		
Child Benefit	All families with dependent children.	Per child age related benefit. Not income tested non-taxable.
Child Tax Credit	Families with child younger than 16.	Almost universal, income threshold close to twice average earnings, tax credit is worth little.
Supplementary Child Tax Credit	Families with child younger than 16.	Income tested, paid to families with earnings close to average earnings.
Combination Tax Credit	Parents in work with child younger than 12.	Paid at 4.3% of employment income up to a maximum of € 100 per parent.

a) Benefits are usually paid to the mother, except for the Dutch (Supplementary) Child Tax Credit that is paid to the highest earner in a family.
b) Australia also has a Large Family Supplement, payable to families with four or more children, and provisions for multiple births. Denmark also has payments for multiple birth and adoptions. All three countries have financial provisions for orphaned children.
Source: Centrelink (2001); SZW (2001), communications with national authorities.

Table A2. **Comparison of family benefit rates**

Programme	Age	Rates: national currency (2001)	Rate as % average earnings	Income tests (annual income levels)
		Australia		
Family Tax Benefit (A)[a]	0-12	A$ 3 204.7	7.4	Assistance reduces by 30%
	13-15	A$ 4 062.45	9.3	for family income over
	16-17	A$ 1 029.30	2.4	A$ 29 857, until the base
	18-24	A$ 1 383.35	3.2	rate is reached, then again at 30% on income over A$ 77 234.[b]
Family Tax Benefit (B)	0-4	A$ 2 752.10	6.3	Reduces on 2nd earner
	5-15	A$ 1 919.90	4.4	income over A$ 1 679 per annum at 30%
Maternity Allowance	Lump sum at birth	A$ 780.00	1.8	Eligible for FTB(A)
Maternity Immunisation Allowance	Lump sum at 18 months	A$ 208.00	0.5	Eligible for FTB(A)
		Denmark		
Family Allowance	0-2	DKK 12 100	4.1	Not income tested
	3-6	DKK 11 000	3.7	
	7-17	DKK 8 600	2.9	
Ordinary Child Allowance	0-17	DKK 3 812	1.3	Not income tested
Extra Child Allowance	One per family	DKK 3 876	1.3	Not income tested
		Netherlands[c]		
Child Benefit	0-5	NLG 1 470	2.3	Not income tested
	6-11	NLG 1 785	2.7	
	12-18	NLG 2 101	3.2	
Child Tax Credit	One per household	NLG 84	0.1	Household income under NLG 120 104
Supplementary Child Tax Credit	One per household	NLG 423	0.6	Household income below NLG 60 053
Combination Tax Credit	Maximum per tax payer	NLG 304	0.5	Must have earnings of over NLG8 673 per annum

a) The rates for FTB(A) are increased by A$ 219 per child (about 0.5% of average earnings) for each 4th and subsequent child, through the Large Family Supplement.
b) Increased by A$ 3 139 per annum for each subsequent child.
c) In addition the Single Parents Tax Credit of NLG 2 779 per annum (4.3% or average earnings) and the Supplementary Single Parent's Tax Credit for working single parents with a dependent child under 12 is paid at a rate of 4.3% of employment income, up to NLG 2 799 per annum.
Source: Centrelink (2001); Socialministeriet (2000a); SZW (2001) and OECD Secretariat calculations.

threshold for Part A and reduced the taper rate from 50 to 30%.[2] With Part B [FTB(B)] – a payment to single income families with dependent children – the reforms also increased assistance and removed an income cut out for the primary income earner that existed in the previous system. As a result of these reforms over 90% of Australian families are now eligible for Family Tax Benefit. Expenditure on the FTB is estimated to be approximately A$ 11 billion per annum.

The importance of family assistance to working families

It is possible to get a feel for the importance of family benefits for households with a parent or parents in employment by looking at those benefits as a share of the household income. For the sake of comparisons several situations have been modelled:

- A lone-parent family with two children, at two gross income points (at ⅔ and at 1 times average earnings); and

- A couple with two children, at three combined gross income points (at ⅔, 1, and 1⅓ average earnings), also looking at different splits of income across the two adults in the couple.

Table A3 shows the value of family assistance paid under these scenarios, as a portion of disposable income at the selected income points. The calculations include cash payments and tax credits and builds in the effects of the tax scale in all three countries. It shows that in both Australia and Denmark family payments are set at significantly higher rates than is the case in the Netherlands. The rates are highest in Australia for those families with income at the ⅔ average earnings income level, reflecting the targeted nature of its family assistance, where the targeting aims to direct relatively more assistance to low-income families. The income threshold beyond which the maximum level of Family Tax Benefit (Part A) starts to reduce is approximately ⅔ of average earnings. The table also shows the role that FTB (B) plays in Australia, in supporting two parent families where only one is in employment. As the income of the parent in employment increases FTB(B) comes to represent a greater share of family assistance and providing a significant margin above two income families on the same income point.

Comparing a lone-parent family with a couple family on the same income, in Australia the level of assistance is the same when there is one income earner in a couple, but drops with the loss of the FTB (B) where the same joint income is earned by two adults in a couple. In Denmark, the assistance represents roughly the same share of take home pay in couple households irrespective of whether there is one or two earners, reflecting the fact that it is a universal payment. The extra provisions available for lone parents in the Netherlands increases the value of their family payments relative to couple families (with a difference between one and two adult households relating to tax credits available to adults irrespective of the presence or children).

Another indicator of how the systems help with the costs of children is looking at the income difference between households with and without children, at the same income. This is shown in Table A4.

Additional children

The equivalence elasticities in Table A5 show the relative value of extra income that an additional person brings to a household with average earnings in the three countries. This provides some measure of the extent to the tax/transfer system accounts for the costs of children for families in employment. The table assumes that the income in a couple household is earned by one adult. It shows that in Australia an income at the average earnings level there is only a relatively small margin provided for extra children, and that there is no differentiation between the children in a lone-parent family *versus* a couple family (except that the assistance for the first child in a couple family is discounted by the payment of a dependent spouse rebate). In the Netherlands elasticity at this income level is also relatively low, with the tax credits for one parent payment showing in the higher margin a lone parent with one

Table A3. **Family assistance as a percentage of take home pay**

1st earner 2nd earner	Lone parent with two children			Couple: one earner with two children				Couple: two earners with two children		
	0.67 APW NA	1.0 APW NA	1.33 APW NA	0.67 APW 0	1.0 APW 0	1.33 APW 0	1.67 APW 0	0.67 APW 0.33 APW	1.0 APW 0.33 APW	1.0 APW 0.67 APW
Australia	25.8	11.4	8.6	26.1	11.5	8.6	7.4	6.2	4.3	3.5
Denmark	21.1	15.9	13.3	13.2	9.7	8.0	7.0	9.9	7.8	6.5
Netherlands	9.7	7.5	5.9	10.1	7.8	6.0	5.1	7.3	6.0	5.0

NA: Not applicable.
APW: Average production worker.
Note: Family assistance rates used are average rates. Actual percentage will vary according to ages of children – see Table A1.
Source: Calculations made using OECD (2002f).

Table A4. **Income difference between households with two children and those without children**
% taken-home pay

1st earner 2nd earner	Lone parent with two children			Couple: one earner with two children				Couple: two earners with two children		
	0.67 APW NA	1.0 APW NA	1.33 APW NA	0.67 APW 0	1.0 APW 0	1.33 APW 0	1.67 APW 0	0.67 APW 0.33 APW	1.0 APW 0.33 APW	1.0 APW 0.67 APW
Australia	NA	13.0	8.6	28.5	8.3	5.8	5.0	6.6	4.5	3.6
Denmark	NA	18.9	15.4	15.2	10.7	8.7	7.5	11.0	8.4	7.0
Netherlands	NA	22.8	17.0	13.8	9.4	7.1	5.9	9.4	7.6	6.2

NA: Not applicable.
APW: Average production worker.
Note: Family assistance rates used are average rates. Actual percentage will vary according to ages of children – see Table A1.
Source: Calculations made using OECD (2002f).

227

Table A5. **Equivalence elasticities for additional children related at APW, 2001**

Family type	Australia	Denmark	Netherlands
Lone parent 1 child	0.09	0.17	0.18
Lone parent 2 children	0.04	0.13	0.05
Lone parent 3 children	0.10	0.15	0.04
Couple – no children	0.04	0.11	0.07
Couple 1 child	0.05	0.07	0.05
Couple 2 children	0.04	0.05	0.05
Couple 3 children	0.10	0.07	0.04

Source: Calculations made using OECD (2002f). For couples, assumes one earner, rates for children are average rates, to take account of different patterns of age differentiation.

child receives. The lone-parent allowances in the Danish system also explain the margin that they receive in that country – and the fact that they have a per-child element.

For working families all countries provide some relief towards the costs of children, with that relief being greatest in Australia for low-income families. From a relative income point-of-view, the systems all recognise the situation of lone parents. It is possible to carry out similar calculations for people with children where they are in receipt of a benefit, but it makes more sense to first look at the nature of the income support systems for those of working age who are not in employment.

Income support systems for those of working age but not in work

The number of children raised in benefit households has become a concern in many countries and has been part of the impetus to re-orient income support towards employment re-integration, for those of working age. Whilst data is not available in this in Denmark, Table A6 shows that trends in Australia and the Netherlands are quite different. In the context of a decrease in the total number of dependent children in Australia between 1990 and 1999, the share that were raised in benefit households increased from under 20% to over 35%. In the Netherlands, the number of dependent children increased over the same period, and the share raised in benefit households jumped about, increasing in the mid-1990s but reducing since, but still representing three in ten children. Such snap shots do not tell us how long these households are on benefit. Many will receive social security or social assistance

Table A6. **Share of children in benefit households**

	1990		1995		1999	
	Number 000s	% all children	Number 000s	% all children	Number 000s	% all children
Australia	705	19.1	983	28.2	1 225	35.6
Netherlands	1 240	37.5	1 317	39.2	1 073	31.2

Source: National authorities.

for reasonably limited durations, however a share will experience longer periods on benefit, or will have repeat spells. It is notable that children of parents where there is a disability or sickness benefit represent the largest single category in the Netherlands – and it is likely that a good share of these will be long term.

The income support systems in the three countries vary considerably, with Denmark and the Netherlands having contributory insurance-based schemes and social assistance for those not covered in the insurance schemes. Australia does not have a contributory social security system but a tax-funded social assistance system open to all. Both the Dutch and the

Table A7. **Social protection systems for those of working age with children**

Type of system	Account taken of children in rates of payment
Australia	
Income tested payments at set rates available to those not in employment. Includes the Parenting Payment – Single for lone parents, and Parenting Payment – Partnered for partners of claimants caring for a dependent child.	Some differences in rates where there are children, but child costs mainly met through FTB system.
Special Benefit: discretionary highly means tested provision in cases of severe financial hardship, and proven need.	Level of grant is discretionary but would take into account costs related to children.
Denmark	
Unemployment Insurance available to those belonging to UI schemes, administered by Unions. Voluntary, but 90% of employees belong. Paid at 90% of previous earnings, with the maximum duration of four years.	No additional payments on account of children (relies on family benefits).
Nationally determined social assistance available from municipality, for those not covered by UI. Funding is 50/50 central/local government. Income tested.	Rates take account of children, by adding a margin equivalent to 20% of the Maximum UI rate per parent.
Netherlands	
Contributory Social Insurance schemes (compulsory). Paid at 70% of previous earnings for five years, followed by an extra two years at a flat rate.	No additional payments on account of children (relies on family benefits).
Nationally determined and funded social assistance available from municipality, for those not covered by social insurance. Income tested.	No difference for couples with and without children [rate is 100% of minimum wage (MW)] Lone parents get 90% of MW, single person gets 70%, so an implicit "family element" of 20% (Couples where one or both are under 21 get lower rates, and in this case, get a premium of the same nominal amount as sole parents, where there are children).
The above are supplemented by locally set poverty relief programmes. Means tested.	Costs can relate to family related needs, such as costs when a child starts secondary school.

Source: Socialministeriet (2000a); SZW (2001) and national authorities.

Danish social insurance systems involve maximum levels of payment and benefits are affected by any income that the recipient earns. Neither makes any additional payment in respect of a partner or children. In all countries social assistance levels are determined by national policy and is tightly targeted on a household basis. In Denmark and the Netherlands, recipients are required to be actively looking for work, and employment services are provided for them (see Chapter 5). In addition, local governments in the Netherlands are also required to administer and fund poverty assistance for anyone in poverty due to certain costs or situations (Table A7).

The Australian system looks similar in some regards to the social assistance systems of Denmark and the Netherlands. However, while social assistance in the two European countries has a residual role, accounting for around 10% or less of social security expenditure, in Australia it plays the main role, accounting for over 90% of social security expenditure (Kalisch *et al.*, 1998). The Australian system involves flat rate income-tested payments. There are some family related payments contained within the Australian income support system,[3] however most of the child related costs are met through separate family benefits. Where there is a couple, both partners income is taken into account, however since 1995 the income test has been modified in order to limit the situation where one partner's benefit is reduced because of income received by the other.

Australia has separate income support provision for lone parents: the Parenting Payment – Single.[4] In the Danish or Dutch systems lone parents not in work are eligible for either work tested unemployment insurance or social assistance. The work test is applied rigorously in Denmark however, in the Netherlands, application varies depending on the attitudes of staff and local politicians, some of who believe the mother should be able to look after their children at home. The Australian provision is currently not work test, but the May 2001 Australian's Working Together package announced the extension, from September 2002, of reasonably gentle obligations to lone parents, and other parents on income support payments in order to promote work attachment.

Each of the three countries also provides housing assistance for people with low incomes. The largest recipient groups for this assistance are pensioners and low income families with children.[5] They also have health care provisions that help parents meet the health costs of children.[6]

Relative levels of income support

A simple comparison of the rates of social assistance benefits (including family assistance) as a share of average earnings shows that they are generally highest in Denmark, but that the Australian system takes greatest account of the costs of children (Table A8). Equivalence elasticities show the relative value of extra income that an additional person brings to a household for those on social assistance. They show that Australia gives nearly the same weight to the first child of a sole parent (*i.e.* the second person in the household) as it does to the second person in a couple household. Denmark is relatively more generous where the second person in the household is an adult and less generous than in Australia when the second person is a child. In the Netherlands assistance to further members of the household (additional children) attract the same marginal increase in income, but this is lower than in the other two countries. The pattern in Denmark reflects the premium couples with children receive in the social assistance rates, and the child benefit payments to single parent families. The Australian system gives the greatest recognition to the costs of additional children on social assistance.

Table A8.   **Benefit income as a share of average wages and equivalence elasticities for additional children, 2001**

Including family assistance

Family type	Australia		Denmark		Netherlands	
	% APW	Elasticities	% APW	Elasticities	% APW	Elasticities
Single person	21.5	–	28.6	–	28.9	–
Lone parent 1 child	39.3	0.82	44.3	0.55	39.9	0.38
Lone parent 2 children	47.6	0.39	49.2	0.17	42.7	0.09
Lone parent 3 children	56.0	0.39	54.1	0.17	45.4	0.09
Couple – no children	38.8	0.80	57.2	1.00	41.2	0.60
Couple 1 child	53.7	0.69	79.8	0.79	44.0	0.09
Couple 2 children	62.1	0.39	83.4	0.13	46.8	0.09
Couple 3 children	70.5	0.39	87.0	0.13	49.5	0.09

Note: Base rate for elasticity equivalence calculations is the single person rate for social assistance. The social assistance rates are those payable where there is no other income. Rates for children are average rates, to take account of different patterns of age differentiation. They do not include housing benefit. Nor do they include childcare assistance.

Source: OECD Secretariat calculations.

Indexing benefits

In each country, social assistance rates are adjusted regularly for price movements, thereby protecting their purchasing power. In the Netherlands this is via a link to the minimum wage, which in turn is linked to price inflation. In Denmark rates are linked to the unemployment insurance rates. There is however an anomaly within the Australian income support system for lone parents, where the Parenting Payment – Single is treated as a pension, rather than a benefit (Parenting Payment – Partnered is a benefit). Pensions are indexed to wages as well as prices, while benefits are indexed to prices only. With wages growing ahead of prices the relative value of the lone-parent payment is increasing faster than the unemployment benefit rate. DFACS estimate that the gap will grow about 25% over ten years. This will distort relativities over time and is difficult to justify on horizontal equity grounds. In principle, a minor change in indexation policy, so that all income support provisions where there was a work focus were indexed in the same manner, would "solve" the problem.

Child support

In all three countries parents have legal obligations to financially support their children whether they are living together or not. Each country has a system for determining the child support payments absent parents are required to make, and for ensuring that payment occurs, with both the Netherlands and Australia taking steps in recent years to ensure more effective systems. The Netherlands, which uses voluntary agreements underpinned by a court system[7] if necessary, introduced a new service in 1997, the National Bureau for the Recovery of Child Maintenance (LBIO) to improve the rate of collection (Columbia). Australia moved in 1988 from a court-based system to an administrative system to ensure fairer levels of liability were assessed, and to improve the collection rates. Denmark also uses an administrative system, but unlike the other two countries, it also guarantees a payment to the custodial parent, provides the most income certainty for the custodial parent, even though it considers the payment *to the child* rather than to the custodial parent.[8]

In each country, the child support liability takes into account the income of the absent parent, so that they pay more if they earn more. In Denmark, this is limited as less than 15% of the maximum rate is income contingent.[9] In the Netherlands the court formula takes account of the capacity of each parent to support their child. In Australia the formula that takes account of the income of both parents, and the living arrangements of the absent parent.

The Danish system, where the absent parents do not meet their liability or paternity is not be determined, a payment is made to the custodial parent by way of a Special Child Allowance (of DKK 9 720 per year). The combination of this and the fact that child support is not charged against social assistance effectively lifts the guaranteed income for lone parents by 7.5% for the first child. In both Netherlands and Australia, the level of income certainty for the custodial parent rests very largely on compliance by the absent parent.

Collection rates for child support in Australia are currently around 90%, and A$ 1.4 billion transferred between parents in the 1999/2000 tax year (Child Support Agency, 2000; DFACS, 2001; communications with DFaCS). In order to reduce the notion of child support as a tax on the payer, Australia has moved its focus from "just enforcement" to facilitating positive post-separation arrangements, so that child support does not get in the way of absent parents retaining a relationship with children. The Child Support Agency is using techniques not previously associated with maintenance collection, such as case management, giving budgeting information, referrals to relationship counselling and parenting programmes. CSA also has a variety of face to face outreach activities, including some pilot programmes in the workplace. AS a whole voluntary compliance in the payment of child support continues to improve.

Benefits to take leave from work to care for very young children[10]

In view of the differences in social protection systems (see above) and employer-provided family-friendly policy measures (Chapter 6) it is not surprising to find considerable variation in the design and use of existing leave arrangements to care for very young children in the three countries under review.

Individual and family-based entitlements

Entitlements to parental leave periods can be individual or family-based in which case parents in dual earner families decide between each other, to what extent each individual parent uses the leave entitlement. Parents cannot both use it simultaneously, hence the use of leave by one parent reduces the extent to which the other parent can make use of the entitlement. For example, in Australia, if one parent uses the full 52 weeks of leave-entitlement following childbirth the other parent cannot take any leave, except for the first week upon childbirth when both parents are entitled to leave. Until 2002, ten weeks of parental leave in Denmark was also a family-based entitlement. In contrast, childminding leave, which can be taken subsequent to parental leave in Denmark, is an individual entitlement. In the Netherlands, entitlement to all leave benefits is individual (Table A9).

Table A9. **Characteristics of parental leave arrangements with employment protection, 2001**

	Aspect	Maternity leave	Paternity leave	Parental leave and childminding leave (if specified)
Australia	Eligibility criteria	According to award.[a]	As for parental leave.	12 months service with employer.
	Duration	According to award[a] (up to 6 weeks before childbirth).	1 week .	Family-based entitlement for 52 weeks until the first birthday of the child.[b] Except for the first week upon childbirth when both parents can take leave.
	Payments	According to award.[a]	According to award.[a]	According to award.[a]
Denmark	Eligibility criteria	All female workers: payment subject to criteria as under parental leave.	All male workers: payment subject to criteria as under parental leave.	*Parental leave*: covers all workers, but eligibility to paid leave concerns those employees with at least 120 hours of work in the preceding 13 weeks, and self-employed persons who have worked at least 18 hours per week during 6 of the previous 12 months.[c] *Childminding leave*: as for *paid* parental leave.
	Duration	18 weeks (of which 4 weeks before expected date of childbirth).	2 weeks.	*Parental leave*: family-based entitlement for 10 weeks. After the 10-week period, the father is eligible for benefit for a further 2 weeks in the 25th and 26th week upon childbirth. *Childminding leave*: concerning children up to their 1st birthday, individual entitlement to 26 weeks, an additional 26 week-period is subject to employer consent. For children aged 1 to 9, individual entitlement to 13 weeks. Leave **cannot** be taken if children aged 0-2 are in public day care.[d]
	Payments	DKK 2 937 per week often topped up to full wage by employer.	DKK 2 937 per week topped up to full wage by employer.	*Parental leave*: DKK 2 937 per week often topped up to full wage by employer. *Childminding leave*: DKK 1 764 per week generally not topped up.

Table A.9. **Characteristics of parental leave arrangements with employment protection, 2001** (*cont.*)

Aspect		Maternity leave	Paternity leave	Parental leave and childminding leave (if specified)
Netherlands	Eligibility criteria	Female employees and self-employed.	Male employees.	12 months service with employer.
	Duration	16 weeks.	2 days.	Individual entitlement to *parental leave* of 13 times the number of hours of the contractual working week to be taken within a six-month period. Per week, employees can only have leave worth half the number of hours they normally work, unless otherwise agreed with employers. For example, workers with a contractual working week of 38 hours can take 19 hours leave per week over a 6-month period. Leave can be taken until the child is 8 years of age.[e]
	Payments	Full wage up to a maximum of € 794.29 per week: € 272.4 for the self-employed.	Full wages.	Unpaid, but public sector employers pay up to 75% of earnings.

a) Award or other relevant workplace and/or individual employment agreement.
b) Subject to employer agreement, part-time leave may be arranged for a maximum period of two years.
c) Persons who have finished vocational training or education of at least 18 months' duration within the last month as well as trainees in paid practical training periods during a training course are also covered, as well as certain groups of unemployed persons.
d) For children aged 3 to 8, it is possible to combine childminding-leave with part-time use of public day care.
e) Subject to employer agreement, the number of hours of parental leave taken per week can be changed.
Source: National authorities.

Eligibility criteria

Around the event of childbirth, Danish workers with some work-history and Dutch workers are entitled to paid leave of absence from work with employment-protection, although payment rates[11] differ can differ for some groups of workers (Table A9). In Australia, if a female worker is covered by an award/employment agreement that provides for leave *prior* to childbirth, it generally covers only those female workers who have been with their employer for 12 months or more. It is estimated that about 72.5% of the workers in Australia are entitled to parental leave (ABS, 1998). Both in Australia and the Netherlands, parental leave is only available to employees who have been with their employer for the 12 preceding months. Eligibility criteria for childminding leave in Denmark are the same as those for *paid* parental leave (Table A9).

Benefits

Australia

In Australia, the statutory right is to 52 weeks of unpaid leave, starting from childbirth. Subject to employment agreements up to six weeks before expected birth date may also be given in leave. Both parents can take the first week of parental leave: this establishes a *de facto* one-week paternity leave period. There is no publicly stipulated income support tied to the leave period. The provision of continued (partial) wage payments during leave is up to employers.

Denmark

In Denmark, a mother is entitled to 18 weeks maternity leave (of which four weeks are before the expected birth date). Thereafter there are ten weeks of parental leave, which can be taken by either parent, but not simultaneously. There is a legal entitlement to childminding leave for 26 weeks (if the child is not yet one year of age), although this can be extended subject to employer consent. Fathers in Denmark are entitled to two weeks paternity leave and 2 weeks "father quota". This is a two-week period following the 10-week parental leave period that is exclusively reserved to fathers on a "use it or lose it" basis.

During maternity, paternity and parental leave public income support is paid at the maximum unemployment benefit rate, which for 80 of workers is topped up to full wages as stipulated in collective agreements. Public income support during Childminding leave is paid at 60% of UI-payment rates, and is never topped up.

As described below, legislation has been passed to change this system: childminding leave will be phased out while the father-quota have been abolished. Reform does not affect paternity and maternity leave, but the family-based entitlement to parental leave of ten weeks has been individualised and extended to 46 weeks for working parents (and 40 weeks for unemployed parents). However, the entitlement to paid leave remains family-based, and is payable to one parent at 100% of the maximum UI payment benefit, for the maximum duration of 32 weeks. If parental leave is taken for 48 weeks, payment rates per week will be adjusted accordingly (32/48*100UI benefit).

The Netherlands

In the Dutch system, there are 16 weeks maternity leave paid up to a relatively high maximum (just over average earnings). Because of this high level, employers do not often have to top up public payments to full wages, although collective agreements provide for this. The employer pays paternity leave (2 days) in full. Parental leave is on a part-time basis, and can be taken up over a 6-month period (see Table A9 for detail). Parental leave is generally unpaid in the private sector, while public sector employers pay 75% of last earnings for the time taken off.

Childminding leave and childcare

Childminding leave in Denmark is the only leave programme in the three countries under review that is directly linked to the use of childcare. Parents on childminding leave caring for children below 2 years of age cannot use public day care facilities at the same time. If parents choose to care for their own child, while the public childcare system is stretched to guarantee childcare places to children after their first birthday (Chapter 3), it is not without reason to restrict access to childcare for those who are cared for at home.

Using leave later during childhood

Parents in both the Netherlands (for parental leave) and Denmark (for childminding leave) are not required to use leave entitlements immediately after childbirth: they can use some entitlement at a later stage during childhood (until the child is 8 years of age in the Netherlands and 9 years old in Denmark). Entitlement to parental leave in the Netherlands is independent of the child's age (thus part-time leave/work for 6 months), while childminding leave entitlement to care for a child at least one year of age is 13 months at maximum (is 26 weeks when care concerns an infant).

Adoption

In all three countries under review, leave arrangements regarding childbirth or care for children generally also apply to adoption and adopted children. Except for benefits granted prior to childbirth, leave benefits are the same in case of adoption in Australia and Denmark. In the Netherlands, adoption leave consists of 4 weeks of leave to be taken within an 18-month period: leave is paid in line with maternity payments. The entitlement to adoption leave does not impinge upon entitlement to parental leave for the same child.

Notes

1. FTB(A) involved an increase of A$ 140 per year in assistance per child, or 4.9% for children aged 0-12 years and 3.8% for those aged 13-15 (Costello, 1998).

2. Approximately 35% receive the maximum FTB(A) rate (DFACS, 2001).

3. For example, the Newstart Allowance (payable to unemployed people) pays a rate that is about 8% higher for sole parents than for single people without children.

4. There is a Parenting Payment – Partnered as well.

5. In Australia, 38% of the around 1 million households receiving rent assistance have dependent children (DFACS, 2001). In the Netherlands, the programme assists around 900 000 (OECD, 1998). In Denmark it covers 170 000 non-pensioner households, of which 83 000 have children (Ministry of Social Affairs).

6. In Denmark and the Netherlands, most services are largely free to the user, with costs being met from taxation (Denmark) and social insurance (Netherlands). In Australia, tax and levy funded Medicare benefits also deal with most costs of visiting doctors, and concession cards reduce pharmaceutical costs to low income families. In all countries most general hospital services are also free to the user.

7. In the Netherlands, courts use a formula for determining the rate, taking into account a range of factors. These include: the capacity of each parent to support their child; reasonable living expenses of the non custodial parent (including costs for setting up a new home and second family obligations); the responsibilities of step-parents; and the nature of the contact between parent and child.

8. In each country there is the option to use voluntary agreements. In Australia, about 10% do so, while in Denmark between 10 and 20% do so. The Netherlands relies more heavily on voluntary arrangements, encouraging them by charging absent parents a fee equal to 10% of their assessed liability to use the LBIO.

9. Denmark has a standard rate for child support of DKK 10 980 per annum per child is made up of a base rate (DKK 9 760) and an income-related supplement (DKK 1 260).

10. The description concerns the situation as in 2001. Benefit reform scheduled to be introduced in Denmark during the 2nd quarter of 2002 are not accounted for (see Chapter 4).

11. Public payments during child-related leave periods are proportional to unemployment insurance payments in Denmark and regulated under sickness insurance in the Netherlands.

OECD PUBLICATIONS, 2, rue André-Pascal, 75775 PARIS CEDEX 16
PRINTED IN FRANCE
(81 2002 11 1 P) ISBN 92-64-19843-1 – No. 52657 2002